T0354757

Dr. Clark has published two other books:

Relationships—Reflection of the Image of God

Being Transformed by God in the Workplace

CALLED ACCORDING TO HIS PURPOSE

A Journey into the World of Parenting Special Needs Children

Dr. Crawford G. Clark

WESTBOW PRESS®
A DIVISION OF THOMAS NELSON & ZONDERVAN

Copyright © 2021 Dr. Crawford G. Clark.

All rights reserved. No part of this book may be used or reproduced by any means, graphic, electronic, or mechanical, including photocopying, recording, taping or by any information storage retrieval system without the written permission of the author except in the case of brief quotations embodied in critical articles and reviews.

WestBow Press books may be ordered through booksellers or by contacting:

WestBow Press
A Division of Thomas Nelson & Zondervan
1663 Liberty Drive
Bloomington, IN 47403
www.westbowpress.com
844-714-3454

Because of the dynamic nature of the Internet, any web addresses or links contained in this book may have changed since publication and may no longer be valid. The views expressed in this work are solely those of the author and do not necessarily reflect the views of the publisher, and the publisher hereby disclaims any responsibility for them.

Any people depicted in stock imagery provided by Getty Images are models, and such images are being used for illustrative purposes only.
Certain stock imagery © Getty Images.

Unless otherwise noted, scripture quotations taken from the Amplified® Bible (AMP), Copyright © 2015 by The Lockman Foundation. Used by permission. www.lockman.org

Scripture marked (KJV) taken from the King James Version of the Bible.

Scripture quotations marked (NIV) are taken from the Holy Bible, New International Version®, NIV®. Copyright © 1973, 1978, 1984, 2011 by Biblica, Inc.® Used by permission of Zondervan. All rights reserved worldwide. www.zondervan.com The "NIV" and "New International Version" are trademarks registered in the United States Patent and Trademark Office by Biblica, Inc.®

ISBN: 978-1-6642-4983-7 (sc)
ISBN: 978-1-6642-4984-4 (hc)
ISBN: 978-1-6642-4982-0 (e)

Library of Congress Control Number: 2021923216

Print information available on the last page.

WestBow Press rev. date: 11/19/2021

DEDICATION

I dedicate this book to my children, Danielle and David, who have been our joy.

I would also like to dedicate this book in memory of my friend Theodore DeShields and his mother, Jewel DeShields, as well as all those who suffer from intellectual and physical disabilities.

FOREWORD

God, the Timeless Creator of all, Lord and Architect of our entire Universe and all that lies beyond it, has gifted humans with a world of astonishingly perfect design, infinite variety, and unique purpose for every one of its inhabitants.

When we consider the vast array of variations within individual life forms, it should come as no surprise to find them among human beings as well. Unfortunately, we may tend to marginalize those whose differences from ourselves are substantial enough to require extra effort on our part to understand or accommodate them, and to categorize people in various ways in an effort to streamline how we relate to them. In doing so, we sometimes try to force square pegs into round holes instead of receiving and experiencing joy from each person as he or she truly is. We may consider it inconvenient to develop new ways of relating to those who arrive in our lives with characteristics we cannot easily fit into our preconstructed categories.

Children with special needs are one good example of this. They present unusual challenges to us and require special diligence on our part to understand them, to find ways of nurturing them, and to help them become all that God designed them to be. However, they are not mistakes!

They are not "less than" just because they do not fit into a chart of the average norms. Instead, like each star in the sky, the mitochondria in the cells of the human body, and every creature in the sea, they have their own glorious purposes; each one is another beautiful color in the vibrant, variegated rainbow of humanity. It is up to us to celebrate their lives and to help them realize and activate their own individual potential and significance in the world: such important work, but not easy!

In this book, Reverend Dr. Crawford Clark compassionately addresses the needs of special needs children, their siblings, and their parents in an open and winsome manner, including transparent accounts of struggles that he and his wife, Beverly, have faced with their own son and daughter, and substantive practical guidance in negotiating legal and financial planning for their futures.

Thanks to their generosity, they invite others to share in what they have discovered and come to understand in the hope that other parents and communities might become more appreciative of just how much joy special needs children can contribute to the lives of those around them and become better equipped with wisdom when facing puzzling difficulties. He points the way to valuable available resources perhaps unknown to many parents. In addition, he encourages parents to mine the treasures of personal skills, gifts, talents, and abilities that might lie hidden and undeveloped in their children without the perceptive eyes and loving guidance of their folks. Their countless insights, accumulated over decades of loving perseverance, are priceless!

It has been such a privilege to participate in helping to take this volume to print. Each page is a treasure, and the entire book is a veritable gold mine!

Soli Deo Gloria!
Bonney Ramsey Scott

ACKNOWLEDGMENTS

I thank my Lord Jesus Christ who once again filled my mind with the ability to articulate what had been percolating in my heart for numerous years.

I thank my incredible wife, Beverly, who has been an awesome woman of God and a great mother to our children for all these years.

I thank my children, Danielle and David, who have been a joy in my life, for giving me the permission to tell our story.

I thank my friend, the late Jewel Deshields, who shared with me the wonderful inspirational story of her son several years ago.

I thank Bonney Ramsey Scott who meticulously went through the book and was able to provide tremendous insight and help in providing the best articulation and clarity possible in telling our story.

INTRODUCTION

According to the census bureau, there are over fifty-four million people in the United States who have either an intellectual or a physical disability. This does not include individuals with disabilities who are institutionalized. That means that at least one out of every five individuals has some type of disability.

How are we to view these individuals? How are we to view those who have the obligation of taking care of them? Does the general population understand what it takes to be a caretaker of one or more individuals who have disabilities? In many instances, a person may have more than one disability. With multiple disabilities, there is the possibility of multiple complications.

Over the years, there has developed a greater public awareness of the difficulties that families with children with disabilities face, but it still isn't as high as it needs to be. There also are individuals who have committed themselves in various ways to the education of those who have special needs as well as to helping with physiological and psychological therapy for those with special needs. Despite those who help in these areas and who provide much needed support, there is also an imperative for support from a wide range of people from various backgrounds. There is need for a community of people to help families who have loved ones with disabilities.

What exactly is needed? You might be surprised by the answer that I personally have to this question. What is really needed has no price tag. What we need is understanding and time. We must take the time to understand the struggle, the emotional investment that produces weariness, the physical exhaustion that is experienced on a regular basis, and the psychological and spiritual turmoil that many deal with regularly who are the caregivers for children with mental and physical disabilities.

What a great help it would be if someone could provide respite for a few hours every day for these families. Most people, because their own lives are filled with all kinds of activities, cannot seem to find the time to help someone get a break for a few hours from the care of a child or children with disabilities.

What does it mean to love your neighbor as yourself? What does neighborly love look like? How many people would look at those around us with children with disabilities as being our neighbors? Do we ask the question, What can I do to help you? The word *love* is used so often and rolls off our lips so easily when we speak to people, even to those we hardly know. What does it mean in practice? Are we willing to get into the messiness of people's lives, particularly those who have children with disabilities? How willing are we to give up some of the things we want to do to help those we know who are struggling in environments of disability?

There is a saying that we hear quite often, especially in Christian circles: They will know that we are Christians by our love. Who will know us by our love? What does that love to look like? Who are the ones we are supposed to be showing love to on a regular basis—just our own families? It is my attempt in this book to share the difficulties that I believe most families who have children with disabilities experience daily. All families have similar issues, but they might be manifested in different ways. I will share what I know to be true for our own family situation as well as that of many others. Those families who do not have children with disabilities will find that our families go through similar issues that their families go through as well.

Often people question why God would allow a child with a disability to be born to their family. They may experience isolation from other people, anger toward God and others, spiritual struggles, mental gymnastics, and tension between spouses and among other family members. The degree of the severity of the disability a child has (or perhaps more than one child in the same family) determines the intensity of the emotional, psychological, and spiritual uneasiness that is experienced by that family. However, for those with eyes to see, it will become evident that even children with special needs can serve the higher purposes of God in this world, each in his or her own special way. And there is joy to be had in sharing that experience with them!

In addition to sharing our journey as a family with two children with disabilities, I would like to share the journey of a woman named Jewel DeShields who was told by her doctor that she would not be able to have a second child. God subsequently blessed her with a child named Theodore, a name that means gift of God. The gift that was given to her was taken away when he was just twenty-eight years of age. Theodore completed the mission on Earth that God had given him, and then he was called home to be with the Lord. Mrs. DeShields shares her incredible story of how God used this child to impact her life and the lives of many others, even though his life was brief. I am reminded of Theo every time I look at my license plate. His license plate read "1 Agape," which means One Love. After his passing, I secured a license plate in Pennsylvania that read "1 Agape 1." (Apparently, someone in the state already had "1 Agape.") It is so fitting that Theo's license plate represented how he genuinely loved people with God's love and also served a great purpose in God's overall plan, even though his life did not match up to the norm of most human lives.

I hope that the story of Theo, which was written by his mother, will be an inspiration to you and that it will help you to see God in a way you never have seen Him before. In fact, I hope that this book will help you to experience God through these two families. We should be able to see God easily through both our children and Theo. We will see that they were all *Called According to His Purpose.*

CONTENTS

Part 1 The Story of Our Children

Part 2 The Story of Theodore DeShields As told by His Mother, Jewel DeShields

PART 1

The Story of Our Children

1

Oh, No! Our Lives Will Never Be the Same

Who plans on having a mentally challenged child or a child who will struggle when it comes to learning? No one expects to have a child who will face a life that is considered to be not normal—at least not when a couple first hears that they are going to have a baby. In our case, we found out there were some possible issues with our child during pregnancy. Finding out that their child possibly will not be born as what is considered to be "normal" can be devastating news for expectant parents.

All parents who have a mentally challenged child can tell you that the journey they have traveled is one that is filled with ambivalent feelings. These feelings can vacillate. One minute you can be excited because of something the child did that made you smile or feel joyful; the next minute you can be angry because the child did something that made you upset and act out of character. This emotional rollercoaster can make life unsettled, and it can cause all sorts of rocky relationships in a family, and even in a community.

One of the questions that is often asked by people who have children on the spectrum is "Why me?" That seems like a logical question to ask even though there might not be an answer. Even if someone might be able to give somewhat of an answer, it will fall short of what parents may expect to hear. Even if there were an answer, it would not be satisfactory for most. Persons of faith might be expected to ask a different question, but because they are human and struggle with life issues, in many instances, they ask the same question.

This question is not aimed at a human being, even though it is usually spoken to one. This question usually is directed toward God. For many people who find themselves parents of children with mental disabilities, the feelings behind the question of *why* are quite intense and may last over a period of years. Can we really find an answer to this question that would be satisfactory? Are we able to accept an answer from the One who can give us a possible answer? Who might that be, you might ask. God Himself!

For us to become receptive to a genuine answer to the question "Why was my child born lacking what are considered to be normal qualities?" we must believe in the existence of a Creator who is supreme, omnipotent, omniscient, and sovereign. These descriptors are part of the attributes of the God of the scriptures. The question then becomes, Can we believe and accept what He has to say about life, including where life comes from? If our premise is derived from this mindset, then a probable answer to our question may be obtained.

The difficulty for most parents who have children with challenges is handling emotions. Emotions play a major part in the way individuals react to various situations. It is no different when it comes to raising children who have challenges from the very beginning. Physical, emotional, and psychological challenges all affect the emotions. In fact, there are emotional situations throughout the entire lives of those who have children or adopt children who are, as we say, "on the spectrum." Some parents or caregivers can master their emotions and learn to control them very well over time. Some may never get to the point of being able to control them. Our differing temperaments contribute to the difficulty of mastering our emotions. Not everybody handles things the same way. Some individuals are very calm under pressure; others are very emotional under pressure; and still others respond differently depending on the situation. There should not be an expectation that everyone will react in the same way in these situations; instead, we should expect people to learn how to manage their emotions.

It is safe to say that dealing with a child with challenges will take up most or all of a parent's life. Some parents choose to institutionalize a child if the disability is severe. There are other variables that will undoubtedly play into the reasons for institutionalization. Each family structure is different, as is the availability of support that is needed for a family to be able to live as normal a life as possible. The day-to-day responsibilities of care range from minor to major; however, at some point, these responsibilities do take a toll on the caregiver or caregivers. Parents who have never had to provide care for challenged individuals on regular basis might not understand the impact that the responsibility has on parents' lives. They might not understand the intensity of the stressors that exist in these types of caregiving situations. Stressors can bring about struggles in a marriage, among siblings, with finances, with socializing, with possible depression or addiction, and so on.

There is major excitement surrounding the expectation of a new child—not just the birth, but also about what the child might possibly become, what he or she might do. All kinds of thoughts run through our minds. We think about the special days our children will experience. We think about what they are going to accomplish in life. We think about the day they will leave our home and live on their own. We can't help having expectations for them as well as for ourselves. We can't help thinking about the future and how they will set fire to the world. These are the dreams we have. These are the thoughts that might be in our heads long before the child is even born. We cannot help it. Dreaming is part of what we do. Dreaming is a big part of the joy. Thinking about the future for them as well as for us is part of the excitement. When we find out that the child that we have been dreaming about might not be able to fulfill these dreams, we are devastated. The joy and the excitement that we were feeling melts away like ice cream on a hot day. The dreams shatter and are replaced with thoughts only of survival—what must be done on a daily basis to keep things going is now the imminent issue at hand. Many times, there is only one parent handling this daunting task.

Raising children with challenges can be exasperating in many ways. It can disrupt the parents' personal dreams as well. They might have had plans regarding education or projects they were looking forward to pursuing. The disability of the child will interfere with that process. Depending on the response of the parents, resentment can enter the picture and bring about friction in the marital relationship. Sacrifice is necessary. However, if one parent is not willing to sacrifice, there is a strong possibility that only one parent will be taking care of the child. This happens time and time again. Unfortunately, you might not hear about these situations because people are often not concerned about these parents' experiences. People have their own issues and concerns to worry about.

Sacrifice is the key word to use when it comes to describing what is necessary in a family with children with challenges, whether physical or mental. There are things that parents must give up—things that they may have been looking forward to, even that they have been waiting most of their lives to do. Sacrifice is something that takes place in these family environments on a regular basis, whether by one parent or both. Sacrifice becomes like a leash that is tied around the neck of a dog. The dog cannot get away no matter how it tries. The sacrifice feels like a prison for many—a prison from which they will never be able to escape.

Please understand what I am saying. I am explaining some of the feelings that some—even many—may have. However, many parents may never express these feelings to others around them. Most parents feel they would be judged or misunderstood if they did so. So they choose to keep silent and hold onto the feelings.

Initially, when parents find out that they are having a child who is going to be mentally or physically challenged, the response is disbelief. What they have just heard is not true. It cannot be true. It takes time to process such information. It is similar to the reaction a person might have upon hearing that someone close to him or her has passed away suddenly. It is difficult to believe what has happened. It cannot be true! People do not want to accept what they have just heard. They think they are having a dream and soon will wake up.

At some point, when the information has sunk into their minds, they begin asking questions. Their minds can begin to go all over the place. They get past the point of rejecting what has been said and move to a place of contemplation. For the most part, people go through the five stages of loss. Most of us know what they are: denial, anger, bargaining, depression, and acceptance. Many individuals go through these stages when they experience loss in their lives. Learning that a child will not be what is to be considered normal is a hurtful loss. Parents might not express that loss immediately or ever at all, but they will feel it.

Life changes in a huge way even with the birth of a child who does not have disabilities. Parents can feel overwhelmed. Once that child comes home, life changes—sleep patterns, socializing, schedules, household procedures, and the interaction of the parents. Everything changes. Life is no longer the same. Stress becomes part of the environment, but it is welcomed.

It is the same for parents of a child who has a disability. However, there are many more mental and emotional issues to deal with. These issues can cause stress levels that can bring about chaos in the family structure. Wondering how to manage this new dynamic can be extremely overwhelming for many couples. It is painful just thinking about how to proceed with taking care of the child and maneuvering through the vast array of social services that might be needed. This is a lot of weight to carry for new parents, even for parents who have had children without disabilities.

Most parents deal with the various complications and struggles as they arise. The potential for many children with mental or physical challenges to ever get better is quite minimal. To be honest, I must say that the expectation is quite high that they will not get better and accomplish things that children without disabilities can do. Parents just hope for the best. They desire the best for their children and pray that they can overcome the disability and that they will be normal, whatever normal may be. Some children are able to improve if they receive early intervention care. But for many, even with intervention, there isn't much improvement because of the capacity for the child to comprehend or to be able to overcome the physical issue. Accepting a permanent situation can be hard to handle. In fact, it can bring about not only disappointment, but depression. This depression can last for a long period of time; if it lasts more than two weeks, it can turn into clinical depression. Clinical depression in a parent is another stressor added to the family situation. Depression can go unnoticed. A person with depression can go through the motions of getting things done, but his or her emotions are numb. Another problem arises when one parent or both parents focus on the child with disabilities so much that they do not pay enough attention to other children. Parents can also neglect the needs of their spouses.

I have been in several houses where people live in an atmosphere of clutter. There are varying degrees of clutter. Light clutter means that things are just out of order and not in place, maybe a few things thrown here and there. Major clutter means there is stuff all over the place; nothing is in order. There might even be trash on the floor and food that has been left out for days. There could be a pile of unwashed dishes in the sink that have been there for weeks as well as papers thrown all over every table in the house. How can people live that way? They get accustomed to it. The situation is acquired, like people who acquire a taste for coffee or beer. They accept it and lose the concept of what order in their environment can be like. In most cases, the environment reflects depression, but in some cases, it can reflect laziness. In other cases, it can reflect a mindset that focuses on what is okay for that person, and that person does not consider how others might feel about the environment. This example of major clutter is an illustration of what can happen in the mind of a new parent who has a child with a disability. The mental condition can become cluttered with all kinds of thoughts. These thoughts are all over the map and produce a mental disorder that can initially prevent the parent from functioning normally. This condition may last for months and may extend into years if not treated.

For others, there are no feelings. This would describe me. I cannot tell you how I felt. All I can tell you is that I was dealt a hand, and I had to deal with it. To be honest, I would not have said it quite that way. I would have been more diplomatic, but this is the straightforward version. *Responsibility* and *duty* would be the key words for me if I had to describe where I was mentally at the time. It was my responsibility as a parent to take care of my child, no matter what the situation was going to be. We can take care of our responsibilities without feelings. A sense of duty doesn't require feelings, only action. We do what is necessary and we continue to do it to the best of our ability. As things happen, we just keep going. We don't have time to think about feelings. "Just do it"—like the Nike commercial says. This is where I was mentally and emotionally at the time. I am sure there are many others who did the same thing that I did.

It is interesting, however, that my wife, Beverly, did not feel the same way. In fact, she expressed her feelings at various points along the journey of parenting. Still, feelings did not emanate from me. I could not even pinpoint what feelings were there. I believe this is quite common for men in this type of family situation with a child with a disability. The way men handle and view the situation can be totally different from the way women carry on.

Another thinking process that is quite present is one that pertains to the future, at least for my wife and me. Since we did not have family members who were able to take care of our children should anything happen to us, we were concerned and under pressure about who would take on the responsibility of looking after them. This was, and still is, a genuine concern. Trying to figure out the future care undoubtedly has been one of the many overwhelming issues we have had to face. The number of considerations in making such decisions is astronomical. Because of all the variables, it is easy to understand why many couples just bury their heads in the sand and forget about trying to figure things out. Some may say, "Just leave it for someone else or even the state to handle it. At least they will be okay." It is the parents' responsibility to figure these things out for their child or children who cannot take care of themselves mentally or physically.

Because of all the different issues that are prevalent for parents with a child who has a disability, they should not suffer in silence or attempt to handle things on their own. They need to work at getting all the knowledge and understanding that is available so that they can maximize the use of potential resources. They should let people know what they are dealing with and consult the various agencies that they might need for their child. They should ask family members who might be able to provide some direction regarding resources.

Despite the difficulties my wife and I had to face, we kept fighting for what we could get for our kids by opening our mouths and letting people know what our needs were. If one door closed, we would look for another door. It is amazing that there are individuals out there who misuse the systems that are in place. They lie and create false scenarios in order to cheat the system. When we have a child or children that are in need, we should never be too proud to ask for what we are entitled to receive. Not asking for what we need is neglecting what rightfully belongs to our children. Pride and isolation can prevent many parents from making their situation a bit easier than what it currently is.

It should be noted that, despite the agencies that are there to help, some might not help and some of the individuals who work for these agencies might be more discouraging than they should be. Their attitudes can keep parents from getting what they should get. Some individuals who work for these agencies look down on people who are receiving help. Many may think that the parents don't need it. Some just hate their jobs, and misery loves company. Because they are miserable, they come across as uncaring and unhelpful. Their attitude can cause parents to not pursue getting the help they deserve. They back off so they don't receive what they rightfully should get for their or children. This should never be. Parents must fight for all they should get. We had to do that.

Despite the emotional rollercoasters, the disappointments, the depression, the struggles, and the relational battles, God is present for those who want Him to be. He can help us in our situation. He can give what is needed for parents. Parents must allow Him to be part of the process. We found out that Jesus must be the source of strength in the entire environment—not just the family structure, but the systems that are being dealt with continually. Dealing with the false shame, the attitudes, and the lack of understanding by people through the entire parenting process can be brutal and destructive if not dealt with properly. Having a strong faith does not prevent these things from happening, but it helps parents manage their emotions and focus on what is important. The biggest thing that faith provides is a perspective that is Christ centered, which helps us to not get caught up with the fact that so many individuals treat children and adults with disabilities inappropriately.

The lifestyle of a family with special needs children often consists of the same routine day in and day out. It could be compared to the movie *Groundhog Day* in which Phil (played by Bill Murray), a jaded weatherman, lives out the same day over and over and over again. Can you imagine caregiving for a person repeatedly without a change of routine, never having a break to do anything different? That is what it is like for many who have this type of family structure. There is never a change in routine. They do the same thing repeatedly without experiencing life outside of caregiving. Think about that for a minute—never going anywhere, no vacation, very little entertainment, very little "me" time, very little opportunity to do anything for fun. This is what life is like for many. No wonder depression and discouragement can set in and steal all the joy a parent could have. No wonder these parents can see nothing but caregiving in their future. No wonder they look at life as something that was taken away from them. No wonder they feel they have been punished, banished to a world of total sacrifice.

For this reason, many men leave or are tempted to leave these kinds of situations; divorce can become a viable option for them. Such a decision is prompted by living with such conditions. Do not get me wrong! Parents should never abandon the responsibility they have regarding their children. Parents should do their best to get the help and support they need. Many choose not to do so.

If a family can learn how to manage the difficulties that are associated with a special needs situation, I believe a change of attitude will follow. Faith can truly play a part in helping families navigate the waters. The wisdom that comes from God and the peace that comes from Him as well can help families deal with such difficult situations. The power of God can work in our lives. With this purview, people can see the beauty that comes through children and adults with disabilities. Many parents are blinded to the beauty because of the struggles. Breaking through the barrier of blindness can bring about a perspective that sees God in the struggles and how God is able to use them. God shows us that.

Initially, even as a person who is involved with ministry, although I did not complain about the situation, I was unable to see the beauty and to fully understand how such individuals like my son and daughter, with their limited abilities, are used by God for His divine glory. God has gradually opened our eyes to not only see, but to experience the unique gifts they have been given by God. It truly is amazing to see it and witness this on a regular basis. God uses them to show us what His love—pure love—genuinely looks like. It is a love of purity as well as of beauty.

[illegible] giving [illegible] their [illegible]. [illegible] they look at life [illegible] something that was taken away [illegible] they [illegible] together [illegible] to [illegible].

[illegible] reason, many [illegible] are [illegible] their [illegible] situation, [illegible] can become [illegible] them. [illegible] is [illegible] by [illegible] such [illegible] wrong. Parents should [illegible] responsibility [illegible] children. Parents should do the best to [illegible] and [illegible] they need. [illegible] not [illegible] do.

If a family [illegible] difficulties that [illegible] with a special [illegible] situation [illegible] will [illegible] may [illegible] comes from God [illegible] come from [illegible] to help families [illegible] situations. [illegible] God can work [illegible] with [illegible] through [illegible] disability. [illegible] to the [illegible] of the [illegible] the [illegible] of [illegible] and how God [illegible].

Initially, [illegible] involved [illegible] ministry [illegible] did not complain [illegible] to [illegible] and [illegible] how [illegible] learned [illegible] God [illegible] purposes [illegible] have been given [illegible] a regular basis [illegible].

2

Voices

Most of us have heard of the mental condition known as schizophrenia. Schizophrenia is a mental health condition that affects a person's ability to function socially. People with this condition may hear voices, experience paranoid or delusional thoughts, social withdrawal and fearfulness or agitation to a severe level in everyday life.

You might be asking why I am bringing up schizophrenia at this juncture. Family members in families with children who are challenged can feel as if they are experiencing a partial state of schizophrenia. Notice that I used the word *partial*. One of the symptoms of schizophrenia is the hearing of voices. It is safe to say that individuals outside of a family who has a child with a mental or physical condition for a lifetime do not realize the number of voices that the challenged family members hear over the years. Different voices communicate different ideas, some good and some are bad. Most people would never describe what families go through as schizophrenia, but in a sense, that is what it feels like to so many. Let us look at these voices. The first voice that appears at the very beginning is denial.

> **The voice of denial**—This is the inner voice that does not want to accept that a child will always be in the condition that he or she was born with. We continue to deny the permanency of the condition. In some cases, a child will get better because of treatment over time, but in many cases, the child will not get better. But still, in the back

> of the parents' minds, that voice still lingers and says that, one day, maybe, the child will improve because of technology yet to be developed. Parents continue to tell themselves that the possibility is there.
>
> **The voice of hope**—This voice is inextricably tied into the fabric of denial. The denial of permanency brings about a belief that things will eventually get better for the child who has the disability. With the treatment that is available, especially with early intervention, the child could overcome his or her condition. Parents tell themselves it is a temporary situation. Parents say with hope, "We know this child will ultimately be able to function in society. It just will take a little longer due to the research that needs to be done."

These voices are almost always present in the beginning years of family life with the child. We all hear that, if a child can get early intervention, he or she can possibly live a productive life. All parents want their children to live productive lives and to be considered by the culture as valued members of society. It is normal for parents to have hope. Hope is almost always the immediate next stage after denial. Parents want the doctors' opinions right away regarding the possible future for the child. What parents are really asking, at best, is for doctors to predict the future for their children. In many instances, this prediction is impossible to make. All the doctors can do is make educated guesses. What will it take to propel a child to be in a better position? What services are available to help move the child and the family in the right direction? Parents want the best services if possible. The voice of hope emerges to counteract the denial.

It is safe to say that both denial and hope can exist at the same time. The length of time they are present in the minds of parents differs. It is not possible to predict how long a person can vacillate between the voice of denial and the voice of hope. Parents must wait it out and see what time will bring. Of course, this waiting period can be excruciating for many families.

Other voices emerge as time goes on. For some, the voices that emerge later might have been present at the beginning but were kept silent due to the other voices being so loud. The next voice that can be present is the voice of anger.

> **The voice of anger**—This is the inner voice that lashes out at someone or something. There is a need to be angry because of the condition of the child. As I stated in the first chapter, no one signs up for the job of caretaker of a person challenged from birth. It is normal for most people to react out of anger when something negative occurs in their lives. Even when something is expected, people can still be angry when it happens. For example, a person can know that a loved one is going to die, and yet, still feel angry because of the death. Anger can impact behavior. That is why one parent can express anger by yelling and screaming while the other can be silent and exercise what is called passive aggressive behavior, which is very subtle. The voice of anger causes people to lash out at the person closest to them or at God. Much of the anger is toward God. The problem is that God is not directly in front of them. The result is that loved ones can catch the wrath of the angry persons. Many godly people have struggled in their relationship with God after having a child that has a permanent disability or condition. It is hard for them to worship God when they believe that the One they worship is at fault.

Closely related to the voice of anger is the voice of rejection.

> **The voice of rejection**—The voice of rejection relates to the voice of anger. When people think about why a child was born with a disability, they can first be angered and place the fault on God. However, after some time, the thought process can change. The voice of rejection can enter the picture and bring about an attempt to justify why the child was born that way. Some might say "God is

getting back at me because of my lifestyle." "God is now causing me to suffer because of what I did to my parents or significant other." "God is now punishing me because I failed to obey what He told me to do." People can feel that God is punishing them because of something they did or did not do. This punishment is directly associated with rejection by God. Lives of sacrifice and suffering are now what is necessary to satisfy what people have done to hurt God. Most of us, because of how we are wired, must have a reason for something that has happened. If we believe it, our behavior will now follow. The voice of rejection impacts the lives of parents for the rest of their lives.

Another voice that raises its head after a period is the voice of abandonment.

The voice of abandonment—This voice can emerge at any time; it can come and go over a long period of time. It can also be present permanently for some people. The voice of abandonment says that no one cares about the situation and no one wants to care. This voice constantly tells people to search the environment for people who seem to not want to empathize with their situation. When family members do not come to visit or call, so-called friends don't ever ask if they can help care for the children, church members don't ask how parents are coping or seem to be concerned about their well-being, or other individuals never ask how they can help, parents feel abandoned. The voice of abandonment causes parents to shut down and not express their needs. They conclude that nobody cares about them, and they can't make people care. They tell themselves, "If they cared, they should ask me." "Why should I have to say anything if they can clearly see what I am dealing with?"

Is it possible that parents with children with disabilities do not vocalize their need for help enough? Should they be putting out a message that they need help with their situation? Should they be specifying the kind of help they need? Are the parents of mentally and physically challenged children too judgmental when it comes to how they perceive those outside their situation and those people do not understand because the parents aren't assertive enough to move toward them? These are some questions we should ask ourselves. The voice of abandonment can bring about isolation from people, bitterness, heightened anger, disappointment, depression, and a buildup of a hatred toward humanity if we are not careful. Along with the belief that people do not care is that people do not have time to care. They are so busy with their own lives and problems that they do not want to take time to help those in need. Parents may think, "I do not want to bother them."

There is another voice that talks to us. This voice tends to start as a whisper but can eventually gain steam and can take over parents' thinking. Sometimes they do not realize that it is even present, but it emerges over time. It is the voice of shame.

> **The voice of shame**—This voice tells parents they do not deserve to have people in their lives because they are damaged goods; their family isn't normal. This voice says that they are useless to everyone. This voice brings about a belief that the family has some missing parts and is unable to function properly in society. In some cases, the family line will not be extended. I think about this one at times because I know that I will not experience grandchildren. The perceived belief of inferiority can come about because of the messages that people articulate when they have conversations with the parents.

On a few occasions, we attempted to get Danielle, our daughter, tested at the local elementary school. We were asked by the educators why she wasn't attending school. We told them that we were homeschooling her. Immediately their response was, "What about her socialization?" We have been asked this question numerous times over the years. We told them that our daughter could socialize better than any kids in the school because of the people she had been around. They looked at us as if we were out of our minds. They felt were hurting our child because she was not in their school; they didn't realize we were helping her by teaching her at home. What was the message that we were receiving from these educators? The message that obviously was coming through was that the educators knew more than we did about our own child's needs and that we were putting our child in a position of disadvantage. As parents, we were hearing that, despite our education, we lacked the knowledge to give our mentally challenged child what she needed. They felt she should be in a class with a teacher who had been trained to teach in a special education class. *Okay!* we thought. *Let us see what it will be like for her.*

Upon hearing this subliminal message, we decided to observe the class for a portion of a day to see the special education teacher's methods. It was quite interesting. To make a long story short, the teacher really could not teach all the children with different mental disabilities. There were approximately twenty-five students in the class. Most of the students were sitting at their desks not even paying attention to what the teacher was saying. We could see that there was not much personal attention given to each child, and the children were not learning much in this type of environment. Yet, to the educators, we lacked sense because we did not want to put our child in that situation and setting. What was coming through was shame, even though we really didn't understand the feeling at the time. We were made to feel that we were not good enough to do what they could do. We had not been trained in their area of expertise. We did not have what it took. Wow. This is what the culture was saying to us. However, God had a different message. We can find God's message in the book of Deuteronomy. In chapter 6:1–9 (NIV), we read:

> These are the commands, decrees and laws the LORD your God directed me to teach you to observe in the land that you are crossing the Jordan to possess, so that you, your children and their children after them may fear the LORD your God as long as you live by keeping all his decrees and commands that I give you, and so that you may enjoy long life. Hear, Israel, and be careful to obey so that it may go well with you and that you may increase greatly

> in a land flowing with milk and honey, just as the LORD, the God of your ancestors, promised you. Hear, O Israel: The LORD our God, the LORD is one. Love the LORD your God with all your heart and with all your soul and with all your strength. These commandments that I give you today are to be on your hearts. Impress them on your children. Talk about them when you sit at home and when you walk along the road, when you lie down and when you get up. Tie them as symbols on your hands and bind them on your foreheads. Write them on the doorframes of your houses and on your gates.

In this we can understand that God gave a command to the Israelites about what they needed to do for their children. Based upon this scripture, we can glean some principles of what we are to do with our children concerning parenting and training them. The responsibility for teaching the child falls on the parent, not the system. If the system, especially in our modern day, cannot give children what we believe is best for them to learn, we need to do it ourselves, if it is possible. I know that this was a lengthy example for shame, but I needed you to see how it plays out in a subtle way. Shame sometimes can be present even though it is not on the surface. To identify the voice, you may need to go deeper. Shame can be present but not reveal itself right away.

Notice something about these voices we have talked about—they all are inner voices; they are within us. These voices are part of the intrapersonal substance of our makeup. There are other voices that people hear that originate from the outside. These voices come from the interpersonal relationships that are centered around people. Let's look at some of these voices.

> **The voice of silence**—This voice can also be subtle. The voice of silence is the voice of those who do not have anything to say about the situation. They talk to parents about everything else but not about the situation they are in. This voice is a relative of the voice of abandonment. The voice of abandonment is an inner voice, whereas the

voice of silence comes from the outside. When people are silent about the situation, the situation feeds into the parents' reasoning pattern that people don't really care about them. Parents are alone on the island of caregiving, never to be rescued. The voice of silence can be extremely loud for those who have mentally challenged children.

The voice of optimism—This voice is overwhelmingly optimistic. This voice emerges from those who believe that the challenged children will be fine. People encourage parents to keep trusting and believing that the children will be able to do things on their own. This voice, though optimistic, can be a voice of false hope. When people are on the outside looking, they do not really know what the inside is like; they cannot possibly have any idea of how a child is going to turn out. They never have taken the time to understand the daily struggles that are associated with the environment that a challenged caregiving family is involved with daily. Their optimism, though genuine, is not realistic. In fact, most parents just want them to be quiet. Their optimism makes things worse because the voice in which they speak goes against the voices that the parents have been living with for years, which are most likely accurate.

The voice of "You are a good parent"—This is a voice that sounds really good. In fact, it is great to know that others feel that caregiving parents are good parents. It feels good to hear a different voice that is positive. However, what does being a good parent mean? Is it the consistency in which they go about what needs to be done with the child? Is it how the child behaves in the presence of others? Is it something that they feel needs to be said to encourage the parents to keep going? Is it that, considering the circumstances, parents appear to be good? Is it that, if they were in the same situation, they could not do it?

These types of questions can go on and on. What is really meant by being a good parent?

The voice of "I am sorry"—The perception of this voice can be unpredictable. It appears on the surface that a person is feeling empathetic toward a person who is in a mentally challenging environment, but the words *I am sorry* may add to the other voices that are negative. What do the people who say these words mean? Are they sorry that the parents must be in the situation in the first place? Are they sorry for the child who has the disability? Are they sorry for both? These words can cause parents to think they and their family are damaged. Parents are led to believe they are different from everyone else. This outer voice can feed directly into the inner voice of rejection.

The voice of Satan—This voice can be one that keeps the negative voices constantly present. This voice encourages the negative voices and even provides a continual lifeline that can cause a parent to experience a breakdown. All the voices speaking at the same time can damage a mind that is already extremely fragile. The purpose behind the voice of Satan is to kill, steal, and destroy. If he can keep the environment in the mentally challenged home disrupted, he will eventually begin to break down the family unit. The voice of Satan forces parents to constantly focus on the lies that are present in their minds as well as those that are being articulated by well-meaning voices on the outside.

The voice of God—The voice of God is the voice that should supersede all the other voices. The voice of God contains truth. His truth can help to minimize the other voices and keep parents and other family members from suffering the schizophrenic condition. The voice of God, if people are open to listen to Him, can bring a calmness and

> strength necessary to deal with the ambivalent feelings that will be present through the entire lives of those who are parents of mentally or physically challenged children. God is the One who designed this unique family unit. He is the One who can help them navigate its choppy waters.

There are a lot of voices that parents must contend with regularly as they travel the river of life with mentally challenged children. Hearing the voices constantly can make people feel they are suffering from schizophrenia. To describe some of the thinking processes that may be part of a parent's experience with the mentally challenging environment through the grid of the mental condition of schizophrenia, I believe is quite helpful in understanding the mental complexity that is associated with parenting.

We can see why schizophrenia is a fitting way to describe what parents of challenged children must experience. Most parents would not be able to clearly articulate what I just laid out for you. Trying to figure out all the voices would be a complicated task for any parent. A lack of reality is present since many parents of children with disabilities cannot experience most of the joys of life that parents of so-called normal children experience such as going to college, marrying, and having children. Some mentally challenged children grow up to be adults who can experience some of these things with supervision. Many, however, cannot.

We have talked about the false information that some of the voices provide. These voices foster false beliefs and confused thinking. All the voices are talking, each battling for prominence in the mind, each desiring to have control, each wanting to rule with a heavy hand that will not let go. No wonder there is a reduced desire for social engagement among many families with challenged children. With all the mental gymnastics taking place, parents do not have the energy to be around people. They are consumed with the task at hand—providing care to the one who is in need. This process can remain in place for a lifetime.

There is only one voice that should stand out among all the voices, and that is the voice of God. His voice is the only one that can bring comfort and hold back the continual bombardment of the other voices maneuvering for supremacy. "If God is for us, who can be against us." This is what Paul stated in Romans 8:31(NIV). What a powerful reminder that God will have the most prominent voice in our lives if we belong to Him and trust Him. That is Jesus, our Savior and Lord. This statement can become a reality for those who know God and have Him as their Savior. He can provide a strong voice that can put the other voices to flight.

3

Solitary Confinement

I recently was talking to a friend with whom I had not spoken in several weeks. He shared with me an experience he had gone through since our last conversation. He had been placed in a correctional facility for two weeks, and while there, he had been placed in solitary confinement. What exactly is solitary confinement?

> Solitary confinement is the isolation of a prisoner in a correctional facility from other prisoners as a form of internal penial discipline.

> A person in solitary confinement receives food through a slot in the door. The inmates are given only one hour to exercise, which takes place in a cage. For most of the twentieth century, a typical stay in solitary confinement amounted to just a few days, possibly several weeks in more extreme cases. Today inmates can spend years at a time in solitary. Persons placed in solitary confinement are totally isolated for whatever period designated. Over a period of time, the person will experience some negative effects, including the exacerbation of existing mental problems, the development of new mental problems, and a decreasing ability to assimilate into prison society or outside society. In everyday life, we require problem solving to stimulate the brain. In solitary confinement,

> there are no problems apart from the confinement itself, which a person is powerless to change. The mind, however, has difficulty accepting the situation, and the person can become overwhelmed by the mind's panic.

Depending on the length of time prisoners are in solitary confinement, they can emerge with the same problems that confinement was meant to prevent in the first place. The isolation from people can bring about aggression, depression, thoughts of suicide, and a range of mental health issues that may not have been there previously. In some cases, inmates might prefer to stay in solitary confinement and will intentionally cause disruptions so that they can go back.

The interesting thing in the case of my friend is that there was no reason for the system to put him in such a terrible environment. After a few weeks, he was released from prison and all charges were dropped. Even though he has been released physically, he will never be able to forget what happened to him mentally. He will always remember what it was like to be in solitary confinement. He will remember being in a dark cell where he was by himself for twenty-three hours a day. All he had were his thoughts. But he had something else. He had the presence of God.

I have taken the time to explain the experience of solitary confinement because caregiving parents of mentally or physically challenged children often feel the same. At various times along the journey, they experience feelings of isolation—the darkness, the lack of supportive people, the long stretches of confinement. The feelings of isolation can be overwhelming at times. In fact, the feelings can begin to take hold of the mind, producing thoughts that may not be quite accurate when viewing the situation properly. The perception of circumstances can be exaggerated by the level of stress; and it can be minimized and not honestly acknowledged. For example, I wrote earlier about how my wife struggled at times with the homeschooling process with the children. During the times in which she was extremely stressed, she would become very emotional, which would begin to impact her thinking regarding her ability to effectively homeschool. She then began to feel inadequate and have second thoughts about whether she was doing the right thing by homeschooling of the children. This situation occurred several times over the years.

These feelings of isolation do not occur only with the parents. They are common in the children for whom they are caring. The level of functionality of a child determines the level of the expression of feelings that the child can share with the parent. The feeling of belonging is such a major factor for many children with disabilities. Even though we might not be able to tell initially if the child is feeling isolated, the child is able to manifest how he or she feels through body language or change of behavior. Just as when any child is not given attention and feels neglected, a mentally challenged child will show displeasure in some type of tangible way. I know that this was the case with my son. He wanted to fit in with everything so badly. He wanted to do what the other kids did. He wanted to experience what the other kids were experiencing. However, it was not easy for him or easy for us. The harder he tried, the more difficult it became for him due to his skill level. I struggled myself just watching *his* struggle and sympathizing with him as he continued to try things without success. My heart went out to him as he desired to play sports like soccer, baseball, and basketball because he loved them so much. I was happy that there were teams available that accepted all kids because the sport was not about the competition; it was about providing the experience of playing and having fun.

Despite David's lack of skill with sports and the struggles he has had over the years with his learning disabilities, he has always exhibited a drive that never allowed him to give up. He has always displayed an attitude that says "I can do it" whether he could or not. In my mind, I would say, *Why does he still want to do this? It isn't working for him.* Notice that is how *I* was thinking. *He* was not thinking along these lines. What is interesting about this example that I am sharing with you about David is that he has gone through feelings of isolation on many occasions, but he has never allowed his feelings to keep him from trying. This is an amazing quality that he has been given by God. It is what helped us to allow him to start taking the bus on his own even though we wanted to transport him in the car. This quality is what led him to apply to Community College of Philadelphia on his own because he wanted to attend. It did not matter if he would struggle with the classes. He was in college and was able to experience being in a classroom setting with others. He had never had that opportunity, though he had tried a few times during the homeschool journey. David has two qualities that many young adults who do not have disabilities lack: persistence and drive. His drive and persistence keep him from being isolated, stuck in a fishbowl by himself just continually going around in a circle and getting nowhere.

There is another example with my daughter that occurred when she was of elementary school age. We felt that she needed to be more involved with girls her age and needed to connect with them at a level to which she was not accustomed. We were attempting to find some community activities in the neighborhood in which she could participate. We found that the Girl Scouts were meeting in one of the local churches. We thought that this would be a great activity for her, so we made the necessary arrangements to take her. Well, to our surprise, during her first day, the girls did not even pay any attention to her. She stood in the middle of the floor looking lost. None of the girls attempted to reach out to her or get to know her. It was also interesting that very few of the adult leaders reached out to her either. We let it slide the first time because we felt that it was just a fluke. The following week, we went back, and the same thing happened. We attempted one more time. That was it! We were done with the Girl Scouts. We went home upset, feeling isolated, and feeling that no one cared. Of course, the fact that Danielle had a mental disability and was quite hesitant when it came to integrating with people should not have mattered. It appeared that the girls had formed cliques and were not concerned about whether the new girl was welcomed or not. Danielle had an intellectual disability, but they would not have known it just by looking at her. It would not be until they spoke to her that they would be able to tell that she was different from them. Just because she was different should not have been a reason for her not to be a part of what they were doing. What were they learning about accepting others who weren't like them? Did they care? These were the thoughts, at least in my mind, that I had when I drove away. My daughter had been isolated, all by herself, even though there had been people all around her.

This is the interesting phenomenon that I am describing about the isolation that occurs in the environment with mentally or physically challenged children, which manifests itself in various ways. I will address these in a minute.

Currently our world is going through a pandemic. Citizens all over the United States as well as in many other countries around the world are required by their governments to be isolated in their homes. This and other measures have been put in place to prevent the spread of coronavirus disease (COVID-19). After numerous months of being shut down in varying degrees, people are tired of the isolation and the social distancing. People are experiencing sadness and depression. God created humans to be relational beings. Being isolated from other people for long periods of time, especially family members, is not normal. We were not designed to live this way. Nevertheless, experts in various fields have concluded that the best way to stop the spread of the virus is isolation and social distancing, which are unnatural. Therefore, we are seeing more and more people across the country protesting and defying the orders to isolate as much as possible.

The longer we stay insulated from others during this pandemic, the more people will come out of it experiencing some issues. Mentally, we all will have to process how to interact with each other again. For extroverts, it may be quite easy, but for introverts, it may prove quite difficult. This is the problem with being isolated for such a long period of time. Isolation can keep us from reality. Notice what has happened with this pandemic: the closure of businesses, the closure of schools, the partial closure of government, the increase of people with a disease at times overwhelming the healthcare system in certain regions, the death of loved ones, and the loss of jobs. These are all physical aspects. What about the mental aspects—the anger and the depression caused by the loss of loved ones; the anger and the depression caused by the loss of jobs and layoffs, the anxiety about the unknown future, and the pent-up emotion that has grown in people. A host of additional issues are also present, but you get the point that I am making.

Parents with children who are intellectually and physically challenged already know what this type of isolation can do. A pandemic does not really bring with it much of a mental shock for most parents who are caregivers of intellectually and physically challenged children because they have already experienced the same kind of emotional and mental impact that has been produced by the pandemic—for years. The feelings that the general population are experiencing are feelings that these parents learned to live with on a regular basis. Through the experience of COVID-19, millions of individuals who are going through physical isolation understand that it brings with it mental disruptions in our cognitive thinking processes.

We know that physical isolation is one type of isolation. In the field of biology there are several kinds of isolation: ecological, temporal, behavioral, mechanical, and geographical. These various forms of isolation are recognized in the research community. They do not apply, however, in the psychiatric community. I believe that there is an isolation that occurs that maybe we never even thought about, especially those who are in environments that involve intellectually or physically challenged children. I have described disturbances that result from physical isolation such as loneliness, anxiety, and depression. Another type of isolation is what I will term "reality isolation." This term does not appear the dictionary or any book. It is what I believe happens to many families with mentally or physically challenged children.

The word *isolation* means "separation" or "seclusion." The word *reality* means "truth." We can say that the meaning of "reality isolation" is "being separated from truth." The environment in a home with a special needs child is quite demanding. In many instances, the children cannot do things for themselves and are always dependent on someone else to help. If there are children in the home who do not have disabilities, isolation can impact them as well because of all the attention that is being given to the disabled child. Resentment can easily set in with every member of the family, including parents who feel that they are being neglected by their spouses who are devoting so much time to the child. So, isolation can occur in the romance area of the marriage, creating disconnection and disaffection.

The demand of taking care of a challenged child can bring about resentment at some point in each member in the household. In addition, there can be anger, confusion, mood swings, frustration, transference of emotions onto other members of the family, and possible memory lapses because of all the pressures and demands. Ignoring the reality of all these situations results in *reality isolation*, which is the willful refusal to recognize what is taking place in the family unit. Do these dynamics sometimes exist in what would be considered normal families? Yes. However, in the family with mentally or physically challenged children, they are more likely to occur to a greater degree because of the disabilities present and the potential mental challenges that impact the individual family members who do not have permanent disabilities. When these issues are present, it might be necessary for the family to seek counsel. Establishing a support system is crucial in maintaining sanity and stability of the family unit.

One of the most intriguing experiences of isolation that a person ever experienced can be found in the pages of scripture that describe Jesus's battle of His life. This battle occurs in the Garden of Gethsemane:

> And when He came to the place, He said to them, Pray that you may not [at all] enter into temptation. And He withdrew from them about a stone's throw and knelt down and prayed, Saying, Father, if You are willing, remove this cup from Me; yet not My will, but [always] Yours be done. And there appeared to Him an angel from heaven, strengthening Him in spirit. And being in an agony [of mind], He prayed [all the] more earnestly and intently, and His sweat became like great clots of blood dropping down upon the ground. And when He got up from prayer, He came to the disciples and found them sleeping from grief, And He said to them, Why do you sleep? Get up and pray that you may not enter [at all] into temptation. And while He was still speaking, behold, there came a crowd, and the man called Judas, one of the twelve [apostles], was going before [leading] them. He drew near to Jesus to kiss Him. (Luke 22:40–47 AMP)

Jesus spent his final hours of freedom in the Garden of Gethsemane. Luke refers to it as the Mount of Olives. Matthew and Mark refer to the place as Gethsemane, which means "olive press." The "garden" was a grove of olive trees on the Mount of Olives. Jesus and the disciples spent a great deal of time at this location, so it had become a place of comfort. This was a special place where Jesus spent much time alone with His Father. It was here that Jesus experienced a great struggle, where He battled with His flesh. His purpose for being on Earth was about to be fulfilled very shortly, and though He knew what was going to happen, He still struggled in His humanity. Jesus felt abandoned. The disciples were supposed to be supporting Him in prayer, but they were asleep. He knew that the most painful moments he would ever experience were quickly approaching: His

Father would turn His back on Jesus because of the weight of sin Jesus would be carrying. The thought of being separated from His Father was overwhelming to Jesus. Jesus would experience separation from the sweet fellowship that He had continually experienced with His Father. The connection between them had never been broken at any time.

How do I know that Jesus was contemplating these thoughts? Jesus gave us a clue on the cross when He cried out in a loud voice to the Father, "Why have you forsaken me?" (Matthew 27:46 NIV). People who are forsaken experience feelings of isolation. Betrayal brings isolation and hurt. Jesus would experience betrayal: losing the support of His disciples who had been with Him for three years, being abandoned by his disciples, and being forsaken by His Father to whom He had always been obedient. We cannot just pass over the fact that Jesus was agonizing over what was coming His way. He was going through mental turmoil as well as emotional agony. Jesus can identify with us when we are struggling mentally with things. Jesus knows how we feel as we deal with the environment in which we are continually immersed. Jesus's anguish was so deep that He had to have an angel come and minister to Him. Jesus needed someone outside of Himself to come and comfort Him at one of the worst times in His life. If Jesus needed help, then what makes us think that we do not need help as we go up and down on the river of our emotional and mental journey that is continually before us?

It is interesting to think how the angel might have ministered to Him in this moment. Since Jesus was about to embark upon His journey through the trials and ultimately to the destination of the cross, the angel could have helped Him by:

- Sharing how His death was an act that would glorify and honor the Father
- Pointing out that He was doing exactly what His Father wanted Him to do
- Reinforcing the fact that He was acting out of obedience, of love and adoration for God, which was the perfect offering to God
- Reminding Him that His death would be the only way humankind could be eternally saved

Also, the angel could have done some very practical things. We can picture the angel embracing Jesus, holding Him ever so tightly. Perhaps the angel wiped the perspiration and blood and tears from His brow. Whatever the scene, we need to see the awful weight and intensity of our Lord's agony.

How does knowing what Jesus went through help us in our present circumstances? We need to realize that our Savior sympathizes with our situation and can know exactly what we are feeling and how we are thinking. He does not get upset because we go through these feelings that are associated with parenting special needs children. He wants to come alongside us to help us to do the parenting as well as to center us on why we are doing it. How are we to do it? We are victorious through His grace, and we do it for His glory. His presence helps us to handle the isolation that we experience from people who marginalize us, and to trust Him to lead us in how we are to maneuver the maze of life with our children. His presence will keep us from remaining isolated from people but will give us the push that is necessary to overlook people's actions and press toward what is best for our children and for ourselves. This spiritual push is powerful and quite necessary for us to accomplish God's will for our challenged children as well as for ourselves. Understanding the bigger picture for our lives and theirs changes our focus and provides for us a degree of purpose that is quite necessary for those who find themselves in environments with challenged children. With God's help, we are able to fight off the effects of solitary confinement and prevent ourselves from sinking into its clutches.

4

Where Is My Identity?

I would venture to say that all people of the world want to feel important and significant. It doesn't matter where they live or where they come from, deep within the fabric of people's makeup lives a desire to want to add something to the world in which they belong. With just under eight billion people in the world, it seems overwhelming to realize that each person has a part to play in it. With personal importance ranking so high in our lives, how does it apply to those who have mental or physical disabilities? It may be hard to imagine how much many of them could contribute, and yet, in some unique ways, they do. The desire to be important is something that is instilled in us by design of the Creator and is rooted in our humanness. This sense of importance is tied into who we are and how we identify ourselves.

Our identity is what makes us who we are and determines how we feel about ourselves. Identity, for many individuals, can be exceedingly difficult to determine, especially for those in their teenage years. The teen years comprise a journey of discovery, one that can take several years, possibly extending into a person's twenties or even thirties. Understanding who we are provides a security that helps us navigate life; it determines the path that we travel as individuals. Identity defines who we are and who we are not. If understanding identity is so important to us as human beings, how do people who cannot comprehend identity or its importance function? How do we determine how they fit into this world where busyness is the backdrop of most people's lives? Those with mental challenges, whether they can comprehend what identity is or not, have been placed on Earth for various purposes.

So many times, I have wished that I was able to enter my daughter's head so that I could know what she was thinking. I would love to know how she is "processing," and if she is able to do so, I would like to understand her interpretation of information that flows in her direction. Knowing how someone who is intellectually challenged, especially those who are extremely "low functional" operate, is a mystery. I wish she could tell me how she feels about things and could express her opinions on the issues of life. To be honest, that is what is so difficult for some of us who are parents of mentally challenged children. We are not able to communicate on a level that enables us to understand each other. I cannot talk with my daughter about the current situation in the world right now with COVID-19 and how it is impacting families all over the world and locally in our neighborhood. I cannot have a conversation with her about politics and how she feels about a particular candidate who is running for office. I cannot talk to her about a man she likes and whether she thinks he is marriage material or not. For parents, these losses of experiences are not expected when they first have children. For the children, especially those who are limited in their cognitive ability, these matters are of no concern.

My daughter does not have to be concerned about what we consider the difficulties of life. She has her own world in which she operates daily; it is free from the issues that bring us pain, struggle, and depression. Some children who have higher functional capacity do experience pain and heartache. I am just sharing where my daughter is in her intellectual ability. What is also difficult for us as parents is not knowing why she feels the way that she feels since she cannot articulate what is going on in her mind. We are left to guess what is bothering or distressing her. Many times, I believe she makes up something just to give us an answer. She lacks the ability to critically analyze things mentally as well as emotionally. However, she can respond to what we tell her to do regarding basic things such as putting the dishes away, taking a shower, or even going downstairs to get something out of the storage room. The fact that she can perform certain basic functions brings about a sense of importance for her as an individual. Thoughts of importance do not appear to be part of her thinking process, but for us as parents, who are the caregivers, a sense of importance should be part of ours on behalf of the children. Whether or not the mentally or physically challenged individuals understand identity or significance, we should treat them in a way that shows that they do.

It is easy to feel that God has robbed us of what we believe to rightfully belong to us as parents. It is every parent's desire to have children who are healthy and have no mental or physical issues, to watch them grow and develop in an environment that will lead them to be productive citizens in the world, and to be able to experience all the experiences that children normally have while developing into adults. We want their lives to be even better than the lives we enjoyed. When children are born with disabilities, especially with low-functioning capabilities, the dreams and expectations that were present in our minds die. Parents may feel abandoned. They may feel that God has intentionally brought struggle into their lives. This can cause them to drift away from the One who loves them the most, God Himself. Accompanying these feelings toward God is possible depression at times that can be tied into the daily grind of caregiving for the mentally or physically challenged child that now is part of the daily routine.

If personal identity and significance are so important for us, how do we establish a mindset that confers that same sense of importance upon our mentally or physically challenged child that can last for a lifetime? How are we able to view them in a different way that can change our understanding regarding their individual significance? Let us look at Psalm 139:13–16 (AMP):

> For You did form my inward parts; You did knit me together in my mother's womb. I will confess and praise You, for You are fearful and wonderful and for the awful wonder of my birth! Wonderful are Your works, and that my inner self knows right well. My frame was not hidden from You when I was being formed in secret [and] intricately and curiously wrought [as if embroidered with various colors] in the depths of the earth [a region of darkness and mystery]. Your eyes saw my unformed substance, and in Your book all the days [of my life] were written before ever they took shape, when as yet there were none of them.

This text speaks directly to everyone who has been born of a woman, which includes everybody on the planet from the beginning of time, except Adam and Eve. Notice the wording that is used by David regarding the presence of God being in the womb at the time of conception. God is the One who was bringing about the development of the child. The way a person is created in the womb is a process that is orchestrated by God Himself. Everything that God creates is for a purpose and is to bring glory to Him. This verse communicates that God is the author of life, and He designs each person uniquely as He weaves them together in the womb. I am not denying the biological aspect of how life is formed through the chromosomal contributions from each parent. God is the One who designed how this natural physical development of life occurs. Since He is all powerful, He can do anything He desires and can even overrule natural occurrences in life if He chooses to do so. If God is present during the formation of life taking place in the womb, then no mistakes are being made. See how this scripture can speak to everyone about identity. All people are unique in their own way with no two persons being alike, even twins. God has designed each person with a unique identity. That means that our identities are derived from God's character, not anything else. Every person is a creation of God and is made in His image, and His image is perfect.

Over the years, I have come to realize that most of us who deal with identity issues struggle with three perspectives that are intertwined:

- What people think of us
- What we perceive people think about us
- What we feel about ourselves

The combination of these three perspectives aids in the formulation of how individuals view themselves. In many instances, the view is not quite accurate. We are to see ourselves through God's eyes. Seeing ourselves through the lens of what He says we are helps us to have an accurate assessment of who we truly are. This is how a proper identity is created in our lives. This perspective applies to people who are mentally or physically challenged even though they are not able to understand it. All people, whether living with a disability or not, are important to God, and their identities are defined through His eyes. Understanding that God begins creating our unique individuality in the womb helps us to see that God has ordained and designed in great detail who each person is to be. With this thought in mind, we should now be able to see intellectually and physically challenged individuals as having divine purpose and significance.

Not only does this verse speak to identity, but it also speaks to self-image, self-esteem, and self-abasement. Notice that the psalmist says that we are fearfully and wonderfully made. When God sees us, He sees the perfection of His design. He has fashioned us and made us all in His image, which does not designate whether our minds and bodies should be a certain way or should all be the same. If He has crafted us in a unique way, it is imperative that we understand that "normal" can now be perceived as inclusive of all people whether they have a disability or not. If all individuals are fashioned by God, that means He has made them to be the way He did for His divine purpose. The question then becomes how to help the mentally and physically challenged children to develop into the people God wants them to be. Maybe that is where we need to understand what we can glean from this scripture—that they already are what God has called them to be.

Another passage that helps us understand how God thinks concerning our identity as well as who He has made us to be is Jeremiah 1:4–5:

> Then the word of the Lord came to me [Jeremiah], saying, Before I formed you in the womb I knew [and] approved of you [as My chosen instrument], and before you were born, I separated and set you apart, consecrating you; [and] I appointed you as a prophet to the nations. (AMP)

We can recognize from the mouth of Jeremiah, who is speaking in the first person, that God formed him in the womb. This is additional insight relative to identity that we gleaned from David. Charles Dyer writes, in *Bible Knowledge Commentary,* that the word *knew* in the text goes beyond the meaning of intellectual knowledge but conveys close personal relationship.[1]

Jeremiah tells us that God knew before he was born that He was separating him to be used for a specific purpose. Jeremiah had a call on his life before he was even in the womb. If God knows us before we are conceived, it is easy to understand that He can know the direction our lives will take and determine how He will use us based on His foreknowledge. Jeremiah says the same thing as David: God had formed him in the womb. I hope that you are noticing the connection of in these scriptures. God also says in Ephesians 2:10 that we are His workmanship:

> For we are God's [own] handiwork (His workmanship), recreated in Christ Jesus, [born anew] that we may do those good works which God predestined (planned beforehand) for us [taking paths which He prepared ahead of time,] that we should walk in them [living the good life which He prearranged and made ready for us to live.] (Ephesians 2:10 AMP)

I know that this verse has to do with believers and how God can use them to accomplish His work, but we can also see another application. I want to point out something that I believe is especially important to understand about the character of God. If He has designed individuals who are mentally challenged to be the way they are, that means that God knows their mental capacity and whether they can understand the gospel message or not, despite whether they show any indication of understanding. If mentally challenged people are not able to understand the gospel message but are in the will of God by operating in the capacity in which they were designed by him, then God is responsible for handling their salvation and knowing what He has for them. We must trust God for that area of their lives if we are unable to know through the communication process where they are with God. We do know through our experience with them that they are doing and being what they have been created and called by God to do and be.

It is essential for us to look at an experience that Moses, at eighty years of age, had with God. I believe we can get some additional information about how we are to look at our intellectually and physically challenged children. It is necessary to include the entire account of this conversation that God had with Moses to capture the fullness of what occurred. It is found in the book of Exodus:

Now Moses kept the flock of Jethro his father-in-law, the priest of Midian; and he led the flock to the back or west side of the wilderness and came to Horeb or Sinai, the mountain of God. The Angel of the Lord appeared to him in a flame of fire out of the midst of a bush; and he looked, and behold, the bush burned with fire, yet was not consumed. And Moses said, I will now turn aside and see this great sight, why the bush is not burned. And when the Lord saw that he turned aside to see, God called to him out of the midst of the bush and said, Moses, Moses! And he said, here am I. God said, Do not come near; put your shoes off your feet, for the place on which you stand is holy ground. Also He said, I am the God of your father, the God of Abraham, the God of Isaac, and the God of Jacob. And Moses hid his face, for he was afraid to look at God. And the Lord said, I have surely seen the affliction of My people who are in Egypt and have heard their cry because of their taskmasters and oppressors; for I know their sorrows and sufferings and trials. And I have come down to deliver them out of the hand and power of the Egyptians and to bring them up out of that land to a land good and large, a land flowing with milk and honey [a land of plenty]—to the place of the Canaanite, the Hittite, the Amorite, the Perizzite, the Hivite, and the Jebusite. Now behold, the cry of the Israelites has come to Me, and I have also seen how the Egyptians oppress them. Come now therefore, and I will send you to Pharaoh, that you may bring forth My people, the Israelites, out of Egypt. And Moses said to God, Who am I, that I should go to Pharaoh and bring the Israelites out of Egypt? God said, I will surely be with you; and this shall be the sign to you that I have sent you: when you have brought the people out of Egypt, you shall serve God on this mountain [Horeb, or Sinai.]And Moses said to God, Behold, when I come to the Israelites and say to them, The God of your fathers has sent me to you, and they say to me, What is His name? What shall I say to them? And God said to Moses, I AM WHO I AM and WHAT I AM, and I WILL BE WHAT I WILL BE; and He said, You shall say this to the Israelites: I AM has sent me to you! God said also to Moses, This shall you say to the Israelites: The Lord, the God of your fathers, of Abraham, of Isaac, and of Jacob, has sent me to you! This is My name forever, and by this name I am to be remembered to all generations. Go, gather the elders of Israel together [the mature teachers and tribal leaders], and say to them, The Lord God of your fathers, the God of Abraham, of Isaac, and of Jacob, appeared to me, saying, I have surely visited you and seen that which is done to you in Egypt; And I have declared that I will bring you up out of the affliction of Egypt to the land of the Canaanite, the Hittite, the Amorite, the Perizzite, the Hivite, and the Jebusite, to a land flowing with milk and honey. And [the elders] shall believe and obey your voice; and you shall go, you and the elders of Israel, to the king of Egypt and you shall say to him, The Lord, the God of the Hebrews, has met with us; and now let us go, we beseech you, three days' journey into the wilderness, that we may sacrifice to the Lord our God. And I know that the king of Egypt will not let you go [unless forced to do so], no, not by a mighty hand. So I will stretch out My hand and smite Egypt with all My wonders which I will do in it; and after that he will let you go. And I will give this people favor and respect in the sight of the Egyptians; and it shall be that when you go, you shall not go empty-handed. But every woman shall [insistently] solicit of her neighbor and of her that may be residing at her house jewels and articles of silver and gold, and garments, which you shall put on your sons and daughters; and you shall strip the Egyptians [of belongings due to you]. (Exodus 3:1–22 AMP)

And Moses answered, but behold, they will not believe me or listen to and obey my voice; for they will say, The

Lord has not appeared to you. And the Lord said to him, what is that in your hand? And he said, A rod. And He said, Cast it on the ground. And he did so, and it became a serpent [the symbol of royal and divine power worn on the crown of the Pharaohs]; and Moses fled from before it.

And the Lord said to Moses, put forth your hand and take it by the tail. And he stretched out his hand and caught it, and it became a rod in his hand, [This you shall do, said the Lord] that the elders may believe that the Lord, the God of their fathers, of Abraham, of Isaac, and of Jacob, has indeed appeared to you. The Lord said also to him, Put your hand into your bosom. He put his hand into his bosom, and when he took it out, behold, his hand was leprous, as white as snow. [God] said, Put your hand into your bosom again. So, he put his hand back into his bosom, and when he took it out, behold, it was restored as the rest of his flesh. [Then God said] If they will not believe you or heed the voice or the testimony of the first sign, they may believe the voice or the witness of the second sign. But if they will also not believe these two signs or heed your voice, you shall take some water of the river [Nile] and pour it upon the dry land; and the water which you take out of the river [Nile] shall become blood on the dry land. And Moses said to the Lord, O Lord, I am not eloquent or a man of words, neither before nor since You have spoken to Your servant; for I am slow of speech and have a heavy and awkward tongue. And the Lord said to him, Who has made man's mouth? Or who makes the dumb, or the deaf, or the seeing, or the blind? Is it not I, the Lord? Now therefore go, and I will be with your mouth and will teach you what you shall say. And he said, Oh, my Lord, I pray You, send by the hand of [some other] whom You will [send]. Then the anger of the Lord blazed against Moses; He said, Is there not Aaron your brother, the Levite? I know he can speak well. Also, he is

> coming out to meet you, and when he sees you, he will be overjoyed. You must speak to him and put the words in his mouth; and I will be with your mouth and with his mouth and will teach you what you shall do. He shall speak for you to the people, acting as a mouthpiece for you, and you shall be as God to him. And you shall take this rod in your hand with which you shall work the signs [that prove I sent you]. (Exodus 4:1–17 AMP)

In this scripture, we witness a conversation that takes place between God and Moses. Moses had been second in command in Egypt for some forty years prior to this encounter with God. For the past forty years, he had been a shepherd on the back hills of the mountains. God was now commissioning him to go and deliver the people of Israel. During this conversation, we recognize that Moses didn't really want to do what God had asked. He was straightforward with God and proceeded to present to God four complaints. The first complaint was his objection to God's command because of his lack of ability (3:11) and his lack of authority (3:13). Moses doubted his ability to confront the new Pharaoh (Amenhotep II) successfully and to lead the nation out of slavery. Moses' second objection was the feeling that the Israelites would challenge his assertion that God had sent him to deliver them. He then posed two more objections: his fear that the people would repudiate his authority (4:1) and his lack of eloquence in speech (4:10).

Moses believed that he was personally inadequate to fulfill the mission God expected of him. This feeling of inadequacy came from a lack of confidence and security within himself. Though being a great leader some forty years prior, he now looked upon himself as inadequate, even though God let him know that He was going to be with him in the endeavor.

When we examine this personal inadequacy of Moses a little further, we observe that he had slipped into a mindset that had developed over time. This had disabled him and rendered him helpless to accomplish anything that was out of his realm of comfort. Many individuals today are disabled mentally, not because they have the incapacity to process knowledge, but because they have allowed their minds to become immobilized by fear, depression, or lack of motivation. When people get stuck in these mindsets, they are rendered helpless; they are just like people who have low-functioning mental capacity. I believe that we can get a major insight into God's mind from Exodus 4:11: "And the Lord said to him, Who has made man's mouth? Or who makes the dumb, or the deaf, or the seeing, or the blind? Is it not I, the Lord?" (AMP).

Once again, we can discern that God is consistent in what He conveys through the mouth of different individuals over a span of years who were not part of the same period. Here in Exodus, God made a statement to Moses that might surprise us. God said that He was the One responsible for creating the dumb and the deaf and those who are blind. Are you able to grasp now that the way we look at disabilities and the way God views them are significantly different? He has created individuals who are born with disabilities, whether intellectual or physical. If God is all powerful, He can change things in the womb and to create a different outcome. Those who are born with disabilities are born that way not because it is their fault; they had nothing to do with their condition when they were born. Their condition, however, can facilitate the accomplishment of God's will through them in the future. Just as a tree or plant that blooms each year at the same time is under the will of God, people who are intellectually or physically challenged are that way because it is the will of God. The question then is, are we able to help them in their journey in fulfilling God's will for their lives? As we endeavor to do this for them, aren't we fulfilling God's will in our lives as caregivers? In understanding that God has uniquely positioned them in our lives, we will also understand how God wants us to help move them in a direction that brings joy to them as well as to ourselves and others.

Now that we can distinguish God's heart regarding viewing our identity correctly, we must learn how to carry out how God wants to use us as parents in the lives of our children with disabilities. In order to see a picture of what this may look like, we must examine the following scripture:

> And David said, Is there still anyone left of the house of Saul to whom I may show kindness for Jonathan's sake? And of the house of Saul there was a servant whose name was Ziba. When they had called him to David, he said

> to him, Are you Ziba? He said, I, your servant, am he. The king said, Is there not still someone of the house of Saul to whom I may show the [unfailing, unsought, unlimited] mercy and kindness of God? Ziba replied, Jonathan has yet a son who is lame in his feet. And the king said, Where is he? Ziba replied, He is in the house of Machir son of Ammiel in Lo-debar. Then King David sent and brought him from the house of Machir son of Ammiel at Lo-debar. And Mephibosheth son of Jonathan, the son of Saul, came to David and fell on his face and did obeisance. David said, Mephibosheth! And he answered, Behold your servant! David said to him, Fear not, for I will surely show you kindness for Jonathan your father's sake and will restore to you all the land of Saul your father [grandfather], and you shall eat at my table always. And [the cripple] bowed himself and said, What is your servant, that you should look upon such a dead dog as I am? (2 Samuel 9:1–8 AMP)

David and Jonathan, son of King Saul, were exceptionally good friends. They were so close in the friendship that they made a covenant of friendship with each other. Both King Saul and Jonathan were killed in battle, and David was not engaged in any conflicts at the time. Things had calmed down and were quite peaceful. It was during this time that David asked Ziba, his servant, if there was anyone in Saul's household to whom he could show mercy and kindness. Ziba indicated that there was one person named Mephibosheth, the son of Jonathan, who was crippled in both feet. Upon hearing these words from Ziba, David immediately sent for Mephibosheth. He restored Saul's personal estate to him and supported him on a royal pension.

David demanded that Mephibosheth go to live with him as well as sit at his royal table. Wow! I believe there is a huge message that can be taken away from this encounter. David, because of his love for Jonathan, wanted to be a blessing to someone from King Saul's family. He wanted to extend kindness to whomever that person might be. Mephibosheth, the son of Jonathan, was the recipient of that kindness. Mephibosheth, as you can see from verse 8, had a major problem with self-image and his view of himself. He had become lame in both feet because of being dropped by a nurse who was taking care of him as she was running away from a conflict when Mephibosheth was five years of age. He now was a man and had a family despite his condition. However, mentally he had a huge inferiority complex.

Depending on the severity of the physical handicap, individuals can view themselves as damaged goods and worthless. This is how Mephibosheth thought of himself. This is the meaning of the expression that he used when he referred to himself as a "dead dog." Many individuals today feel the same way, and many are treated as though they are as well. Those with mental disabilities may realize this to a certain extent, but may not, depending on the severity of their condition. The story of Mephibosheth shows us that people with physical disabilities can also suffer with mental issues that develop because of the perspective they have with respect to their physical limitations. Though mentally capable of thinking properly, their minds can become filled with thoughts that cripple them and prevent them from functioning at their highest mental potential.

David showed a love that was unconditional. He was not deterred by Mephibosheth's condition. He spoke directly to him and invited him to the royal table. He was going to be adopted into the family as one of David's sons. Mephibosheth had access to the king at any time, and he was given a place of honor. What a picture of what God does for us!

We are adopted as sons and daughters into the family of God through Christ, given access to everything in the kingdom, given the privilege of entering His presence, and are invited to sit at the table with Him! This picture of love and kindness that God gives to us is what we see in the story of David and Mephibosheth. David shows us that we are to approach our children with disabilities with the willingness to seat them at a place of honor and to extend kindness to them. By implementing such practices, we are giving them what is necessary to combat what they may feel about themselves. The love that is being extended elevates them to be what God has called them to be. Because David was keeping a commitment to his friend Jonathan, Mephibosheth was the recipient of blessings. He was given dignity, significance, an identity, and honor. David received something also. He experienced the privilege of being blessed by blessing someone who, undoubtedly, at that time, would not have received it from anyone else.

God can change the trajectory of our lives as we submit to His will through our obedience. It is not easy to raise children with disabilities in challenging environments. However, when we can adopt God's perspective, which is much higher than our own, and are willing to accept the will of God for our lives, though the challenge might be difficult, the journey can bring with it great joy.

NOTE

1 Charles H. Dyer, "Jeremiah" in *Bible Knowledge Commentary*, ed. John F. Walvoord and Roy B. Zuck (USA: Victor Books, 1988), 1130.

5

Journeying Through the Idiosyncrasies

There are many kinds of movies—drama, romance, action, mystery, horror, comedy, and documentary. The billion-dollar movie industry will keep making movies as long as people desire to see them.

Some movies will leave you scratching your head. Some movies are strange, having elements that are quite peculiar. In fact, the website hiddenremote.com has identified Tim Burton as one of the most prolific directors and producers of weird movies. Some of his movies are *Mars Attacks, Beetlejuice, Charlie and the Chocolate Factory, Alice in Wonderland,* and *Big Fish.* You can find the top ten weird movies by Tim Burton on the hiddenremote.com website. Some movies just do not make sense and are filled with unpredictable oddities. We must remember that the person who wrote the screenplays or the books from which the movies are derived are the ones who came up with many of the elements that are strange or peculiar to us.

Life for parents of children with intellectual or physical disabilities can be like a movie that they live every day. The type of mental or physical disability the children have will determine the types of "movies" the parents will experience on a regular basis. It is safe to say that the environments for these parents are filled with idiosyncrasies. The word *idiosyncrasy* means "a mode of behavior or way of thought peculiar to an individual" (www.dictionary.com). Synonyms include *quirk, oddity, mannerism,* or *peculiarity.*

I can say as a parent, as well as someone who has known over the years several families with children with disabilities, that all these families have experienced idiosyncrasies with their children. But I can also say that all people have idiosyncrasies. They do things and say things that may be considered strange to other people. The difference with children who are mentally or physically challenged is that the family environment is filled with these idiosyncrasies on a daily basis. For example, I remember that our David, as a little boy, was always moving my shoes from what he considered to be *his* spot on the shoe shelf. In our house, we have a set of shelves that we use for storing our shoes when we come into the house. There are three shelves, and we place our shoes in any available location. One day when I came home from work, I put my shoes on one of the shelves. When I came back later, I noticed that my shoes had been moved and my son's shoes were in the spot where my shoes had been. This happened on a regular basis. I thought to myself, *This is really strange.* But I accepted it. For him, that spot was for his shoes, and his shoes only.

Having to have a specific location for a pair of shoes would be considered peculiar, wouldn't you say? It reminds me of what used to occur in church on Sundays when I was growing up. There were some older church attendees who felt compelled to sit in the same pew every week. If they saw that someone else was sitting in what they considered to be *their* seat, they would become upset. It did not matter whether it was someone they knew or a visitor, that seat belonged to them, and they were going to sit there if possible!

My daughter exhibits more severe idiosyncrasies than my son. One of her oddities is to stay in her room all day by herself. She lives there. She is perfectly content to stay in her space watching her videos, listening to her music, and playing with her Barbie dolls. This is not considered to be normal behavior, but for her, this is the norm, and she is content with it. She has been staying in her room ever since she was a little girl. The only time she comes out is for dinner and to see if anyone is around now and then. When Bev was homeschooling, Danielle came out of her room every day for lessons.

One of the biggest issues when integrating some mentally challenged children into various social situations is behavior. The social competence range of children is dependent upon their level of autism. Behavior of children in public is most likely one of the biggest problems for parents and definitely plays into the decision for many to stay isolated at home. There are quite a few peculiarities in the behavioral realm. The specific behavior manifestations in each child determine how often, as well as how long, a child can stay in public. Other issues might have to do with cognitive understanding and the ability to process information that is received by the child from someone, whether out of the home or in the home. Some mentally challenged children freeze when they do not understand what has been asked. They are slow in processing the information if they can do it at all. So, there may be a blank stare without a word being said. The other person is left wondering why the child did not provide an answer to a direct question. I have encountered this repeatedly with both my children.

When we had our son tested in elementary school, we found out that he had a mild case of Asperger's syndrome (also known as Asperger's disorder). We learn the following from the Autism society about Asperger's syndrome:

> [Asperger's syndrome] was first described in the 1940s by Viennese pediatrician Hans Asperger, who observed autism-like behaviors and difficulties with social and communication skills in boys who had normal intelligence and language development. Many professionals felt that Asperger's Syndrome was simply a milder form of autism and used the term "high-functioning autism" to describe these individuals. Uta Frith, a professor at the Institute of Cognitive Neuroscience of University College London and editor of *Autism and Asperger Syndrome*, describes individuals with Asperger's as "having a dash of autism."[1]

Other features include clumsy and uncoordinated motor movements, social impairment with extreme obtuseness, limited interests and/or unusual preoccupations, repetitive routines or rituals, speech and language peculiarities, and non-verbal communication problems. Our son did not have all these characteristics, but he exhibited some of them. The way that the clinician described it to us was that he had a *touch* of Asperger's syndrome. Well, that explained the shoe rearrangement and some of the other repetitive things that he had been doing on a regular basis.

I will share another situation that occurred several years ago when we started attending Epic Church in Philadelphia. David was interested in working with the production team, which was responsible for handling the setup of the camera and sound equipment. He had become interested in sound equipment and electronic devices when he was a teenager. Shortly after he signed up for the production team, the leader approached me to talk about some concerns he had regarding David. David had been given tasks to do but wasn't doing them very well. The leader noticed that David was not able to perform several tasks simultaneously. I told the leader that David had to learn one thing at a time. He would be able to do a task but would have to do it repetitively until he was comfortable. The leader then changed the way he worked with David, assigning him something that he would work on for a while and then switching him to something else for a while until he was able to "get it." As a result, David has become one of the most reliable volunteers on the production team. He gets there on time and is always ready to do whatever assignment he is given. With a little patience and proper direction, what had been a struggle became a personal strength. Once he felt comfortable with one task, he could move to another. As he learned the different assignments one at a time, he was able to remember how to do them. The tasks were no longer overwhelming.

For me, to do something over and over the same way every day without change is exceedingly difficult. Maybe that is why it has been challenging for me to be a day trader in the stock market. It is tedious to apply the same technique every day, not deviating from what can work every time. Methodology must always supersede emotion. I am way too emotional when it comes to trading. Yet, if I were able to exhibit what is a peculiarity for David in trading, who knows how much money I could have accumulated by now! By the way, I do not have very much money in the account. David probably would be way better at it than I am!

David had multiple issues to deal with: diabetes, fragile X syndrome, obesity, and Asperger's syndrome. As parents, we were mentally overwhelmed that our child had to deal with these issues so early in life. Parents never want to see their children go through struggles, whether intellectual or physical. There is a feeling of helplessness knowing that, in most cases, we can do only so much to help them.

At this point, I would like to bring to light a verse in scripture that tells us that God's people are peculiar: "But ye are a chosen generation, a royal priesthood, a holy nation, a peculiar people; that ye should show forth the praises of him who hath called you out of darkness into his marvelous light" (1 Peter 2:9 KJV).

Please note the specific description of the word *peculiar.* Believers become a "peculiar people"—a people for God's own possession—"a people saved to be His own." Isn't it an unbelievable thought that God would make us His special possession? Something that is special is adored or admired and is well taken care of. It is cherished because it is of great worth. God considers us to be worth more than any treasure that exists. We are His possession, and He will make sure that we are secure and well protected. He has promised that for all those who are His.

I felt it necessary to use this scripture to show that, when people become believers in Christ, they are called *peculiar* people. In this context, the word *peculiar*, when translated from the Greek, means "God's own possession"—a *special* possession. Individuals who do not know Jesus personally as their Savior, in most instances, think that people of God are peculiar. They do not understand the things that genuine Christians do, such as living their lives in an extremely strict way, being sacrificial in extreme ways, and finding joy in what others consider deplorable situations. Those who are not believers view us as having idiosyncrasies that are "out of this world," When we use principles from scripture, we see they are not from this world. They come from the Kingdom of God, which is another world.

We use the term "special needs" to refer to individuals who have physical or intellectual challenges. Most of society see these individuals as not fitting into the category of "normal." *Special*, as it is used for those with mental disabilities, is a term that indicates that the person is deficient in intellectual ability or cognitive understanding. If we look at the way God uses the term, it carries with it a different connotation. The word *peculiar*, then, is a word that does not minimize a person's ability; rather, it describes them as being of value to God. We all have some kind of deficiency, yet the "special" tag is not attached to us. If we can take what God says about believers being special to God, meaning that they are God's treasured possessions, and apply it to those who are intellectually and physically challenged, just think what having God's view would do for us in the way we handle the idiosyncrasies that are exhibited by them, as difficult as they may be!

On several occasions, we also have had to deal with David's anger. He would get upset over seemingly insignificant things at times. Sometimes he would be angry, and we would have no understanding about the cause. To me, this anger was a peculiarity, especially because there appeared to be no reason for it. One of the reasons his anger was so frustrating was that he would never tell us *why* he was upset. We had no idea what was going on inside of his head. Without this information, it was quite difficult for us to help him. This kind of scenario would take place on a regular basis. There have been times over the years when he would come into the house from work with an attitude. When we'd ask him what was wrong, the answer would be, "nothing." Seeing David feeling this way impacted us because we were then drawn into his situation emotionally without knowing why he was feeling what he was feeling. Many times, we never did find out. Sometimes he would give a little bit of information to his mother.

Anger, I believe, is one of the emotions that mentally and physically challenged children experience automatically. The anger that is exhibited by the child might be delayed at times, until the child recognizes the disability. Children might be perfectly fine with their disabilities until they reach a certain age—the age when they are able to distinguish that they are different than their peers, that they are treated differently, or other people say thing about them.

It is possible that children with intellectual and/or physical challenges have a difficult time processing their emotions and identifying different emotions. If they do not have a reservoir of understood emotions from which to draw, they might not be able to know exactly what they are feeling. Anger is a natural emotion that also occurs among individuals who do not have disabilities, and it is predictable that this anger response occurs in children with disabilities. This anger can pop up at any time for no apparent reason, at least in our minds. I have no idea what goes on in David's mind when he becomes angry.

One time, we were at the airport getting ready to leave on vacation to Florida. We were standing in the Transportation Security Administration (TSA) line waiting to go through security. As we were approaching the area where personal items like shoes, cell phones, bags, and so forth are to be placed, David was trying to take his shoe off with his foot. After numerous attempts without success, I said to him, "Just reach down and pull your sneaks off please." Out of nowhere, like a hot rushing wind, David yelled in my face and said, "Leave me alone!" The anger displayed on his face was on the edge of rage. We were close to each other, so it might have appeared that I was ready to grab him. Bev jumped between us because the scene appeared to be getting out of hand. Can you imagine getting into a fight at the airport with your son while TSA officers and countless people are standing around watching? It would not have been pretty, especially because of my position as a minister of the Gospel. Thank God nothing physical happened between David and me. We went through the line with some looks from bystanders, but that was about it. His anger had just risen out of nowhere like lava from a volcano. Still to this day, I do not know why he was so angry just because I asked him to take his sneaks off properly.

I can share another story from my college days at Penn State. It was my second summer there. The school at the time operated on a term system as opposed to a semester system. I had just finished my fourth term and was entering my fifth, which was to start in a few days. I had moved my things from East Halls to South Halls, the dorms where students would stay for the summer. I was first to arrive at the dorm room, so I unpacked my things and set up the room in a highly organized way. I had a large stereo system that extended slightly into my roommate's "space." I did not know who my roommate was yet, but I was soon to find out. Later that day, he arrived. After pleasantries, the war began. He demanded to know why my stereo was on his side of the room. He did not even wait for an explanation. He just slid my stereo to my side of the desk and yelled, "You keep your stuff on your side, and I keep my stuff on my side!" I thought to myself, *What is wrong with this guy?* I stood there in shock. This was only the first day of a term that would be my worst with regard to roommates.

Jerry (the name I will use here for him) had a physical handicap. He walked with a limp, and one of his arms did not function properly; it hung down from his shoulder without any motion. Jerry always seemed to have an attitude and was very sarcastic. At the time, I was only eighteen years of age, and I did not understand things the way I do now. Even though I did my best to be nice to Jerry, he constantly displayed anger for what appeared to me to be no reason whatsoever. This was peculiar behavior that I did not understand. As I think about Jerry some years later, I believe that his condition played into the way he acted. He was angry at his condition and took it out on people who had nothing to do with it. Talking to him was extremely difficult because of his constant sarcasm, arrogance, meanness, and anger. I learned to just be quiet and try not to say much to him. I also did not touch anything on his side of the room. I was on edge the entire term and could not wait until he was out of my life. It was peaceful when he was not around, and I valued my time alone. I believe Jerry's physical disability encouraged his nasty attitude toward life and people and played a major part in the reason he behaved so badly and kept people from trying to get to know him. He isolated himself from people who could possibly become his friends. Apparently, he did not desire that. He was in his world by himself, hurting people because he was hurting.

This cognitive behavior emanated from a mindset that had been established because of a physical disability. It appeared that he had not received any kind of counseling. I have no idea whether he wanted any or not, or whether his parents had attempted to facilitate it. Maybe they had tried but had no success. This is my assessment as I look back at the situation. Could I be wrong? I could, but as I think about the hundreds of people whom I have come across over the years who have had physical disabilities, I have seen similar behavior displayed, especially the anger. This anger fits into the category of idiosyncrasies that are exhibited in intellectually as well as physically challenged individuals. These behaviors, as you can see in the examples that I have provided, are present during the earlier stages of development. Once again, depending on the severity of the disability and what type of disability an individual has, the anger can be coupled with aggression. In some cases, medication must be implemented to bring calm to the mentally challenged person as well as peace to the family unit.

A friend mentioned to me something that she had recently read about anger and young children and her experience as a young mom. She said, "I wish I had realized something as a young mother concerning young children who throw tantrums out of anger. The article pointed out that toddlers who 'act out' do so because they, one, do not have the vocabulary to explain the emotions they are experiencing, which sometimes are immensely powerful emotions! And two, so many times toddlers have not been raised by parents who take the time to sit with them and gently try to reflect to them what they think the child may be feeling so that the child feels understood. So, instead, the child may just fling himself on the floor in the grocery store and kick and scream because he is frustrated about something, overly tired, in need of physical affection and reassurance, hungry, or coming down sick, but he doesn't know how to express exactly what it is bothering him because he doesn't have the vocabulary."

She brought up some remarkably interesting questions. Is it possible that some of David's unexplained anger came from the same frustration that causes young children to throw tantrums? She suggested, "Maybe he just doesn't know how to verbalize what he is experiencing, and so it comes out as an amorphous agitation that he doesn't know how to communicate." She then asked another question: "Do you think there is a common experience there between incredibly young children without a lot of vocabulary yet and even older children who may display anger without words because they just don't have them? It is highly possible and probable that children with mental disabilities have difficulty knowing how to properly decipher their emotions. There is also a strong possibility that part of the disability is that they are not able to understand completely how to merge a proper feeling with their thinking process. If parents can get their children to understand how feelings work and get them to identify what feelings they need to convey, they will have accomplished a tremendous feat. Success in helping mentally challenged children to understand their feelings is dependent on the degree of cognitive ability."

People are created by God with a uniqueness that makes them who they are. No one else can claim to be them because of this uniqueness. Just think, if everyone who has ever existed was lined up and their fingerprints were examined, the fingerprints of no two individuals would be the same. The possibility of fingerprints matching is impossible. God did create so there is a possibility that we might have some *similar* characteristics. These characteristics are what enable us to identify things that are in common as well as those that are not in common. How should we view idiosyncrasies when it comes to our children with mental and physical disabilities? We are to see them in the same light as we do with those who do not have a diagnosed disability.

Since everybody is born into an imperfect world, can we say that everyone has a disability? Spiritually, we know that all are born with a spiritual disability: the state of being without God. Spiritually, those who are operating without God in their lives are living in an environment that is disabled. There is an inability to have intimacy with God and the impossibility of being able to experience His presence in their lives. Spiritually, we can be completed only by God, not by a person. We all might not have the same kind of disabilities that those who are mentally and physically challenged have, but we all have at least one disability. It is quite simple to explain. Wouldn't any person who has an incurable physical condition be considered to have a disability? Among the most common incurable diseases are acquired immune deficiency syndrome (AIDS), Parkinson's disease, and Alzheimer's disease. Diabetes and multiple sclerosis are other diseases that often cannot be cured. Wouldn't those who have conditions such as depression, dementia and Alzheimer's be considered individuals who suffer from disabilities? What about people who suffer from concussions or who have to take medicine that keeps them physically alive but causes memory loss over time? This is what happened to my mother-in-law. At any given time, any person who is impacted or impaired mentally, whether temporarily or permanently, has experienced a disability. Even people who go through mood swings are experiencing a disability.

Let us consider the definition of disability:

> The lack of competent physical and mental faculties; the absence of legal capability to perform an act. The term disability usually signifies an incapacity to exercise <u>all</u> the legal rights ordinarily possessed by an average person. Convicts, minors, and incompetents are regarded to be under a disability - a condition which prevents one from performing all usual physical or mental functions. This usually means a permanent state, like blindness, but in some cases is temporary. In recent times society and the law have dictated that people with disabilities should be accommodated and encouraged to operate to <u>their</u> maximum potential and have the right to participate in societal and governmental activity without impediments.

> Hence, access by ramps, elevators, special parking places and other special arrangements have become required in many statutes. 2) A legal impediment, including being a minor who cannot make a contract, or being insane or incompetent, as determined by others.[2]

A disability is any condition that makes it more difficult for a person to navigate through and interact with the world. These conditions or impairments may be cognitive, developmental, intellectual, mental, physical, sensory, or a combination of multiple factors. Impairments that cause disability may be present from birth or appear later during a person's lifetime. If we apply this definition to all people, we see that we all have had a disability or will have one during our lifetimes. Along with the acknowledgment that we all have some type of disability is the recognition that we have idiosyncrasies that go along with these disabilities. Idiosyncrasies can exist without a disability. However, idiosyncrasies can be exacerbated because of a disability. If we can understand that idiosyncrasies are part of the uniqueness of people in general, regardless of the presence of a disability, we can begin to see all people through the eyes of Christ. The idiosyncrasies should not dissuade us from accomplishing God's will, which is to love Him and to love people as He has created them.

NOTES

1 Autism Society, "What is Autism?" accessed April 15, 2020. (www.autism-society.org/what-is/aspergers-syndrome).

2 A Law Dictionary, Adapted to the Constitution and Laws of the United States. By John Bouvier, "disability," retrieved September 8 2021 (https://legal-dictionary.thefreedictionary.com/Disability)

6

The Food Battle

Christmastime has always been a wonderful time of year for me. It has been since I was a kid. Not only was it exciting to receive gifts, but the food we ate at the time was also part of the experience. The food parade would last for over a month, commencing on Thanksgiving Day. Thanksgiving was really the beginning of the Christmas season. On Thanksgiving Day there would be a huge meal with all kinds of food. I recall my aunt staying up most of the night fixing dinner for the next day—a meal that would be eaten in less than half an hour. There was the turkey that was filled with stuffing. Then there were cranberry sauce, mashed potatoes and gravy, string beans, corn bread, macaroni and cheese, potato salad, and so much more. To top off the meal, we would have dessert which was a choice between sweet potato pie and pound cake that had been made from scratch. The food from Thanksgiving Day would last for the remainder of the week. Shortly after Thanksgiving, we consumed dozens of cookies that emerged from everywhere. At school, the teachers would bring cookies into the classroom. Parents and relatives would bake cookies for students to take to class. At home, my aunt, sister, and mother would bake more cookies. I would go back and forth between two houses. My mother lived around the corner from my aunt, with whom I was staying. There were cookies all around me. Cookie Monster from Sesame Street would be in heaven with all the cookies. Then there was the meal on Christmas day, which was quite like the one on Thanksgiving Day, except there were even more sides from which to choose. We must not forget the candy that would also be provided along with the food during the Christmas season.

Every year the tradition was the same, and along with this cycle of food was the weight gain that came along with all the eating. I would put on five to ten pounds every Christmas season without question. The problem was that I would find it difficult to lose the weight once I gained it. The tradition of eating like this throughout my childhood years continued into my adult years, even after I was married. The tradition of Thanksgiving still exists with the same kinds of food. I can say that there has even been more variety added. There are now more vegetables as well as a special punch, and brownies have been added to the dessert menu.

Food is a major part of all our daily lives. Some may consume less than others, but we all need food for survival. The kinds of food that are available to us, whether in supermarkets or restaurants, are endless, and our children, whether mentally or physically challenged or not, usually adapt to the parents' diet. Parents are in control of the food that is brought into the house. Children, even as babies, may not like certain foods, but most learn to eat what is given to them. At a certain age, children's palates might change, making them able to determine what they like and do not like. Flavia Scalzitti, in her article about food, says:

> If you think about life's different occasions, food is most likely at the center of each one. We use food to mark special occasions, such as birthdays, anniversaries, baby showers, graduations, and weddings. Food is used to offer comfort to people who are mourning and to those who need extra help while recovering from illness.[1]

I think it is necessary to understand how food impacts the family and can become part of the struggle within families. There may be certain foods that are always given to mentally challenged children. They will desire these foods all the time without deviation. For example, my daughter, as a baby and even growing up, always loved hash browns and plain Cheerios. At some point in time, she decided that she did not want the hash browns anymore, and she determined that she did not like the plain Cheerios anymore either. We tried giving her other cereals, but she would not eat them. We finally tried Honey Nut Cheerios, which she liked, and continues to eat every now and then. She now loves beef sausage links and toast, which is her breakfast of choice almost every day.

In a previous chapter, I talked about idiosyncrasies that mentally challenged children have. It appears that, when it comes to food, many may exhibit other peculiarities also. My daughter, when sitting at the dining table, does not like us looking at her. If we look at her directly, she will turn her head to one side or the other, so she does not have to face us. I must say, however, that she avoids eye contact almost all the time and not just at meals. She finds it difficult to look at people's faces, including her family members. We must tell her to look at us when we are speaking to her. Since mealtimes are great times to connect with each other, we had to get used to her not wanting to look at us or speak to us, even though she has a very limited vocabulary. Eating with Danielle is a totally quiet experience.

For our son, it was and is a different experience. At the age of nine, we almost lost him to diabetic shock. His body had gone into ketoacidosis:

> ... a serious complication of diabetes that occurs when your body produces high levels of blood acids called ketones. The condition develops when your body can't produce enough insulin. Insulin normally plays a key role in helping sugar (glucose)—a major source of energy for your muscles and other tissues—enter your cells. Without enough insulin, your body begins to break down fat as fuel. This process produces a buildup of acids in the bloodstream called ketones, eventually leading to diabetic ketoacidosis if untreated. The most common cause of ketoacidosis is diabetic ketoacidosis, but it can also be caused by alcohol, medications, toxins, and rarely starvation.[2]

We had no idea what was happening to him. He was in what appeared to be a trance after suffering for a few days from what we thought was a cold. It was at this juncture that we found out he was a diabetic. He had just had a check-up some weeks prior to this almost fatal incident. We had to enlist an endocrinologist to be part of his life every three months after we found that he was a diabetic. He has been taking insulin ever since that horrifying day some fourteen years ago. Along with the insulin came the weight gain. Since David's diet was like ours, his love for sweets was off the chart while Danielle favored snacks that contained salt.

It is not unusual for individuals to like salty snacks or sweet snacks. David loves sweets, and Danielle loves things salty. Danielle will eat certain kind of cookies and hard candy, but this is her limit when it comes to sweets. David loves all kinds of sweets and will also eat salty things as well without hesitation. Danielle loves potato chips, corn chips, crackers, pretzels, and other salty treats. She couldn't care less about most cookies, cakes, pies, and ice cream. Her preference in every situation is a bag of microwave popcorn, which she has almost every night except for Sunday when she has the popcorn that is popped in a pot. When examining Danielle's diet, we can easily see that her preferences are extremely limited. Her lunch consists mostly of hot dogs. She eats rice at dinner just about every day as well, and her meat selection is mainly chicken and meat loaf. When we go out to eat, her one and only choice is chicken fingers and French fries. David, on the other hand, will eat just about anything; however, he does not like mashed potatoes or tomatoes.

Most children are finicky when it comes to food. If everyone in the house has a different taste, parents must buy different foods to satisfy everyone. The cost of purchasing food this way on a regular basis can be high. You may have noticed that I have not mentioned any vegetables. Neither of our children eats a lot of vegetables or fruit. Danielle must be made to take what we refer to as a "no thank you portion," while David will eat lettuce and broccoli. Danielle does not eat fruit at all except for green grapes while David prefers apples. We must provide a supplement called Juice Plus so that they can get their daily nutritional value of vegetables and fruits:

> Just for kids, Juice Plus+ offers child size servings of Fruit and Vegetable Blend Chewables. Juice Plus+ Fruit and Vegetable Blend Chewables deliver added whole food-based nutrition from 20 different fruits, vegetables, and grains in a tasty, soft chewable form. The appealing taste

> comes from two all-natural sweeteners - tapioca syrup and organic cane syrup - with absolutely no high fructose corn syrup. It contains no artificial flavors or artificial colors and is 100% vegetarian. The 'chewiness' comes from fruit pectin, not gelatin.[3]

It is obvious that many individuals whom we encounter who have special intellectual or physical disabilities have other issues as well. My children are no exception. Danielle not only has fragile X syndrome and scoliosis, she also has a weight problem. Why? Because we gave her the food that she likes while she was growing up and continue to do so. We know that hot dogs and chicken fingers are not wise food choices, but we continue to give them to her because that is what she wants. We, as parents, desire to please our kids, so we give them what they like. In our minds, we feel that it is okay since they can enjoy what we would consider to be things in life that normal children or adults their age would experience. All the carbohydrates—bread twice a day and rice every day—have caught up with her. For a while, she was the person in the family without a weight problem; now she has joined us. David not only has to deal with the cognitive issues, but he must also deal with physical issues. We, as parents, have our own physical issues that we must deal with, including obesity, which has been a lifelong battle for me, and for Beverly.

There is another tension that rears its head in our lives as parents. It really does not matter if the children have a disability or not, parents want their children to be happy. We lean on the side of giving them what they want, whether it's food or anything else. Danielle and David like certain kinds of food, and we provide it for them. The rationalization that occurs in our minds is that they are going through enough problems without adding another by taking away the foods they like. We know that it is probably not the best thing to do, but we give in to our emotions and let it go. The children are the ones suffering the consequences because of what it is doing to their health. We are really compounding their problems. To insist that they eat a healthy diet that includes only periodically some of the things that they enjoy is the best solution for both the parents and the children. By not helping them to establish a good diet, we have added additional issues to their lives that most likely will remain with them the rest of their lives. We have then passed our issues with eating on to them without considering the costs.

The tendency for many individuals in general is to turn to food for comfort. Grabbing snacks when you are not hungry is the easy thing to do. Eating ice cream after experiencing disappointment appears not to be harmful, or grabbing a handful of cookies after hearing bad news is no big deal. If we are eating ice cream and grabbing cookies at some point during the day every day, we, indeed, have a problem. We do not like to use the term *addiction* for food, do we? Yet, many of us are suffering from food addiction, and our children are also suffering the same way. If we think about the relationship we have had with food over the years, what can we say about it? If we are honest, we can say that food has become our go-to, our cure-all. We turn to food for comfort to help us handle difficult situations emotionally. Many of the foods we eat become comfort food. What is comfort food?

> A term that has been variously defined as (1) A simply prepared food that gives a sense of well-being—typically a food with a high sugar or carbohydrate content associated with childhood or with home cooking, the psychological benefits from which usually outweigh its nutritional benefits; or (2) A hearty or deliciously satisfying food Examples: Ice cream, grilled cheese sandwiches, pizza, cookies, warm milk, chicken and dumplings.[4]

How might the stress that is brought on by the difficulties of taking care of a mentally or physically challenged child impact the family's eating habits? The family members, both parents and children, might turn to a great deal of comfort food, and consuming comfort food on a regular basis can turn into emotional eating. What is emotional eating? Consider the following statement:

> We don't always eat just to satisfy physical hunger. Many of us also turn to food for comfort, stress relief, or to reward ourselves. And when we do, we tend to reach for junk food, sweets, and other comforting but unhealthy

> foods. You might reach for a pint of ice cream when you are feeling down, order a pizza if you're bored or lonely, or swing by the drive-through after a stressful day at work. Emotional eating is using food to make yourself feel better—to fill emotional needs, rather than your stomach. Unfortunately, emotional eating doesn't fix emotional problems. In fact, it usually makes you feel worse. Afterward, not only does the original emotional issue remain, but you also feel guilty for overeating.[5]

Some emotional triggers or common causes for emotional eating may be manifested in the family unit, especially in families where there is a great deal of stress derived from caregiving for intellectually or physically challenged children. Here is a summary of these triggers:

Stress—Have you ever found yourself being hungry after a stressful situation? It's not just in your mind. Stress that is experienced on a regular basis is called chronic stress. Because we are driven and often live fast-paced lives, it is easy for our bodies to produce high levels of cortisol, which is a stress hormone. This condition triggers cravings for all kinds of foods—especially foods that are high in sugar, salt, and fat. These foods give us a burst of energy. When stress is uncontrolled, we turn to these kinds of foods to find emotional relief.

Stuffing emotions—Just we can "stuff" our anger to avoid venting it on someone or something, we can use food to temporarily hold back our uncomfortable emotions. Food can help us numb feelings that we particularly do not like. The food, however, only serves as a temporary fix. Some of the emotions that are uncomfortable are anger, fear, sadness, anxiety, loneliness, resentment, bitterness, uneasiness, and shame. Eating, however, will not help us avoid the difficult emotions we don't wish to feel.

Boredom or feelings of emptiness—Do you ever eat just to be eating? Often, when there is nothing to do and we are sedentary, we can experience boredom or emptiness. But we can use food to fill those areas that are unfulfilled and empty. Food is a way to occupy our mouths as well as our time and minds. We can use food in the moment to distract us from the underlying feelings of purposelessness and dissatisfaction with life.

Childhood habits—I am sure that you can remember those times as a child when your parents bribed or rewarded you with food. They probably used candy, ice cream, pizza, potato chips, cookies, and any food that was your favorite. Food was used to accomplish what needed to be done or to help change your mood. Many of the habits that were formulated throughout our childhood become part of what we do as adults. Patterns become rituals for us. Some of these eating habits can be driven by nostalgia.

Social influences—Socializing is a major part of most people's lives. Food is the center of that socializing, whether eating out for dinner, participating in a backyard barbeque, or mingling at a church function. Getting together with people has and always will be a great stress reliever, especially when we eat food that we have not prepared. When such events occur, it's easy to overindulge simply because the food is there or because everyone else is eating. On many occasions, the people whom we are with encourage us to eat more. We overeat to please them, not because we are hungry. We do it because we can easily feel peer pressure, and afterwards, we may not feel too good about ourselves.

Isn't it safe to say that, for many of us, this is the type of eating pattern that we have established in our homes over the years? We eat when we do not need to eat, we eat the wrong kinds of food regularly, we eat when we are not hungry, we eat out of emotion, and we eat foods that we should eat only minimally due to health concerns. We have passed many of these habits on to our children, whether they have disabilities or not. We control, for the most part, what they eat because we purchase the food, bring it into the house, and make it available to everyone who lives there. We help to establish their diet by giving them what they like and holding back what they do not like. We think that we are doing them a favor, but we are doing them a disservice and are not helping them. We have started them on a journey that is extremely difficult to stop. If it is hard for me as a parent to stop, I can imagine what it is like for the children, especially for those with disabilities, and even more so for those who show several idiosyncratic desires for certain foods. How do we identify whether we are emotional eaters?

According to the Help Guide, we need to ask the following questions.

- Do you eat more when you're feeling stressed?
- Do you eat when you're not hungry or when you're full?

- Do you eat to feel better when you're sad, mad, bored, or anxious?
- Do you reward yourself with food?
- Do you regularly eat until you've stuffed yourself?
- Does food make you feel safe? Do you feel like food is a friend?
- Do you feel powerless or out of control around food?"[6]

How many of us can truly be honest about how food is impacting our lives, particularly in homes that include children who have disabilities? As I think about how food has impacted my life, I am able to say that eating has been an exceedingly difficult personal struggle for me. My parents both had a weight problem for many years. It was not until my mom was older and started losing her appetite that she lost her weight. My weight has been up and down my entire life, most of the time higher than it should have been. There has never been a time when my weight was steady for a sustained period. Even though the kinds of nutritional foods have changed over the years for us, the junk foods, which are the comforts, have been there continually. The patterns of eating can be passed on to our children without us even recognizing it. There is a passage in 1 Corinthians 6 that mentions about our bodies. For the believer in Jesus, it really can and should have a direct bearing on how we eat:

> Do you not know that your body is the temple (the very sanctuary) of the Holy Spirit Who lives within you, Whom you have received [as a Gift] from God? You are not your own, You were bought with a price [purchased with a preciousness and paid for, made His own]. So then, honor God and bring glory to Him in your body. (1 Corinthians 6:19–20 AMP)

In context, this verse has to do with how the body should not be used sexually in a way that displeases God. As believers in Jesus, we are members of Christ, representatives of Him on Earth; therefore, we are not to be joined to a prostitute or to any illicit partner. We are not to become one flesh with anyone other than a legitimate spouse, for we are members of Christ and His cause upon this earth. However, we can glean another principle from this verse that pertains to our bodies. Our bodies belong to God, and we should, to the best of our ability, maximize their use and efficiency. What we put into our bodies has an impact on what our bodies can do. We know through scientific evidence that our diet can have a major influence in whether we contract any number of diseases. What we eat, the amount of water we drink, the amount of exercise and sleep we get all play important roles and influence our bodies.

Through these two verses, we can understand that the body is designed to be the temple of the Holy Spirit. This is one of the glorious truths of both scripture and the Christian experience. The word *body* is singular; each believer is a temple of the Spirit of God. The Holy Spirit dwells *within* the body of the believer. God lays claim to the body when He dwells in it through His Spirit. Believers do not own their bodies—not anymore! Jesus Christ bought our bodies through the shedding of His blood on the cross. Therefore, we are now the servants of God. One commentator described it like this:

> The body and spirit are both designed to glorify God. Note that a temple has no other purpose for existing except to house God's presence. It has but one function—receptivity. Note that the function is not activity. All activities of a temple should be to merely prepare for the reception of God's presence. The case for taking care of the human body has been stated as clearly as it can be. The body and the spirit of man have been created by God to glorify God. They both belong to God through the redemption that is in Jesus Christ.

When adding a spiritual component to the family unit that has children who are intellectually or physically challenged, a new approach to eating can be formulated. If our minds can receive the truth of the Spirit and be convinced to change our beliefs about eating, our behavior will be altered. If we can appropriate this new way of thinking for ourselves as parents (that is, if we have a problem with food or have contributed to our children's problem with food), we then can begin to implement new practices that can dramatically change our approach to eating, which will have a dramatic impact on the entire family.

Here are some scriptures that might be helpful in both physical and spiritual nutrition:

> And God said, See, I have given you every plant yielding seed that is on the face of all the land and every tree with seed in its fruit; you shall have them for food. (Genesis 1:29 AMP)

> Then said Daniel to the steward whom the chief of the eunuchs had set over Daniel, Hananiah, Mishael, and Azariah, Prove your servants, I beseech you, for ten days and let us be given a vegetable diet and water to drink. Then let our appearance and the appearance of the youths who eat of the king's [rich] dainties be observed and compared by you, and deal with us your servants according to what you see. So [the man] consented to them in this matter and proved them ten days. And at the end of ten days it was seen that they were looking better and had taken on more flesh than all the youths who ate of the king's rich dainties. So the steward took away their [rich] dainties and the wine they were to drink and gave them vegetables. (Daniel 1:11–16 AMP)

> And He humbled you and allowed you to hunger and fed you with manna, which you did not know nor did your fathers know, that He might make you recognize and personally know that man does not live by bread only, but man lives by every word that proceeds out of the mouth of the Lord. (Deuteronomy 8:3 AMP)

> Beloved, I pray that you may prosper in every way and [that your body] may keep well, even as [I know] your soul keeps well and prospers. (3 John 1:2 AMP)

> Everything is permissible (allowable and lawful) for me; but not all things are helpful (good for me to do, expedient and profitable when considered with other

things). Everything is lawful for me, but I will not become the slave of anything or be brought under its power. (1 Corinthians 6:12 AMP)

They gave Him a piece of broiled fish. (Luke 24:42 AMP)

Do not associate with winebibbers; be not among them nor among gluttonous eaters of meat. (Proverbs 23:20 AMP)

I appeal to you therefore, brethren, and beg of you in view of [all] the mercies of God, to make a decisive dedication of your bodies [presenting all your members and faculties] as a living sacrifice, holy (devoted, consecrated) and well pleasing to God, which is your reasonable (rational, intelligent) service and spiritual worship. (Romans 12:1 AMP)

These you may eat of all that are in the waters: whatever has fins and scales in the waters, in the seas, and in the rivers, these you may eat. (Leviticus 11:9 AMP)

Whatever parts the hoof and is cloven-footed and chews the cud, any of these animals you may eat. (Leviticus 11:3 AMP)

And he took curds and milk and the calf which he had made ready and set it before [the men]; and he stood by them under the tree while they ate. (Genesis 18:8 AMP)

And taking the five loaves and two fish, He looked up to heaven and, praising God, gave thanks and broke the loaves and kept on giving them to the disciples to set before the people; and He [also] divided the two fish among [them] all. And they all ate and were satisfied. And they took up twelve [small hand] baskets full of broken pieces [from the loaves] and of the fish. And those who ate the loaves were 5,000 men. (Mark 6:41–44 AMP)

From these verses, we can conclude that the body is talked about quite a bit in the pages of scripture, as are various kinds of food and the importance of having a relationship with God. There is a correlation between the spiritual and physical components of life. We need the spiritual to feed that part of us that connects with God—the part that needs to understand Him and receive guidance from Him. But then there is that other part—the part that is the physical that needs to be in the best shape possible to accomplish whatever God needs to use us to accomplish. The instructions come through the spiritual. When we are physically in shape—eating properly, being emotionally healthy and psychologically stable and astute—we are in a good position to hear God clearly. He then feeds us in the areas that we need nurturing. He can go deep and bring healing to those areas of our lives in which He is the only one who can do so. If we can maintain good eating habits, get proper exercise, and get into the Word of God, God will help us to be prudent in our efforts to take care of our mentally or physically challenged children properly.

> I mentioned in the beginning of this chapter how food plays a big part in our lives, especially during holidays. Food provides other things in our lives besides sustainability physically. Flavia Scalzitti says the following about how food communicates: "When I talk to people about food, I find out so much more than ingredients and recipes. I learn about traditions, cultural differences and similarities, relationships, and I start to hear stories that give me a glimpse into people's lives"[7]

My wife and I often watch shows on the HGTV network that feature different houses. We see people who want open-concept houses with large kitchens that are visible from many angles. Why do people desire this type of design? Is it because they desire to be relational as they prepare their food? I would say yes! The kitchen area is where life takes place, but more especially it takes place at the table. The table is where people sit and relax, enjoy their food, and talk about their experiences, disappointments, conflicts, and even their hopes and dreams. It is at the table where connection occurs through conversations and discussions. It is at the table where children can be trained, people can learn, disagreements can be solved, discipline can be administered, traditions can be preserved, memories can be created, and relationships can be nurtured. It is around food that our lives can grow and be enriched. We can see throughout various cultures, even in the scripture, that food is an important ingredient in connecting people. Hospitality is one of the greatest ways that we can connect with people. Food plays a major part in being hospitable and can be one of life's greatest joys.

What are we communicating indirectly with our children through food? If food communicates in nonverbal ways, what are we saying to our children through our relationship with it? Our children, whether they have disabilities or not, might very possibly take on the same relationship that we have with food. Let us, as parents, be cognizant of what we are communicating to our children, be it verbal or nonverbal. Everything that we do has an impact in ways that we might not realize. How can God change how we look at food? I believe it starts with the scriptures I have included here. God is concerned about every aspect of our lives as well as our children's lives. He has provided a blueprint for us to follow: the Bible. It is left up to us to do what we should with that blueprint. If we implement the principles that are in it, we will see positive changes. If we do not, we will experience the same things that we are currently experiencing. The choice is ours. Who will win the battle?

NOTES

1 Flavia Scalzitti, "Connecting Through Food," Mom it Forward, July 12, 2018 https://momitforward.com/connecting-through-food.

2 Mayo Clinic, Diabetic ketoacidosis - Symptoms and causes, accessed April 20, 2020, https://www.mayoclinic.org/diseases-conditions/diabetic-ketoacidosis/symptoms-causes/syc-20371551.

3 Juice Plus, "Our products," Accessed April 3, 2020. https://www.juiceplus.com/us/en/products/capsules/...

4 Segen's Medical Dictionary © 2012 Farlex, Inc. All rights reserved. "Comfort Food." Retrieved September 8, 2021, https://medical-dictionary.thefreedictionary.com/Comfort+Food.

5 Melinda Smith, M.A., Lawrence Robinson, Jeanne Segal Ph.D., and Robert Segal, M.A., "Emotional Eating and How to Stop It," Helpguide, accessed May 2020, https://www.helpguide.org/articles/diets/emotional-eating.htm.

6 Smith, Robinson, and Segal, Helpguide, accessed May 2020 https://momitforward.com/connecting-through-food

7 Scalzitti, "Connecting Through Food," July 12, 2018 https://momitforward.com/connecting-through-food

7

What Kind of Education Is Needed?

For patents, the education of their children is an important topic, and for many, it can be exceedingly difficult to figure out. Through the years, the educational system has changed in many ways and on many levels. Some of these changes have occurred in methods of teaching, of how children are tested, and how children should be dispersed in classrooms. The curricula as well as materials used also have changed over the years.

My wife and I decided how we would educate our children before we were married. We had several conversations about homeschooling the children. Beverly did not wait until after we were married to express a major desire that was on her heart. I think that it is necessary to highlight the importance of expressing desires to a potential future spouse. Learning how to talk about major expectations early in a relationship can prevent difficulties in a marriage and can possibly be the key element that will prevent the marriage from occurring between two individuals, which can be a good thing. Exposing expectations prior to marriage will bring about a large degree of harmony in the marriage. Everyone will be on the same page, and there will not be any surprises.

Because I knew ahead of time that Beverly wanted to homeschool our children, my mind was prepared to get ready for what would undoubtedly be a major challenge for both of us as parents. Do you find it interesting that we were thinking about education long before the children were even born? This is not unusual. Many couples choose where to purchase their homes based upon the school system in the area. Couples want their children to experience the best education that is available in the neighborhood. It is natural for parents to desire the best for their children even if they did not have the best for themselves. However, because we must operate in reality, not everyone can live in a location that can provide the best education. We are then left with a decision to put our children in the best possible situation.

Some might wonder how parents mentally prepare for homeschooling. For Beverly, it was not much of a problem because she had witnessed a family who was actively engaged with the process of homeschooling their children. Therefore, she had developed in her mind the possibility of doing it with her own children. I never experienced it or known anyone who was doing it. For me, it was more of a financial issue; I knew that we had to be able to live on my salary alone. When we were about to get married, my annual salary was a little north of $20,000. If we were to homeschool the children, I would need a major increase in salary. We had seven to eight years before we would be facing this homeschooling dream of hers. Not only was there a financial aspect, but there was also a supportive aspect that needed to be addressed. How would I be able to support Beverly with this mission of homeschooling that she felt so strongly about? Obviously, she felt her desire to educate the children was given to her by God. For me, since everything was in the future, as a believer in Jesus, I had to trust that God would provide. If we were going to homeschool the children, God would have to increase my salary in a big way and give me the ability to know how to support my wife emotionally in this endeavor.

Danielle, our first child, was born in 1993. She was born shortly after midnight right before a major ice storm started. I recall driving home in the snow in the wee hours of the morning. Shortly after her birth, we heard from the doctor about the possible complications she most likely would have. The question then became for us, how do you homeschool a mentally challenged child? We would not know the extent of her mental disability until she started developing. It would begin to manifest in different ways over time.

In the previous chapters, we addressed what occurs in the thinking processes of the parents. These cognitive elements were operating in our minds as we went through this time of development for Danielle and for us. All we could do was to wait and to treat her as if there was nothing wrong with her until the symptoms started to manifest. Beverly, at the time, was working as the pastor's secretary at the church we were attending, and I was a park manager with the Fairmount Park Commission. By this time, God had blessed me with a position in management at my place of employment. The possibility of Beverly leaving the workforce to be home with our daughter was closer to becoming a reality. During this time, until she was approximately two years old, our daughter spent her days with a caregiver.

Shortly after Beverly resigned from her job to care for Danielle, she became pregnant with our son, David. Our children are a little more than three years apart. At this point in time, we had been seeing some delays in our daughter. She was not talking very much or soaking up information as most children do at age three and four. We were now experiencing the symptoms that were beginning to manifest because of her condition. After having her tested, we found that she was on the autism spectrum. What was so surprising for us was that she was not supposed to have the condition known as fragile X syndrome. She was to be a carrier since the female with fragile X possesses the X chromosome:

> According to the United States Library of Medicine, (FXS) Fragile X syndrome is a genetic condition that causes a range of developmental problems including learning disabilities and cognitive impairment. Usually, males are more severely affected by this disorder than females.[1]

Affected individuals tend to have limited intellectual functions. However, in our case, Danielle was considered to be moderately mentally challenged. Bev, despite our daughter having this diagnosis, did not deviate from her decision to homeschool. Within a few years, the doors of Beacon Light School—our school—opened. Bev was the teacher, and I was the principal. Our school journey was about to begin.

In the state of Pennsylvania, a homeschool teacher must have at least a high school diploma. The requirements are different in each state with the rules in some states more rigid than in other states. Beverly designed the curriculum and provided the required information to the school system of Philadelphia: an affidavit (legal documentation showing responsibility of the child's education) and an individual education program (IEP). She would also have to hand in a portfolio at the end of the year containing all the work that Danielle had done throughout the year. Homeschooling a child brings with it a wide range of learning possibilities that cannot be obtained in a traditional schoolroom. The homeschool classroom consists of the entire world. We were ready to begin our journey, and Beverly was at the helm. The homeschool journey would be a long one, and the driver would experience potholes, wrong turns, crashes, traffic jams, and several incidents that would almost deter the journey, but she would keep driving.

The decision to homeschool children who are considered normal is daunting for many parents. Many do not desire homeschool and quite honestly do not have the patience for it. Many cannot do it because both parents must work to make ends meet. The purpose of writing this chapter isn't to push homeschooling, but to bring an awareness of it being a viable option. We homeschooled because it was what we believed to be the best for our children. The point I want to raise, especially for people of faith, is that the responsibility to educate our children is given to us by God, and the process ultimately falls into our hands. To dismiss our responsibility is to disobey the Lord whom many claim to follow. So many parents abdicate the responsibility to other people, many of those being outside of the family as well as outside of the family's belief system.

Whether children have mental disabilities or not, parents should decide on a standard of education that is based on an accurate perspective of what God expects rather than on what any school system says. What God expects is not based upon academics, though that might be a part of the expectation because of the intelligence level given by God to them. God expects education to bring glory to Him by maximizing the potential of the gifts and talents that He has given to the children. This perspective changes what we should be doing for our children and how we should do it. What is the potential of our children? What have they been given by God that will make them a blessing to people, even if it is to change us as parents? That means all of us, whether we have a disability or not, can have an impact on another person.

There is a proverb in scripture that I believe is appropriate at this point: "Train up a child in the way he should go, and [or even] when he is old he will not depart from it" (Proverbs 22:6 AMP). At first, this *sounds* like a wonderful promise to parents. This is exactly what every God-fearing parent would love to have as a promise from the Creator with regard to marriage and family. Knowing that our children will faithfully serve the Lord by the end of their lives, even though they might struggle along the way, would bring peace to parents. Naturally, Christian parents possess an unquenchable hope that their children will remain with the faith in which they are reared. Or, if the children depart for a while, the parents cling to the belief that they will return. Is Proverbs 22:6 a guarantee from God to parents that their children will stay in the church? Unfortunately, it is not. I am amazed by how many modern commentators, counselors, preachers, teachers, and public speakers explain this verse as a guarantee. But, regrettably, this is a misunderstanding. Promises of God include numerous benefits for obeying His way of life. However, they do not include a guarantee to parents that children reared faithfully will keep the faith as adults. To understand what Proverbs 22:6 means, we need to consider free moral agency, the background or culture of the day in which the proverb was written, as well as the meaning of the words used for "train up" and "a child." Albert Barnes, in his *Notes on the Old Testament*, says that

> "Train up" is derived from a Hebrew word for "education." In the way he should go literally is "according to his way." The text doesn't apply to being upright or exhibiting good living but implies the way that a child is to spend their life with regard to an occupation. Preparation is necessary in the early years so that they can develop the proper habits necessary to be successful.[2]

Other commentaries add to this understanding of Proverbs 22:6. Consider *Dr. Constable's Notes on Proverbs* (2006 edition):

> Train (Heb. *hanak*) means to dedicate (Deut. 20:5; 1 Kings 8:63; 2 Chron. 7:5; Dan. 3:2). It has the idea of narrowing and in this verse implies channeling the child's conduct into the way of wisdom. That guidance might

> include dedicating him or her to God and preparing the child for future responsibilities and adulthood. "In the way he should go" is literally "according to his way."

When we apply this understanding of Proverbs 22:6 to our parenting situation, how is the purview changed. As we combine what we learn over time from developmental professionals with what we learn from our own observation of our children, how do we help them use whatever they have, whether limited or not, to the best of their limited ability? Whatever they can do, we are to help them to get there. If that means getting a severely mentally challenged child to smile because it brings joy to them and us, we have accomplished something that is extremely valuable to God. If we can align our perspective with God's, just think how transforming that would be for the family.

In chapter 2, I wrote about our observations of a classroom in a school near where we live. Due to the size of the class, Danielle would never have received the individual attention that was necessary for her to understand the basics as well as to understand how to do some things that were possible for her to do. Let me be honest. Danielle could have received help from people other than us, but at a cost. I will explain shortly. We asked the school what type of services would be available to Danielle. According to them, she would receive speech therapy once a week and possibly occupational therapy. She would be sitting in the classroom just staring into space for most of the day, almost every day, like many of the children that we had observed, because she would not be able to have specialized attention that would target her areas of need.

Unfortunately, this is the problem when it comes to educating mentally challenged students. Some children who are extremely bright are placed in these cookie-cutter special education classes. They end up being bored, unfulfilled, and untaught. Such an environment does not benefit any of the students that are in the class. The students end up not reaching their potential because they learn differently than the other students. Mentally challenged students need individualized attention in their learning processes. If it is not made available by the regular school system, unfortunately, their potential might not ever be reached, no matter how limited that potential might be. It took less than an hour for us to recognize the insufficiency of the environment that existed in that school.

Since so many parents depend on the school system and because the parents are busy trying to make ends meet financially, many mentally challenged children do not have a chance to go beyond a certain point in their development. At least this was the situation over twenty years ago. There are more resources as well as more awareness today than there has ever been before, and parents should take advantage of these resources. Please keep in mind, as I stated earlier, that many mentally challenged children may not have the capacity to learn very much. Parents cannot know their children's potential for learning if they are not intimately involved with their development.

Now to the point that I was making earlier about cost. Early in the homeschool process, Beverly began to struggle. She was going through an emotional rollercoaster because of her ambivalent feelings about whether she was doing the right thing homeschooling the children. All I could do at the time was to explore other options in case she could not do it. My position was to basically allow her to decide what she wanted to do. I would support whatever decision she made. After considering our options and discussing the matter, we decided to check out Elwyn, located in Media, Pennsylvania. Elwyn is a facility that provides a source for education, treatment, and support services for children and adults with autism, intellectual and developmental disabilities, and related behavioral health challenges. We learned that, in order for Danielle to be accepted into Elwyn, the school system of Philadelphia would have to refer her to them. For the school system of Philadelphia to make such a referral, they would have to relinquish all possible resources for helping her. In other words, the possibility of her being recommended by the school system of Philadelphia would be an absolute zero. Danielle's disability was not severe enough. If I recall, I believe the cost to send Danielle to Elwyn would have been over $40,000 a year (this was in the early 2000s). I can imagine what the cost would be today. No way on God's green Earth could we afford that fee. We continued with the homeschooling.

Many families with mentally challenged children face this dilemma over education that we faced during those early years and throughout the process. Education and other services for mentally challenged children provided outside the public school system are astronomically costly. Most families cannot afford such services. We couldn't then, and we cannot afford it now. Because most families cannot afford to place their children in private schools, they end up sending the children to the public school system, which provides only limited resources.

I do understand that it is extremely challenging to establish an educational system that best fits any child. With this challenge, however, we must be willing to think outside the box. If the public school system does not provide what we consider the best possible opportunity for our children, what should we do? We must ask a lot of questions and find some possible alternatives. There are options, especially in today's world, that can help us determine the best course of action for our children.

Homeschooling does not necessarily have to be carried out by the parent. It can be done by a relative, friend, or anyone who has the credentials to do it—a high school diploma in some states and a college degree in others.

One possible educational avenue is a combination of elements that are provided by the school system, other organizations, and people who are willing help the family with the task of education. For instance, children can be involved with a co-op of other homeschoolers, with programs at the local library, with programs at the local recreation centers or youth organizations, and with services the school system must provide.

We found out that the school system does not provide information to parents voluntarily; parents must be proactive in getting the information, and we usually had to fight for it. We had to be relentless in our efforts to find out what we had a right to receive from the system. Many parents are not able to take up this fight because of work obligations and the everyday struggle of caring for their children who are mentally challenged. It is nice to know that homeschooling these days is not frowned upon as it was when we were doing it years ago. There is much more support available, and there are organizations that provide information for parents about all the rules and the resources available.

For parents to receive all the possible help from all the sources that might be available to them, they must be willing to let go of pride and the feeling that no one out their cares. More resources are available today, but we must be willing to reach out and tell people what they can do to help.

Education is just one aspect of what we need to provide for our children. There is no reason for parents in today's world to suffer in silence.

Beverly was well on her way in teaching Danielle after things had settled down and we had established a daily routine. Once Beverly got into a routine with Danielle, she had to begin the same process with David. He too was placed in a preschool so that he could be around other children. Part-time daycare was just one aspect of socialization for the children when they were young. The main concern expressed by educators was how we were planning to socialize our children.

David appeared to be on a higher intellectual level than Danielle. However, as time went on, we noticed that he was not able to learn quickly. He was having difficulty in math and reading comprehension. After a while, Beverly began to go through another bout of questioning our decision to homeschool. So we attempted to find a school for David when he was of elementary school age. We enrolled him in Holy Family School in Manayunk, a neighborhood in Philadelphia that was not far from our home. Holy Family was a Catholic school. This seemed to be a better option since we did not have any affection for the public school system. After he started attending, we received several calls from the school about their concerns about David. He was not faring very well; he found the new environment overwhelming. He began to go through bouts of anxiety and was struggling with the classwork, which was apparently way over his head. Once again, Beverly and I knew that we needed to take him out of school. He needed to be in an environment he was accustomed to and comfortable in.

We learned something from this experience. Whenever we tried to put the kids in educational situation outside of homeschooling, something happened to keep the experience from being successful. We had attempted to place David in Penn Christian School, located in Plymouth Meeting, a few years prior to placing him in Holy Family. He lasted there for only a few weeks. He was not able to do the work and was not able to acclimate to the surroundings. We will never forget the morning we took David out of Penn Christian School—9/11. We had just come home from removing him from the school when we turned the television on and could not believe our eyes. One Trade Center tower had been hit by a plane and was on fire.

We then saw the other plane fly into the other tower, and we watched it collapse. What a terrible day that was.

Bev made it through that difficult phase and went on to have a good run at homeschooling. She was able to teach David to read. However, she noticed that he still was not doing well with comprehension, so we began to seek help. As I began to search for possible help with David, I stopped in Cedar Grove Christian Academy to see what they had available for students outside of the school. I ran into a wonderful caring person who was so encouraging when I told her our situation. Her name was Mrs. Rank. Still to this day, I appreciate how she was able to encourage me and provide hope for David. We enrolled him in a program there at the school. He attended twice a week for an hour during the school year. He worked with a woman named Mrs. Kuleck who was instrumental in accelerating his learning process. These two ladies, sent by the Lord, accompanied us on our journey for several years and provided us with some great insight about David's learning process that aided him and us immensely.

We learned from Mrs. Kuleck's work with him that he learned in three different ways. He processed ideas things in different ways depending on how they were communicated; reading silently to himself, reading out loud, or hearing someone read to him. Knowing how David took in information was helpful to us. Unfortunately, he was and still is limited in his ability to process information. Anyone who meets David for the first time is unable to tell that he has a disability. In many cases, this is a problem for many mentally challenged individuals. There are so many ranges of cognitive impairment. When you meet our children, at first glance, there is no indication that they have any issues; it does not become evident until they respond—or do not respond—at some point in a conversation. Many people do not know how to respond to Danielle, for example, because she rarely talks, so they just walk away.

When it comes to the education of mentally challenged children, it is important to get all the help necessary. I cannot stress the importance of getting support. It is also necessary to know what help is best for each child. The values of the parents should also play a part in what to allow in their children's lives. An agency might provide services that are good, but their educators may want to give your children information to which you do not want them exposed. It is not only your right as a parent but also your responsibility to God to protect your children from things that might be harmful to them emotionally and cognitively. For example, I would not want my children exposed to any sexual topics, even now when they are adults. Danielle is cognitively at a three- or four-year-old level, and she does not need to be exposed to anything along those lines. My child represents an innocence that is rarely exhibited in an adult. Her world consists of Disney where princesses live in perfect worlds. She does not experience things in the "outside world" and is not usually impacted by human negativity and harmful behavior. Hers is a world in which there is no constant bombardment of sin that rips away her innocence and her love of humanity. In her world, everything is perfect. It is an innocent world that we can learn from.

As I mentioned earlier, homeschooling is not for every family. I would suggest, however, that parents must consider what is the best possible environment for their mentally challenged children? If it is within the parents' capacity to make it happen, they should do it. If it is not possible, they attempt to come up with a system of education that is close to it.

There used to be a show on the HGTV network that featured people who wanted a room remodeled in a particular style. The designer would show them a potential design and would provide the cost of each item. The designer would then design a room that was similar in style but much less expensive. In fact, it would be approximately one quarter of the cost in many instances. The designer accomplished the goal that was desired by the homeowner at a price the homeowner could afford. Is this not the way we should look at what is needed for our children, and not just our mentally challenged children? If we cannot attain the absolute best environment, let us get as close as possible to the best. A room can be remodeled in a short period of time, but we need more time to put a team of people together to accomplish the goal of educating our children. If we are willing to do the work and to ask for help, the quality of education can even surpass that of a school like Elwyn, and it will be attained for less money and with more love. We express our love for our children in various ways; what greater way to love them than to provide an environment where they can fulfill God's purpose and will?

NOTES

1 Medline Plus, "Fragile X Symdrome," U.S. National Library of Medicine, accessed May 2020, https://medlineplus.gov/genetics/condition/fragile-x-syndrome.

2 Barnes, Albert. *Barnes' Notes on the Old Testament.* WORD*search* CROSS e-book.

8

Discipline is Part of the Training

I love all types of fruit. The vast array of fruit that is available is truly amazing. Look how colorful it is—red, yellow, and green apples; red strawberries; blue, black, and red berries; green, red, and purple grapes; red and white grapefruits. I can think of ten varieties of "oranges"! My problem is that I do not eat enough fruit. Even though they are available to me, I do not seize the opportunity to include them in my diet.

Our children are our fruit. Just like each variety of fruit is unique, our children, whether mentally or physically challenged or not, are uniquely different. It is the variety of people in the world that makes it so colorful and interesting.

Fruit grows on trees, vines, bushes, and ground plants. In the early stages of a fruit plant's development, a lot of work is required. Many plants must be pruned on a regular basis, and in some instances, must be pruned severely. We can describe the pruning process as providing training for the plant. Pruning is the process of removing branches from the plant that are crossing one another or have been damaged or are dead because of disease, insects, wind, or human interference. It is necessary to remove these branches to maximize the development of the plant; in other words, so the plant can produce the maximum amount of fruit. The only difference between the training of young plants and mature plants is how often they need to be pruned and how much of the plant must be removed.

The idea of training a tree to maximize its production applies to our children, whether they are intellectually or physically challenged or not. Today's culture places such a negative perspective on the disciplining of children that most parents are afraid to implement discipline when necessary. The disciplining of children is part of the training of children just like cutting branches from the tree or vine is the training that is necessary for that plant. We give our culture's voice too much power when it comes to the way we train our fruit—our children. As parents, it is necessary to understand the role that discipline plays in the early development of our children. Discipline, in all its forms, including spanking, is necessary when it comes to the training of our children, whether they have a disability or not. Not to use discipline shows a lack of love for our children and deprives them of what is necessary and needed for their growth.

If we visited homes across the country, we would probably find that most parents are very tentative when it comes to disciplining their children, especially in today's world. Some parents who have children without disabilities are relinquishing the use of necessary disciplinary measures in their homes, and some parents of children with disabilities are creating similar environments. The total lack of discipline in the home is a major problem today in our culture and is possibly contributing to the lack of maturity in our children without diagnosed disabilities as they transition into adulthood. Undoubtedly, the same can be said regarding the discipline, or lack thereof, of mentally challenged children.

I must admit that raising mentally challenged children was initially difficult, especially trying to figure out when and how to discipline them. Over time, we were able to determine the differences in the way they responded to instruction and some of the behaviors that each of them exhibited. Since my wife was homeschooling, she was the one who experienced most of the negative behaviors of the children. We had to discipline them at times and would use all the discipline tools that were available. Most of us are familiar with the tools—discussion, time-out, taking away a privilege for a certain period, taking away a favorite toy or activity for a certain period, handing out a difficult assignment that must be done in a certain time frame, spanking, and so forth. Spanking, of course, is the elephant in the room. I am amazed at how many parents do not use spanking when appropriate. Our culture has "thrown the baby out with the bathwater"—the expression used when something is discarded without taking into consideration the good results that come from it. Spanking has been given a bad rap because some parents have crossed the line into abusive behavior. Spanking, when used properly and at the right time, can produce good results. The scripture provides for us a specific verse with respect to spanking: "He who spares his rod [of discipline] hates his son, but he who loves him disciplines diligently and punishes him early" (Proverbs 13:24 AMP).

Solomon let us know that a loving parent inflicts temporary discomfort on his children (by spanking with a rod) to spare them the long-range disaster of an undisciplined life. Refusal to discipline our children when they need it shows that parents' genuine love and concern are questionable. Here are some other verses from Proverbs on child discipline: 23:13-14; and 29:15.

> Discipline your son while there is hope, but do not [indulge your angry resentments by undue chastisements and] set yourself to his ruin. (Proverbs 19:18 AMP)

> Foolishness is bound up in the heart of a child, but the rod of discipline will drive it far from him. (Proverbs 22:15 AMP)

> Withhold not discipline from the child; for if you strike and punish him with the [reedlike] rod, he will not die. You shall whip him with the rod and deliver his life from Sheol (Hades, the place of the dead). (Proverbs 23:13–14 AMP)

> The rod and reproof give wisdom, but a child left undisciplined brings his mother to shame. (Proverbs 29:15 AMP)

I recall a situation that happened with my son years ago when he was of elementary school age. He started stealing money out of my top dresser drawer. The first time he did it, I gave him a pass and had a conversation with him about what he had done. When it happened again, I had a more serious conversation with him, and I explained what the consequences would be if he did it a third time. He appeared to have understood the significance of our discussion, and I believed he would not repeat the behavior. However, he did. Because I had discussed with him the consequences, I was forced proceed with the discipline—a spanking. This behavior should not be tolerated by any parent because it can lead to major problems later for the child. It was not time to feel sorry for him, time to coddle him, time to have another conversation, or time to give him a time-out. The offense warranted a strong response. I was not angry when I administered the spanking. I was totally in control and was able to explain to him why the spanking was taking place. I never had a problem with him stealing again.

In many households today, you will probably find some essential tools such as a hammer, a pair of pliers, a few screwdrivers, and maybe some garden tools such as a trowel, loppers, or a pair of pruners. These tools are used for minor jobs such as hanging a picture, pulling out a nail in the floor, putting together a piece of furniture, or planting a shrub. If there are major jobs to be completed, additional tools are needed. In other households there may be a huge assortment of tools, but they are never used. These households have the tools available to them, but no one in the home has the skill to use them to do a major job. Instead, the family calls on someone who has the expertise to do the work they need done. It is this last type of home that many parents have when it comes to the tools for training and disciplining their children. They have tools in their toolbox that are given to them by God to use, but they allow current societal culture to take over and permeate their homes because there is an unspoken acceptance that the culture knows more than the God of the Universe who created them and their children. Spanking is a tool that needs to come out of your tool bag when necessary.

Scripture is filled with information on how to train our children, whether they are intellectually or physically challenged or not. We are to pull out the appropriate tool that is necessary in any given situation. When we allow the culture to bring in its own tools and tell us that our tools shouldn't be used, we allow the culture to render us impotent of authority and power given by God to train our children. In Proverbs 3:12, we can recognize how God feels about the administering of discipline to those He loves: "For whom the Lord loves He corrects, even as a father corrects the son in whom he delights" (Proverbs 3:12 AMP).

If we examine Proverb 3:5–6, we see that God can be trusted to take down obstacles and deliver us to his appointed goal. Then in verses 9 and 10, we see that God is also able to supply our material needs. This same God demonstrates His love by discipline. There is a caveat that is given to the son. This admonition carries with it two parts. The first is not to reject the Lord's discipline. The second is not to resent the Lord's rebuke. We all struggle when it comes to receiving correction or discipline. However, we must understand that, through them, God is demonstrating His love toward us. This is equally true when parents discipline their children. They do not enjoy giving punishment, but they do it because it is necessary for the children. Viewing God's discipline as benefit rather than pain is essential in understanding how God strengthens us and demonstrates His love.

What we can establish immediately in this text is that divine discipline is evidence of divine love. Let us now consider what the writer of Hebrews says in the following verses:

> Therefore then, since we are surrounded by so great a cloud of witnesses [who have borne testimony to the Truth], let us strip off and throw aside every encumbrance (unnecessary weight) and that sin which so readily (deftly and cleverly) clings to and entangles us, and let us run with patient endurance and steady and active persistence the appointed course of the race that is set before us, Looking away [from all that will distract] to Jesus, Who is the Leader and the Source of our faith [giving the first incentive for our belief] and is also its Finisher [bringing it to maturity and perfection]. He, for the joy [of obtaining the prize] that was set before Him, endured the cross, despising and ignoring the shame, and is now seated at the right hand of the throne of God. Just think of Him Who endured from sinners such grievous opposition and bitter hostility against Himself [reckon up and consider it all in comparison with your trials], so that you may not grow

weary or exhausted, losing heart and relaxing and fainting in your minds. You have not yet struggled and fought agonizingly against sin, nor have you yet resisted and withstood to the point of pouring out your [own] blood. And have you [completely] forgotten the divine word of appeal and encouragement in which you are reasoned with and addressed as sons? My son, do not think lightly or scorn to submit to the correction and discipline of the Lord, nor lose courage and give up and faint when you are reproved or corrected by Him; For the Lord corrects and disciplines everyone whom He loves, and He punishes, even scourges, every son whom He accepts and welcomes to His heart and cherishes. You must submit to and endure [correction] for discipline; God is dealing with you as with sons. For what son is there whom his father does not [thus] train and correct and discipline? Now if you are exempt from correction and left without discipline in which all [of God's children] share, then you are illegitimate offspring and not true sons [at all]. Moreover, we have had earthly fathers who disciplined us and we yielded [to them] and respected [them for training us]. Shall we not much more cheerfully submit to the Father of spirits and so [truly] live? For [our earthly fathers] disciplined us for only a short period of time and chastised us as seemed proper and good to them; but He disciplines us for our certain good that we may become sharers in His own holiness. For the time being no discipline brings joy, but seems grievous and painful; but afterwards it yields a peaceable fruit of righteousness to those who have been trained by it [a harvest of fruit which consists in righteousness—in conformity to God's will in purpose, thought, and action, resulting in right living and right standing with God].So then, brace up and reinvigorate and set right your slackened and weakened and drooping hands and strengthen your feeble and palsied and tottering knees, And cut through and make firm and plain and smooth,

> straight paths for your feet [yes, make them safe and upright and happy paths that go in the right direction], so that the lame and halting [limbs] may not be put out of joint, but rather may be cured. (Hebrews 12:1–13 AMP)

What an amazing scripture. It describes how God loves us! His love is demonstrated through the discipline that He exercises toward us. It is necessary that we understand the discipline being described here as having to do with believers: those who are disciples of Christ and who believe in Jesus as their Savior. These are the individuals who receive discipline by God when appropriate. This is how we are to discipline our own children, whether they have disabilities or not.

Now that we understand *who* God disciplines, we need to understand the *how* and *why* He disciplines. God chastens, corrects, and rebukes all those who belong to Him through faith. What does chastise mean? To punish, as for wrongdoing, to criticize severely; reprimand or rebuke."[1] Another definition for chastisement is to train, teach, and instruct.

We are encouraged not to despise discipline; we must not make little of it or treat it lightly. When we are being taught, disciplined, or corrected, there is always the danger of despising it or treating it too lightly. Most of us generally do not stay abreast of the small things that are happening around us. This mindset of ignorance exists for many who do not consider those things that may bring about God's discipline and correction to be of importance. Most likely, we do not look at things that may not work out for us in many instances as being the discipline of God. God speaks through His Spirit, through circumstances, through His Word, and through people. Many times, He speaks, and we continue with our behaviors, those things that please our flesh. Many times, God allows the same consequences to occur until we finally get it. And even when we get it, we may continue to keep doing what we were doing without acknowledging that God desires us to go in a different direction or to make a change. A great deal of our suffering is caused by our own irresponsibility and sinful behavior and attitude. Much of the discipline and correction that we suffer could be avoided if we heeded the discipline of God the first time. Life, then, would be so much better for all of us. We can honestly say that it would be more victorious.

What does God desire from us when it appears that He has a strong hand on us which we believe is His chastisement? The trials and sufferings we are experiencing seem to be unbearable at times, making us ready to give up. We are encouraged through the Word of God not to faint or to give up. The word *faint* means "To sink into dejection; to lose courage or spirit."[2]

We are to look to the One who is able to help us to be sustained in the midst of our experiences, and that is God. We are to look to Him for direction, help, and strength. Even though He might be allowing it, He is there with us and will not leave us without His comfort. On the other side of the experience, we will be made stronger and will be able to share how God is able to provide for us during difficulty.

We can recognize that the purposes for discipline are fourfold:

1. God disciplines us to assure us that we are His children. People who only professes to belong to God and do not truly live a life that God intended for them to live may not truly be family members. Unless people are instructed, disciplined, and corrected by the Spirit of God, they are not sons and daughters of God according to the scripture.
2. God disciplines us to save us and to stir us to live truly redeemed lives. Discipline, training, instruction, and correction create order and protection of life on Earth. This is the reason earthly parents who love their children discipline them. The point is this: God's discipline brings greater life to humankind—an abundance of life in this world and an eternal life in the next world.
3. God disciplines us for our good, to make us partakers of His goodness. Remember that holiness means to be different, to be completely and wholly set apart and separated from imperfection and impurity. God is holy, righteous, and pure—perfectly so. The more sin and evil we practice, the less like God we become. The less sin and evil we do, the more like God we become. Therefore, God is bound to discipline us when we begin to faint under trials and sufferings and when we begin to move toward sin. God wants us to become more and more like Him.

4. God disciplines us so that we can bear the fruit of peace and righteousness. The less sin and evil there is, the more peace and righteousness there is. If the sin and evil of anger and division do not exist, then peace and righteousness prevail. Therefore, when we let sin and evil into our lives, God disciplines us. Why? So that we will correct ourselves and do all we can for the sake of peace and righteousness. The discipline and correction may be grievous and painful to bear at first, but it will bring peace and righteousness if we will only bear it.

From the examination of Hebrews 12:1–13, we can discover why discipline is so important to God and how and why He disciplines those He loves. Several scriptures, especially in the Old Testament, clearly recognize the discipline of God being manifested in different ways: God destroyed the entire population leaving only Noah and his family (Genesis 6); God destroyed the two cities of Sodom and Gomorrah because of the wickedness that was at work within them (Genesis 19); God raised up heathen nations to capture His people to take them captive for numerous years (2 Kings 18, Isaiah 36); and God struck Ananias and Sapphira dead for deception (Acts 5). Why did God do these things? Because He loved, and He actively works to cleanse all impurity from those He loves. In some cases, He make examples of those given over to sin as warnings to others.

Discipline from our human perspective is difficult to understand, especially for those who do not know Jesus as Savior. Even those who know Jesus have difficulties when it comes to discipline. We have just mentioned some of the disciplinary actions that God took with His people. God's discipline is attached to His love and holiness. To say it another way, God is Love, and God is Holiness. We are made in His image, and that image is reflected through those who know Him as their Lord and Savior. God, because He is Holy and because He is Love, acts out of love when it comes to us. His discipline is designed to bring us back to Him when we stray away, just as a shepherd used to break the leg of a sheep that kept wandering away for the purpose of protecting it. If the sheep kept wandering, it would soon be destroyed by a predator who was always lurking around. The sheep with the broken leg had to be carried by the shepherd until it is healed. During the time that the sheep was being carried, it bonded with the shepherd. The sheep learned that the shepherd loved her because of the care that she was receiving from the shepherd. God shows His love through discipline, and that ties into His care of us.

Discipline is necessary for the purpose of keeping us protected from the enemy—Satan—who wants to destroy us. When we understand how the Shepherd (God) cares for us, we can appreciate that He comes chasing after us when we stray. Isn't that what love does? It comes after us when we have gone too far out of the realm of safety. We must believe that God provides these discipline stories in His Word so that we can learn how to genuinely love our children and to exercise the disciplinary techniques that are carried out by God Himself in our own lives. We must always remember that God knows best, and He desires us to bring glory to Him by being the best reflection of Him.

As we understand genuine love, which evolves from knowing God in a personal way, we can understand who He is and how He operates in our lives. God's love for us is so radical that many people live their lives never understanding it. When we can genuinely understand God's discipline in our lives and know that His intention is always to keep our lives aligned with His will and with His purpose, we should be able to demonstrate the same qualities and actions toward our intellectually or physically challenged children. As we understand more and more, we will experience a closeness with God that is beyond imagination.

Not only has this closeness been a transformative element in my life, but the mindset that comes with it is also transformative. The question to ask, then, as parents, is how are we to allow this understanding of God to translate into the way we love our children, whether they are mentally or physically challenged or not? We are to be willing to administer whatever is necessary at any time. We are to love in the moment. To love in the moment is to determine what needs to be done, if anything, in the circumstance that is before us. What is the loving thing to do or to say at the time? If it is discipline, in whatever form is necessary, it should be given. If what is given is in the best interest of the other person, then that is what should be applied. As we learn how to love and to prune in this way, we will see tremendous growth in our fruit (children) as well as in ourselves.

Trusting God when we are in uncomfortable circumstances can be difficult, but not impossible. We are to make every effort to be obedient in all the things that God is telling us to do. I do not need to pray to God to ask him if I should discipline my children. I do not have to ask any entity of the culture around me to give me permission to discipline my child. God has already communicated to us that it is our responsibility as parents to discipline them and that if we do not, we are not genuinely loving them. Who should we believe—God, or the voices that are yelling out as loud as possible in the culture? "Let God be true but every man a liar" (Romans 3:4 KJV). We must decide whom we will believe. If God created the Universe and can exercise complete power over it, why is it so difficult to believe in the Bible blueprint that He has provided for us upon which we are to develop and build our lives?

Back in the fifties, there was a TV series called *Father Knows Best*. I have included several descriptions of the show. From one of the descriptions, we can get a sense of how popular this show was then and continues to be today on cable stations.

> The popular radio show comes to life in this hit sitcom about a wise family man, Jim Anderson, his common-sense wife Margaret, and their children Betty, Bud, and Kathy. Whenever the kids need advice on anything at all, they can always turn to their father, because father knows best.[3]

> Father Knows Best is a wonderful classic television show with a great look into American Family life with mom, dad, and their growing children in Small City USA. From 1954 - 1963 audiences enjoyed and tuned into the 206 episodes created.[4]

From these descriptions, we can understand the popularity of the series, which dealt with family matters. The father was able to speak wisdom into any circumstance thrown his way and could handle it with a confidence beyond imagination. He was trusted and well respected for displaying such character. God is our Father. He can handle everything we bring to Him. He can give us insight and wisdom in every situation. The question is whether I believe the truth about God and what He can provide, not only for me, but for every member of my family, including my intellectually or physically challenged children. *Father Knows Best* provides us with a picture of what a family was like when the father was connected and present. Our Heavenly Father can provide way more and way beyond what the father in the TV series was able to provide. He can know us intimately, go deep inside of us to heal us, provide His thoughts to us, and use us in ways we never thought possible. We can trust that our Heavenly Father can do the same for our intellectually and physically challenged children. What a great relief to know that we have a Father who can love us in such a way. Let us all receive that love that He offers and desires for us to have!

NOTES

1 *American Heritage® Dictionary of the English Language, Fifth Edition*, "chastise," retrieved September 8, 2021, https://www.thefreedictionary.com/chastise.
2 AV1611, "KJV Dictionary Definition: faint," accessed May 2020, https://av1611.com/kjbp/kjv-dictionary/faint.html.
3 IMDb, "Father Knows Best," accessed May 2020, https://www.imdb.com/title/tt0046600/plotsummary.
4 Plot Author Matching, "Father Knows Best", accessed May 2020, https://www.imdb.com/title/tt0046600/plotsummary.

9

Prom Night

For most teenagers, high school is a period of transition. It is a time when they are attempting to figure out not only who they are, but what they are planning to do with their lives. While they are navigating those dynamics, two events occur that most high school students look forward to experiencing: the junior and senior proms. The proms are special events. The kids dress up in fancy clothes, and some are even chauffeured to the event. Prom is an event that is highly anticipated by the participants, especially two to three months before it is to occur. As the time gets closer, in April or May, the excitement builds and the talk about it becomes more and more a part of the daily routine.

Prom provides a night of fun and enjoyment that can include music played by a band or a DJ, dancing, and a catered meal. Prom is an opportunity for the kids to experience a night that is indeed something special. Everyone takes pictures, capturing the moment in time. The senior prom, most likely, is the next-to-last big event for seniors, with graduation being the last, and it creates memories for the students that can last for a long time.

Since my children were homeschooled, they did not experience prom. Even if they had been attending the local high school, I honestly don't know if they would have attended anyway. I really don't know how many special education students go to proms. The level of their disabilities, I am sure, comes into play when determining whether they would have fun attending such an event. I would guess that many mentally and physically challenged students would feel uncomfortable attending, especially those who might be impacted negatively by large crowds or who are sensitive to loud noises. We took Danielle to the UniverSoul Circus one year, and she totally lost it because of the noise. We never went back again. We had no idea that she would have a problem with noise until then. A few mentally or physically challenged students who are well liked or who might be extremely popular for some reason might go to prom, but the majority probably will not.

The mindset of not "fitting in" or of being different from everyone else can easily slip into our minds. This can become part of the thinking of the ones who are challenged and also of the parents. The need for parents to protect their children can also be a driving force that might prevent a child from attending such an event. Parents may not want their children to have bad experiences, so for them it may make sense to forego this type of gathering, especially if the children have been having issues with students not accepting them during the school year. There could be a host of other reasons parents could cite for not allowing their children to attend prom as well. As I mentioned in an earlier chapter, many families stay isolated for a variety of reasons.

Three years ago, Epic Church, a large nondenominational church in Philadelphia, along with the Tim Tebow Foundation, held an event for special needs adults entitled A Night to Shine. It was designed to be a prom for those who were mentally and physically challenged. In fact, there were several such proms taking place at the same time in many locations across the United States, and even around the world. The purpose of these events is to provide an evening out for those with special needs. The night consists of a lot of fun with dancing and dinner in the company of a partner or buddy who is provided for them. In order for the church to manage the logistics of such an evening, hundreds of volunteers were required. They were placed at various locations to perform different tasks. We signed our daughter up for the event. After we described what the event was for and who it was for, she began to get excited. She looked forward to getting dressed up for an evening out, wearing an outfit in her favorite color along with her jewelry and a little makeup. This would be her night, and all the attention would be on her. What was so nice about the event was that the parents and caregivers who took the participants to the event would be taken care of as well. A place was provided for them to relax, hear music, and have a meal. Because a volunteer buddy was assigned to every participant for the night, the caretakers did not have any responsibilities.

We were able to experience this event as observers and not as caregivers. We had fun watching all the participants were enjoying themselves. It was an incredible scene. Hundreds of intellectually and physically challenged young adults were laughing, dancing, and enjoying everything that had been prepared for them. The event had been designed specifically for them, and they were the individuals of honor. Upon arrival, they were celebrated by a crowd of people cheering and clapping for them as they entered through the door. A long red carpet had been laid out for them on the floor. This gave them the feeling of walking down the red carpet at the Academy Awards like celebrities. All the guests walked down the carpet separately so that they could receive their own special shout-out from the crowd who were lined up along each side of the carpet. Our daughter, just like the other adults who were there—some in wheelchairs, some limping; some who were severely mentally challenged—was given her moment in the spotlight as if she was a movie star. The smiles on all their faces were just priceless.

The excitement leading up to this event was amazing for all of us to experience. Danielle loves Disney, and every time we tell her that we are going to Orlando for vacation, she knows that we will be going to Disney World. She starts to talk about it, walking around the house with pictures of previous trips, and playing all her Disney princess movies to prepare herself for the trip. She does these things despite having been there numerous times. For her, every time we go is like the first time.

Danielle was totally excited about going to prom, and we were able to see her mentally prepare for it. She walked around wearing the jewelry that she would wear at the event. She loves clothes and jewelry so much; she usually pulls out of the closet what she plans to wear to church a week ahead of time. This pattern of preparing to go to church has been a part of her life since she was a child. It was this excitement that she was exhibiting with regard to prom. Seeing her wearing her dress and jewelry, with her hair all jazzed up, made her father proud.

For the past three years, we have taken Danielle to Night to Shine. It has been a wonderful evening for her to experience along with hundreds of others who are like her. She dances the night away nonstop with her buddy, who isn't able to get a rest because Danielle doesn't want to get off the dance floor. What an evening for her and the other individuals who very rarely get the opportunity to have a night dedicated to them, which makes them feel so very special! There is something about their smiles and laughter that just gets to me when I see them getting out of their worlds for a little while to experience something that is magical for them. There is an escape from their reality of life to something that provides temporary pleasure and a long-lasting memory. The memory is captured through pictures.

I am reminded of a portion of scripture that depicts an interaction between Jesus and His Father:

> Then Jesus came from Galilee to the Jordan to John to be baptized by him. But John protested strenuously, having in mind to prevent Him, saying, It is I who have need to be baptized by You, and do You come to me? But Jesus replied to him, permit it just now; for this is the fitting way for [both of] us to fulfill all righteousness [that is, to perform completely whatever is right]. Then he permitted Him. And when Jesus was baptized, He went up at once out of the water; and behold, the heavens were opened, and he [John] saw the Spirit of God descending like a dove and alighting on Him. And behold, a voice from heaven said, This is My Son, My Beloved, in whom I delight! (Matthew 3:13–17 AMP)

This verse, at first glance, might have you scratching your head as well as thinking, "How does this apply to anything that we are talking about in this chapter?" Behind this text is something unbelievably beautiful for all of us to experience. This verse provides understanding that can change our perception of our challenged children as well as of ourselves. We find Jesus approaching John for baptism. John knew who Jesus was at this point and told Jesus that he did not want to baptize Him because he felt unworthy to do so. Jesus explained to him that the baptism was necessary for both of them for righteousness' sake. Why was it necessary for Jesus to be baptized if He had no sin? John had been baptizing those who wanted to repent of their sins. Since John's message was a message of repentance, those experiencing it were looking forward to a coming Messiah who would be righteous and who would bring in righteousness. Jesus, being without sin, had no reason to be baptized. This is where the beauty entered the scenario. Jesus had been preparing to enter His work, which was to move toward the cross for our redemption, for thirty years. At that point He was getting ready to move into the ministry phase of His life. With His baptism, if the Messiah were to provide righteousness for sinners, He had to be identified *with* sinners. It was therefore in the will of God for Jesus to be baptized by John to be identified with sinners!

Jesus was identifying with humanity, which was the key that unlocked the mystery of the incarnation (God coming in flesh). It was more than Him coming in a physical body; it was Him *identifying with humanity*. Jesus was going to fulfill everything that was required by the law to be the perfect sacrifice. His identification with us as humans signaled His ability to know the pain, suffering, agony, and the tribulations that are part of the human experience of living under the debilitating effects of sin. The identification of Jesus with our humanity helps us to know that He can understand our struggles with our challenged children. It also helps us to understand that God knows our children's struggles as well. Jesus can meet them in the areas where we cannot. Having the confidence that Jesus can go where we cannot, helps us to settle in a rest that is necessary for us. To be anxious keeps us on edge and forces us to be reactionary to everything that takes place.

When Christians are baptized, they are identified with Jesus in his death and resurrection so that His death becomes their death and His resurrection their resurrection. It was necessary to explain the first part of the scripture so that we could really understand Jesus and the comfort He is able to provide for us, but the second portion of the text is what I want to highlight. As Jesus came up out of the water when He was baptized, something quite amazing happened—a dove descended from heaven, and a voice spoke from heaven. We see the presence of all three persons of the Trinity. There was Jesus who is God in the flesh who had just been baptized, God the Father who spoke from heaven, and God the Holy Spirit who was represented in the form of a dove. We see pleasure that was demonstrated by the Father. He was authenticating that Jesus was the

Messiah, the One who had come to save the people from their sins; but He was also showing pleasure in what Jesus was doing. He was displaying how He felt toward His son and doing so publicly. The public display of pleasure by the Father for His Son Jesus showed the significance of the Son and how special He was to the Father.

The prom experience made my daughter feel special, and we felt special because of what was being provided for her. The attendees felt "special" because they were authenticated as persons and as being worthy of being celebrated. The tag of "special needs" was not part of anyone's thinking when they were out on the dance floor. They were experiencing something magical that made them feel valued. It didn't matter if they were in wheelchairs or couldn't talk—they were just having a great time. Jesus was being made to feel of value when God spoke up at the baptism event. The event was for Jesus and provided pleasure for the Father. It also provided pleasure for Jesus because He was doing something that was pleasing to the Father.

This verse has raised a question for me: What can we do or provide for our mentally and physically challenged children that will help create pleasure for them as well as for the parents? What resources can we tap into to make this happen? Seeing our mentally or physically challenged children smile and laugh is something that may somewhat minimize the pain that we can feel almost daily. Should I wait for that *once a year* when Danielle can look forward to something that produces joy for her? Or should I attempt to create special times for her in various ways on a regular basis? Could creating a schedule for her for experiencing events that could bring her excitement have an impact on her psychologically? I do not know the answer to this question, but I have recognized that she gets excited when there is a major event that she is looking forward to attending like Night to Shine and Disney World visits.

We know that Jesus received validation from His Father at the time of His baptism. This is documented in the pages of scripture. If it was a blessing for Jesus to receive such attention from His Father, wouldn't similar situations apply to us as human beings also? To be approved by those who love us is of utmost importance and goes a long way in making us feel significant. Not only is it important for those who would be considered normal to be validated, it is also important for those who are intellectually and physically challenged. Zephaniah, a minor prophet, wrote something quite interesting:

> The Lord your God is in the midst of you, a Mighty One, a Savior [Who saves]! He will rejoice over you with joy; He will rest [in silent satisfaction] and in His love He will be silent and make no mention [of past sins, or even recall them]; He will exult over you with singing. (Zephaniah 3:17 AMP)

In this text, God encourages His chosen people, Israel, and lets them know that He will grant them victory because of His presence. He will also deliver them from their enemy. He delights in them as well as loves them. He rejoices in them, so much so, that He will sing with delight and joy. This verse provides for us a sense of how God looks at those who are in Him (believers in Jesus). He rejoices in the fact that we have chosen Him to be part of our lives. In choosing Him, we need to understand that He has chosen us. I believe that God rejoices over those who are mentally and physically challenged. Though it may be difficult for us to accept, their condition is part of His will for their lives. During their struggles, those who have the cognitive ability to understand the gospel will enter a joy that is beyond their imagination. For those without the capacity to understand, I believe that God knows best and will handle them accordingly. It is still our responsibility to see that they can experience the joy that God wants them to experience.

Parents can make that joy possible only if they can see things from God's perspective. That means that parents must experience the light that comes only through the Gospel. Are we able to then rejoice over the children as Jesus rejoices over anyone who belongs to Him through faith?

Prom night truly is special in the moment. As the years go by and the event recedes further and further into the past, the memories become fainter and more distant. Everything that occurred might not be remembered. However, Jesus can provide for us a joy that can last no matter what the circumstances may be. Our hearts and minds, though physically exhausted, can still rejoice in the Lord for what He has done and continues to do in our lives through our mentally and physically challenged children. Why? It is because He gives us the power and the ability to do so through His Spirit. If we as parents can live through the power of the Spirit, and genuinely serve our children with joy, isn't it possible for that joy to be infectious? If the frustration in our lives can be minimized and the joy in their lives can be maximized, it is possible that the environment within the household will be changed. There is no guarantee that the environment will change, but the attitude of the parents can be changed, which undoubtedly will have a positive impact on the mentally or physically challenged child. Giving God the opportunity to work on our behalf is the only way to shift our perspective in such a way that will bring hope as well as a purpose that will produce dividends in the kingdom of God!

10

How Community Should Work

In 1996, Hillary Rodham Clinton wrote a book entitled *It Takes a Village: And Other Lessons Children Teach Us.* Clinton proposes in her book a vision for all children in America. She places emphasis on individual and group involvement in their lives. She concludes that those outside of family play a huge role in their development and well-being. This societal involvement helps to meet all of the child's needs.

We must be careful not to merely accept all that she wrote in this book, and genuinely scrutinize the meaning behind it. Clinton includes the government as a primary participant in the process of raising children. From her perspective, the government should have a say in what we do with our children and how they are taught. It is quite apparent that the elites who are in government believe that they know best when it comes to our children. Isn't it true that the experts in education believe that they know best when it comes to the education of our children? Isn't it true that they think that parents know the least? This is the impression I am left with after talking with many of them.

It takes a village to raise a child is an African proverb that means that an entire community of people must interact with children for those children to experience and grow in a safe and healthy environment. This does not really mean an entire village is responsible for raising your children or the children of a crowd. It is a premise that was used among indigenous people. The premise can be appropriate when used in the context of genuine community. Support is provided through different members of the community to help in the process of child rearing without any attempt to take ultimate control of the responsibility away from the parents. But sometimes social service and educational agencies lend more credence and authority to children themselves than they do to their parents!

For example, I have heard many stories over the years of how social services and educational systems have slowly stripped the authority of parents away from them by believing children's accusation of parental abuse over the word of the parents, who are sometimes automatically presumed guilty instead of innocent of all charges. Children have been given power merely by opening their mouths and stating that one or both parents have abused them. The Department of Health and Human Services can even take a child out of the home without any physical evidence that supports the accusation. The word of the child is enough.

There is an abundance of scientific evidence that shows that children's brains do not fully develop until they are close to the end of their teen years, and in most instances, not until they reach their mid-twenties. That is not to diminish the fact that there are many intelligent teenagers, but it does place emphasis on the time frame in which children's brains mature. Prior to twelve years of age, a child's thinking is concrete in nature and not abstract. Many children are discovering who they are during these years, and they interpret many things incorrectly, including various things that occur in the home if their perspective is fully based upon what they have learned in school. For example, a child might have heard in a lesson at school that spanking or touching in a way that causes any type of pain by a parent is abusive. Children may be disciplined for doing something that defies the authority of their parents. At school the next day, they might communicate the experience to their teachers. Since teachers are mandatory reporters, they must report the incident to social services, which launches an investigation. Notice that the investigation is prompted by the words of a child. The parents are not contacted by the school to inform them of what they are about to do. Isn't it interesting that it is much harder for the parent to be believed than it is for the child to be believed? How is it that the child has been given such authority over the parents and is able to use the threat of accusations to manipulate and control them? Many parents are literally afraid to physically discipline their children out of fear of being arrested or having their children taken away from them. Because the government has developed laws that minimize how parents may discipline their children, parents have been immobilized.

The government does not want to be just one of the participants in the village, having an equal say; rather, the government wants to call the shots and be head of the village. It is necessary to understand how "it takes a village" is to be interpreted when used by those in positions of control such as the government. There are those, however, who truly use the term as it should be used, in connection with community.

When I was in elementary school, I once said something inappropriate to a girl. One of the teachers heard it and proceeded to call my home and tell my aunt what I had done. Of course, when I entered the house that afternoon, I was met at the door. Shortly afterwards, I received my just reward—some much-deserved attention on my backside with the belt of correction. Another incident happened at a local corner store in the neighborhood where I lived. At some point I decided to use the five-finger-discount method of obtaining some candy. I had no idea that the owner of the store had been watching me the entire time. When I got home, my mother asked me some very pointed questions about what I had purchased at the store. She already knew what I had done because the store owner had already spoken to her over the phone. Again, I received some kisses on my rear end with the strap. In both incidents, someone who was part of my community—the teacher at the school and the store owner—showed concern about my behavior. The necessity for me to learn what was acceptable and not acceptable with respect to my behavior had to be instilled in me. Those spankings helped to shape my thinking process and change my unacceptable behavior. Developing character in a child was part of the fabric that everyone in the community believed in. The teacher and the store owner did the appropriate thing by contacting my family members to communicate what I had done. I then received what was, at the time, the appropriate punishment.

Community can play a major part in the lives of our children. In fact, when I look back at the neighborhood where I was raised, I remember a lot of interaction among neighbors in the community. They looked out for one another by watching each other's houses when the owners were not home or watching us kids while we played in the street. If one of us was doing something we had no business doing, you better believe that one of the neighbors would say something to us directly or make sure our parents were informed. It felt as if we had parents all over the place. That is why my aunt used to say, "I can see what you are doing." It really felt that way! On many occasions while growing up, I was confronted by my parents about something, and I never knew how they found out about it! This concern of people outside of my immediate family was part of the fabric of the community and contributed to the development of my character. The community concept during the time I was a child was different than it is today. Government, the media, and the educational systems were not as intrusive back then as they are now. If you really examine the climate in our culture, you will understand that the government, the media, and the educational systems aren't genuinely concerned about helping you raise your children; they want to control your children and instill a thought process by which children have the same rights that you have as a parent. This concept of parents and children being equal gives children a power that subverts the authority of the parents as well as the children's respect for their parents.

What is community? I will use the definition that Wikipedia uses because I think it provides us with a broad perspective.

> A social unit with a commonality of norms, religion, values, customs, or identity. Communities may share a sense of place situated in each geographical area or in virtual space through communication platforms. Durable relations that extend beyond immediate genealogical ties also define a sense of community, important to their identity, practice, and roles in social institutions such as family, home, work, government, society, or humanity at large. Although communities are generally small relative to personal social ties, "community" may also refer to large group affiliations such as national communities, international communities, and virtual communities.[1]

According to this definition, commonality is a major component of communities. What does this mean when we use *community* in the context of our intellectually and physically challenged children? What this should mean is that we are able to invite different entities and people into our situation to help us with our children, including the care, concern, compassion, and the desire to see them reach their full potential, whatever that is for them. The community brings with it the expertise, support skills, care, and whatever it can provide on our children's behalf. Different people as well as different entities can help in the developmental process if they are invited to do so. The difficult thing for parents is to invite them into the process without allowing them to have control over the processes that rightfully belong to parents. On several occasions, we turned down help from certain entities because we didn't like the way they ran their operations, or we didn't think that their offering was a good fit with our personal situation. We needed to be able to choose the best approach for our children and not allow someone who didn't know them on an intimate level to make decisions for us. We had to listen closely, pray, and exercise wisdom when it came to our children.

After listening to what any entity or person can provide, if you detect any inkling of a desire to control you, you must exercise discernment as you decide whether you want to receive the help that is being offered or not. The severity of a child's disability will also help determine how much help is needed for the child. The greater the severity of the disability, the more help and support are most likely needed.

Paul, in 1 Corinthians, expressed the need of community in the following text.

> You can easily enough see how this kind of thing works by looking no further than your own body. Your body has many parts—limbs, organs, cells—but no matter how many parts you can name, you're still one body. It's exactly the same with Christ. By means of His one Spirit, we all said good-bye to our partial and piecemeal lives. We each used to independently call our own shots, but then we entered into a large and integrated life in which He has the final say in everything. (This is what we proclaimed in word and action when we were baptized.) Each of us is now a part of His resurrection body, refreshed and sustained at

one fountain—His Spirit—where we all come to drink. The old labels we once used to identify ourselves—labels like Jew or Greek, slave or free—are no longer useful. We need something larger, more comprehensive. I want you to think about how all this makes you more significant, not less. A body isn't just a single part blown up into something huge. It is all the different-but-similar parts arranged and functioning together. If a foot said, "I'm not elegant like a hand, embellished with rings; I guess I don't belong to this body," would that make it so? If an ear said, "I'm not beautiful like an eye, limpid and expressive; I don't deserve a place on the head," would you want to remove it from the body? If the body was all an eye, how could it hear? If all an ear, how could it smell? As it is, we see that God has carefully placed each part of the body right where He wanted it. But I also want you to think about how this keeps your significance from getting blown up into self-importance. For no matter how significant you are, it is only because of what you are a part <u>of</u>. An enormous eye or a gigantic hand would not be a body, but a monster. What we have is one body with many parts, each its proper size and in its proper place. No part is important on its own. Can you imagine the eye telling the hand, "Get lost; I don't need you"? Or, the head telling the foot, "You're fired; your job has been phased out"? As a matter of fact, in practice it works the other way; the "lower" the part, the more basic, and therefore necessary. You can live without an eye, for instance, but not without a stomach. When it's a part of your own body you are concerned with, it makes no difference whether the part is visible or clothed, higher or lower. You give it dignity and honor just as it is, without comparisons. If anything, you have more concern for the lower parts than the higher. If you had to choose, wouldn't you prefer good digestion to full-bodied hair? The way God designed our bodies is a model for understanding our lives together as

> a church; every part is dependent on every other part, the parts we mention and the parts we don't, the parts we see and the parts we don't. If one-part hurts, every other part is involved in the hurt, and in the healing. If one-part flourishes, every other part enters the exuberance. You are Christ's body—that is who you are! You must never forget this. Only as you accept your part of that body does your "part" mean anything. (1 Corinthians 12:12–27 MSG)

Paul used the body metaphorically to describe how those in Christ were to interact with one another. Each part has a function that is necessary for the entire body to operate properly. We can apply some principles that can be derived from this Scripture to help us as parents to function better in our environment with our intellectually or physically disabled children. The text, in its context, stresses the unity of the church. The church is designed by God and provides a model that can be used in designing our family structure, especially with regard to our children with disabilities. Think about the following statements that pertain to the text:

1. Each member is necessary. The foot may not be as gifted as the hand in handling things, but the foot is still part of the body with its own important function. The ear may not be able to see things as the eye can, but the ear is still part of the body with its crucial purpose as well.
2. Each member has an essential function. The eye, the ear, and the nose—they all have their functions.
    - o None can do the function of the other. Each member has its own special purpose.
    - o If the whole body were only an eye, it would be considered abnormal: inoperative, nonfunctional, and useless.
3. There are three significant applications:
    - o The body of Christ, the church, can operate only if enough members function as they are gifted to do.
    - o The body, the church, becomes handicapped if some members do not do the work they are gifted to do.

- o The ability of the body to operate is determined by the number and efficiency of its members. The more the members of the body (church) function efficiently, the more the body (church) can accomplish.

Each member is distinct, but *together* there is only one body. If only one member existed, where would the body be? Of course, there would be no body. So it is with the church. If there is only one member in the church, he or she would be significant, the most important person around. But where would the church be? The point is clear: the church is not one significant and important person. The church consists of many members—all significant and important. But note: despite the diversity, the church is still one body. The church is only as effective as those who are functioning in the capacity properly and are doing it effectively. How do we apply this in our home environments where there are one or more disabled persons? We are to search out all the necessary entities and people who can give us what we need and to seek the help from those who are gifted in the areas in which we need help.

When we look at the body in this text, we can see how all its parts are necessary for it to function properly. This example of how the body is to function not only can apply to the church, but to the parts of the community that exist that can help us along our journeys. To say it another way, the communities of which we are a part can provide for us what we need if we are actively and aggressively seeking it. We should never stop seeking to find what we need from the community. The reason some families do not have access to enough resources is that they don't ask for them or they don't make their needs known. Here is a list of some of the resources that helped Beverly and me while our children were in their developmental stages of their lives:

The doctors—There were several types of doctors involved in our lives, especially in the beginning. We worked with a geneticist who conducted the testing and interpreted the results. There were medical doctors and psychologists who were involved at various points along the way. Every three to five years, we would have testing to see if there were any changes occurring and to determine where our children were cognitively, whether good or bad. We have consulted with an endocrinologist for the past fourteen years for David's diabetes. A nutritionist is now part of the team of doctors whom David must see every three months. There has also been a chiropractor involved with Danielle to help with her back.

Speech therapist—We needed to have a speech therapist involved because Danielle was not talking. She can talk a little today but does not have an extensive vocabulary.

Occupational therapist—The occupational therapist was needed to help with Danielle's walking. Her gait was off. She has scoliosis and tends to have bad posture.

School District of Philadelphia—Every year, Bev had to turn in a portfolio for each of our children that contained all the schoolwork they had completed throughout the year. We also had to have a certified teacher sign off on the work each year.

Neighborhood homeschool co-op—The co-op consisted of families who were homeschooling. The co-op met twice a week so that the children could have some socialization and be taught by a parent in his or her area of expertise such as science, math, social studies, and so forth. Having other parents involved with teaching a specific course helped provide variety in the students' lives.

Cheer—This was a large co-op that provided an entire day of activities and classes for children who were being homeschooled. These classes were for high-school-aged children and provided a day for parents to get a break from teaching.

Grandparents—During the early years, our children's grandparents afforded us the opportunity to have some weekends without the children as well as evenings for date nights.

Church—The family of faith was a major part of our lives. Church provided the opportunity for socialization, learning the scripture, and for the children to develop relationships. Unfortunately, during that time, many of the children who were the same age as our kids did not desire to be friends with them because their disabilities made them different. Please note that church can provide a great deal of help if parents are willing to put their needs out there and to ask for help. There most likely will be people who will desire to help you if they can. Don't allow discouragement to keep you from opening your mouth. Do not allow your pride to keep you from asking for the help you need.

Neighborhood sports teams—David has always loved sports. We were able to find an organization that provides kids the opportunity to play organized sports without the stress of trying to win a trophy, but which still were competitive. There are several organizations that are available for children with severe disabilities that will afford them the opportunity to play sports: Easter Seals, Special Olympics, and the City of Philadelphia Recreation Department.

Reading specialists—These teachers provided additional help with reading skills.

City of Philadelphia—The city provided part-time summer jobs for teenagers.

Neighborhood newspaper—This newspaper provided David's first job. He was able to make money and learn how to appreciate a job.

Neighborhood youth groups—These groups provided opportunities for our children to connect with other children their age as well as to participate in fun activities. David went to several of the groups that were being held at different churches in the neighborhood.

Salvation Army—This charitable organization provided an opportunity for David to learn music and to be with other children his age.

Neighbors—During the latter part of David's high school years, he was able to connect with a few neighbors who were younger than he was. It provided some socialization for him.

Cedar Grove Christian School—Teachers provided help in sharpening David's reading comprehension and math skills.

Community day care centers—These organizations provided preschool services during the early years of our children's lives.

Social security lawyer—This lawyer helped to secure Danielle's Supplemental Security Income.

Friends—We met people along the way from whom we were able to glean advice or ask if they knew anyone else from whom we could get advice.

Caregiver—This is a family member who currently takes care of Danielle on an everyday basis.

I am sure you can get a picture of all the entities and various people that were involved in our lives. I did not actually remember all the help that we had along this journey until I was writing this chapter. Most likely

I have missed some. All these individuals and groups have helped us and have been part of our *community*. They all brought something into our lives as well as the children's lives. They all have played a part in some way and have had a positive cumulative effect on us as parents and on our children. Could it possibly be that we have not valued all the ways that we have been helped by those who make up our community? Maybe we need to assess who helps us and how they help us. Then we should offer up to God praise and thanks for those who have helped us. Maybe that will aid us in being more consciously thankful for the people who actually do come alongside us to help!

The various areas of the community are like the parts of the body that are able to perform various functions. There are many obstacles that we may have to step over and around because everyone isn't sensitive to our needs. There are those, however, who are sensitive to our needs and are willing to do whatever they can for us. The journey with our special needs children can be a long and difficult one. If we can somehow get all the parts of the body (community) that are in our sphere to cooperate, the task just may become lighter.

Mrs. Clinton is right about the village being necessary for us to raise our children, but not in the sense that the village to which she is alluding, which includes the government and the educational systems, should have total control over what we do. Rather the village should be one that is creative with plenty of entities and people who come along to support us in our journey in a way that we deem best for our own children. The journey may be long, but with their help, we can reach the end.

NOTE

1 Wikipedia, the Free Encyclopedia, "Community," accessed May, 2020, https://en.wikipedia.org/w/index.php?title=Community&oldid=1041565595.

11

What About the Other Siblings?

There was a time in history when couples anticipated having big families with lots of children running around. The psalmist wrote the following:

> Behold, children are a heritage from the Lord; the fruit of the womb is a reward. As arrows are in the hand of a warrior, so are the children of one's youth. Happy, blessed, and fortunate is the man whose quiver is filled with them! They will not be put to shame when they speak with their adversaries [in gatherings] at the [city's] gate. (Psalm 127:3–5 AMP)

The psalmist indicated here that children are evidence of God's providence. Providence is the means by which God directs all things, animate and inanimate, seen and unseen, good and evil toward a worthy purpose. So, what, exactly, is the psalmist saying about children? Children have been part of God's divine plan from the beginning. God told Adam to "go forth and multiply" (Genesis 1:28 KJV). That command was given to him directly for the purpose of populating the earth with people. "Children are a reward from the Lord," says the psalmist. This scripture lets us know that sons help defend the family for they are like weapons (arrows) in the hands of a mighty man. Sons can defend the family in civil cases. In the Old Testament, the city gate was where civil cases were heard and handled. An example of this can be found in Ruth chapter four. The imagery of arrows of defense "in the gate" was natural for a nation endangered from without and within.

Having children was not only for the purpose of proliferating humankind; children also served as protection for the family. For us today, it is through children that we can learn, grow, and develop our understanding of God. As parents, the experiences that we have with our children bring out in most of us a desire to impart what we have learned in our own lives to the generations after us. That means that the decisions we make as parents today with our children will have a major impact on the sort of persons they become and how they will interact with the world. The question, then, is how do we as parents apply this in an environment with a child that is mentally or physically challenged? We might also ask how the environment surrounding a special needs child impacts the other children in the family. How are their lives changed and challenged?

In 2001, when our family went back to a church that we had left four years prior, we met a family there that had, if I recall correctly, nine children and two parents. Of the nine, there was one who was severely autistic. He, of course, needed special attention because of his condition. In this situation, it wasn't just the parents who were involved with his care. His many siblings took the time to help with their brother. He was a family member, and they had grown up doing things for him that the parents expected of them. Does that mean that they liked it? Not necessarily! I am sure that, during their teen years, because they had their own agendas and plans, the siblings did not want to be home caring for their brother. Because of the number of children in this family, it was a little easier for the family to function. There were enough individuals who could help with the arduous tasks, and that made the care of him less overwhelming for each individual.

Not all families are made up of that many children! Some may have only one or two children in addition to the mentally or physically challenged child. This makes the situation more difficult and even contentious at times. For siblings without a disability, helping to take care of a family member with a disability can be overwhelming and even bring about resentment due to the constant attention that is devoted to the child with the disability. The stress and the tension placed on the parents can be extremely difficult and can even create fractured relationships for several years. Sisters and brothers in this type of environment need not be selfish and self-absorbed. Balance is essential. To be able to handle the multiple issues that permeate this type of family structure is a major undertaking not only for parents, but also for the teenagers in the family.

Because there are various ranges into which a mentally *or* physically challenged person can fall, the degree and type of care needed is determined by the functionality of the challenged person. If a person is both mentally *and* physically challenged, the situation may be even more difficult. The cognitive and emotional challenges for siblings in an environment that includes a mentally and/or physically challenged child can be significant. Their lives are different from those of their peers who don't live in the same type of environment. In fact, their peers can put a lot of pressure on them because they don't fully understand why they may not be socially available as much as their other friends. There are numerous sacrifices that are made not only by the parents, but also by the siblings: sacrifices that go way beyond what may be required in what is considered a normal family environment.

One issue with which brother and sisters of children who are mentally or physically challenged must deal is their own mindset. Their thinking about their sibling who has the disability determines what they do and how they respond to the everyday struggles that are part of the family dynamic. Their temperament—the way that God designed them to respond to people, places, and things—comes into play as well. It is so important that the siblings have self-awareness. Siblings, as little children, may not totally understand what is going on with their challenged sibling and readily do the small things that they are asked by parents to do to help. However, as they get older, their thinking process becomes different and more abstract, and they will begin to ask questions. Then, as they move into their teen years and their involvement with their peer group becomes more important to them, they will have more things with which to deal, mentally as well as emotionally.

Siblings must come to grips with the reality of the environment in which they find themselves because they can become a major problem for the parents if they are more focused on themselves and the things they want to do instead of the needs of the family. However, there must be a clear understanding by the parents that their special needs child is not the child or the responsibility of their other children. Parents need to be aware that the responsibility to care for the special needs child ultimately falls on them. They can request help from the other children at times but should not require it all the time. If they do, the siblings can become angry and full of resentment, and exhibit a rebellious attitude. The parents can expect the siblings to do too much of the caring for the brother or sister who has the disability, which prevents them from experiencing the activities in which they desire to take part. It is crucial that the parents and the other siblings who are part of the family structure surrounding the child with the disability communicate and make necessary adjustments when needed. If the communication is not there or if parents force their other children to disproportionately care for the child with a disability, damage can be done to the parent-child relationships that may never be repaired.

There are also questions that the siblings might have that are spiritual in nature: Why did God allow this to happen to our sister or brother? Why do I have to be in this situation? Why can't our family be like other families?

If the parents are believers, they should be able to help their children process these questions or any other questions they may have. Helping them to wrestle through the thinking process is a crucial part of their understanding of who God is as well as how He sees the world. For families who do not have Christ as the center of their lives, the answers to the questions will come with more difficulty. The way in which they answer may not include absolutes that are clearly articulated in the pages of scripture. The mental challenges that can come along with being in a family with a child with a disability can, and most likely will, be more of a challenge for siblings in this situation.

Another issue among siblings in a family with a child who has a disability is the emotional component. The age and maturity level of the siblings influence the degree of understanding that they will have about environment in which they live. They experience what is not considered the norm by others but is the norm for them. Caregiving is done on a regular basis. Caregiving for the other siblings was provided until they were able to care for themselves. Care for children who have disabilities most likely will never stop. Caregiving is draining and can bring about emotions that some people consider undesirable or unhealthy. When people spend hours and hours each day doing the same thing with very little help or support, emotions can reflect the tiredness and the depressed mental state. If teenagers are a major participant in the caregiving and are getting very little time to do what they want to do during the years of their development, they may display attitudes that otherwise would not be present. The pressure that they feel helps to bring about what is going on in their hearts and minds. The push and pull between the desire to be with their friends and the need to stay home and take care of their siblings is a constant battle that they fight every day. This dynamic is likely to occur with most siblings as well as with parents who find themselves in the situation. These mindsets do not discriminate by age.

Siblings may bottle up emotions and carry them inside without revealing them to anybody or may be sharing them with friends but not with their parents. This is not good! Not being open with parents about their feelings can bring about negative emotions toward the parents. It is of great importance that the siblings tell their parents how they feel. If parents ignore what they have expressed, it may be necessary to get wise counsel from someone outside of the family or from family members who can be trusted and who may be able to intervene because of their awareness of the family environment. The ambivalent feelings and emotions surrounding the caregiving by the siblings can be added weight, especially if they are teenagers. As teenagers, they are dealing with a host of things emotionally including, in most instances, trying to figure out their own identities.

From a spiritual perspective, teenagers already wrestle with trying to figure out who God is to them. They may have received Christ at church or at camp or even vacation Bible school, but it is likely that they haven't wrestled with the tough questions of how to live out their faith in practical ways. Actually, many teenagers have not yet grappled with having their own personal walk with God. They may have made decisions to please their parents or teachers that were hollow without completely understanding what they were committing to. The spiritual aspect of understanding the sovereignty of God in light of the condition of their sibling can be profoundly overwhelming for anyone their age.

Other issues such as a parent who is no longer present due to death or abandonment, a parent on alcohol or drugs, or one who is experiencing financial setbacks can bring about additional emotional concerns. The dynamics at work in a family *without* a child with a disability can create many difficulties. For a family dealing with a child *with* a disability, these added issues can be devastating, especially if outside support is not available.

Another issue with which siblings must deal involves getting their friends to understand why they can't always be available to do things with them. Time is a major investment that the siblings must invest into the life of challenged sibling. In a single-parent family, the dependency upon siblings may be a major dynamic. The expectation of the parent for the siblings to be available at the parent's beck and call may be way over the top. The siblings can be made to feel obligated to take care of their sibling due to the pressure that the parent is placing upon them. Many times, this pressure comes in the form of guilt. The parent will exercise his or her ability to use words to manipulate a child through guilt to take care of the child with the disability. The parent does not want anyone else to do it because the child knows exactly what kind of care is needed and also knows the desire of the parent. The parent could possibly have someone else help, but the sibling is preferred. The care is done the way the parent likes, and the service is free. Suspicions of being taken advantage of can now enter the mind of the sibling and can bring about even more hostility toward the parent.

Giving up the teen years is a sacrifice. Some siblings do not mind doing it, but others do not have the desire to do it. Parents should not place an unreasonable burden on their children. As I stated earlier, the responsibility of caring for the child with the disability falls on the parents, not the siblings. It is fine if the siblings do not mind helping, but they should not be expected to help. Figuring out ways to have other people help with the caregiving is an excellent way to show love toward the siblings. To have the siblings help on their own terms is a great win for the parents. The siblings will be willing to help if they are not forced and if they know that their parents understand that their lives are as important as the life of the child who needs extra care.

The constant care of a child with a disability can bring about feelings of abandonment, resentment, bitterness, unforgiveness, and the feeling of being unloved in the minds of the other children. They have needs and desire the parents' care as well. With all the attention being given to the child with the disability, the other siblings can feel left out and used. They may see the parents as just babysitters and not as children with their own lives to live. They have their own issues with which they are dealing—at school, with another siblings and friends, a homework project, or just needing quality time. And they need attention from their parents. This, of course, puts more pressure on the parents. In their minds, they may think that their children are being selfish, but they really are not. All the children need their parents, but their parents may not be available to them. If there is a lack of attention by the parents toward the other children, the door will open for them to get that attention from someone else. Once their attention is diverted from the parents, the parents will have difficulty getting the children to want to be around them. The parents should do their best to stay involved with all their children so that they do not lose their relationships with them.

Siblings who continually care for a child with a disability can become overly responsible and independent. In giving attention to the child with the disability, siblings may neglect their own issues. They end up being like the parents. In some instances, siblings experience what some psychologists call parentification. They are expected to take on many responsibilities for themselves and their sibling, and they undertake duties similar to those of a parent while overlooking their own need to be children. This responsibility may seem positive to parents but may be a precursor to emotional distress.

If the siblings can begin to see their brother or sister with the disability through God's eyes, their lives can be drastically different because of what they can learn. I stumbled across these quotes with regards to people with disabilities.

- Sometimes the things we can't change end up changing us.
- There is no greater disability in society, than the inability to see a person as more (Robert M. Hensel).
- The only disability in life is a bad attitude.
- Your disability will never make God love you less.
- Put a "go" in front of "disabled." It spells: God is abled (Nick Vujicic).
- My disability has opened my eyes to see my true abilities.

As I was perusing the University of Michigan Medicine's website, I came across two questions that people had asked. They are as follows along with the answers.

What's the upside of growing up with a sibling with special health or developmental needs?

Siblings of children with special needs have special needs themselves. Their sister or brother with special needs *will* get a bigger share of attention. While having a special needs sib presents challenges, it also comes with opportunities. Kids who grow up with a sibling with special health or developmental needs may have more of a chance to develop many good qualities, including:

- patience
- kindness and supportiveness
- acceptance of differences
- compassion and helpfulness
- empathy for others and insight into coping with challenges
- dependability and loyalty that may come from standing up for their brother or sister.

What kinds of difficult feelings might a sibling have?[1]

Your child may, at times, have trouble coping with being the sibling of a child with special needs. They may have many different and even conflicting feelings. For example, they may feel:

- worried about their sibling
- jealous of the attention their brother/sister receives
- scared that they will lose their sibling
- angry that no one pays attention to them
- resentful of having to explain, support, and/or take care of their brother/sister

- o resentful that they are unable to do things or go places because of their sibling
- o embarrassed about their sibling's differences
- o pressure to be or do what their sibling cannot
- o guilty for negative feelings they have toward their sibling or guilty for not having the same problems.[2]

When parents tune in to the *individual needs of each child* in the family, they can help ease the difficulties.

The issues with the siblings may get so bad that the parents might need guidance to help the siblings who are struggling with the mentally or physically challenged child and the environment that has been created. The University of Michigan Medicine website also addresses this issue:

What are the red flags, or signs that my child needs more help?

Sometimes the feelings can be so intense or disruptive, that a child may need professional counseling to help them cope. Meeting and talking with other kids going through the same thing can also be extremely helpful—even if it is just online. Below, you will find resources to help your family find connections with other siblings going through similar things.

Talk to your doctor if you see any of these warning signs:

- o changes in eating or sleeping (too much or too little)
- o physical symptoms like headaches or stomachaches
- o hopelessness
- o perfectionism
- o poor concentration
- o poor self-esteem
- o talk of hurting themselves
- o difficulty separating from parents

- o loss of interest in activities
- o frequent crying or worrying
- o withdrawal

> You can expect some degree of sibling rivalry, even when one child has an illness or developmental disability. But sometimes the rivalry crosses the line into abuse. If there is a chance the sibling relationship has become abusive, you should seek professional help. Talk to your health care provider about options.[3]

Luke says the following:

> Jesus also said to the man who had invited Him, "When you give a dinner or a supper, do not invite your friends or your brothers or your relatives or your wealthy neighbors, lest perhaps they also invite you in return, and so you are paid back. But when you give a banquet or a reception, invite the poor, the disabled, the lame, and he blind. Then you will be blessed (happy, fortunate, and to be envied), because they have no way of repaying you, and you will be recompensed at the resurrection of the just [upright]. (Luke 14:12–14 AMP)

This verse clearly shows a demonstration of humility. Jesus addressed His words to the chief Pharisee, the most proud and ambitious man present. What He said was forceful; it served as a strong warning, for no man can enter the Kingdom of Heaven without true humility. Humility is not serving or centering one's life on those who can repay. Jesus used the banquet as an illustration. If the host engages the presence of only those who can repay him for his favor, then the host has received his reward. He will receive their favors, but that is all he will receive. He will not have God's favor; he will be left with only human favor. It wasn't that Jesus was downgrading normal social life and Christian fellowship; He was saying that the host had not shown humility and lowliness of mind, the giving of himself and his goods to those who really needed his gifts and services.

The host served only those who could repay by adding to his welfare. He had not humbled himself to help anyone who really needed help.

To demonstrate genuine humility means to be sacrificial and to be willing to give up what might be important to us for the sake of others. Humility involves, to a certain degree, serving those who are less fortunate such as those who are poor and those who have disabilities. Jesus, in the context of the verse, identified a person who was able to assist those who were in need because he had the means to do so. A willingness disperses what he had without any expectations to receive is an example of humility. There is no expectation in return. Is not this what Jesus demonstrated throughout His interactions with people on Earth? He was the essence of humility. We are to be like Him.

This is a reminder to us to know that, when we serve others out of a heart of humility, God takes notice and is blessed. Our reward might not be realized here on Earth, but it will be by God at the resurrection. That means that, when siblings help to care for their challenged siblings, they are not doing it out of futility. If they can do it out of humility and understand that they are receiving something from it that is of spiritual value, what a difference it makes with their approach! The attitude from which they operate will be one that brings pleasure not only to God, but to their parents. It is through God's sovereignty that they were placed in a particular family. That means that they have a purpose in that family along with the child who has the disability. That purpose can only be found through having a relationship with God through Christ. If they are able to recognize their need for salvation and then allow God to give them a new set of eyes, their experience with their sibling will be reframed and transformed.

Finally, it is necessary to state that siblings need support in addition to the parents when it comes to being in a family with a child with a disability. I came across a Brookes Blog that can be found at https://blog.brookespublishing.com/12-ways-to-support-siblings-of-children-with-disabilities/. It gives twelve ways to support siblings who have a brother or sister with special needs. They are as follows.

- Acknowledge siblings' complex emotions.
- Set and support high expectations—but watch that siblings do not take it too far.
- Expect and allow for typical sibling conflict.
- Create a safe environment.
- Give siblings opportunities to connect with peers.
- Provide access to accurate, age-appropriate information.
- Carve out one-on-one time with siblings.
- Actively involve siblings in the educational team.
- Advocate for services that support siblings.
- Learn more about life as a sibling.
- Address siblings' concerns about the future.[4]

Children who have siblings with special needs can go one of two ways. They can grow up being sensitive to their brother or sister and love in a way that is amazingly Christ like, or they can grow up having emotional issues that stem from their family of origin. If the parents are aware of their other children and give them what is needed, the siblings can adjust to the family dynamic and be extremely helpful in many ways. However, if the parents ignore their needs, the siblings might be headed for a difficult life. The parents need as much help as possible to navigate the difficult waters in which they find themselves. This help can come in the form of people, but it also must come by way of God. The help that is most greatly needed is that power that is given by the Source that is outside of ourselves: the help that comes from God Himself. Allowing God to be in the process to aid and strengthen the entire family will help all to walk in their calling, which is according to His purposes.

NOTES

1 Fritz Chery, "Disabilities," Biblical Reasons, accessed April 2020, https://biblereasons.com/disabilities.

2 Rachel Zeichman, "Thrive with Your Family: Supporting Kids with Special Needs and Preventing Sibling Fights," Michigan Health, May 7, 2020, www.med.umich.edu/yourchild/topics/specneed.htm.

3 Rachel Zeichman, "Thrive with Your Family: Supporting Kids with Special Needs and Preventing Sibling Fights," May 7, 2020, www.med.umich.edu/yourchild/topics/specneed.htm.

4 Brooks Blog, "12 Ways to Support Siblings of Children with Disabilities," May 2, 2017, https://blog.brookespublishing.com/12-ways-to-support-siblings-of-children-with-disabilities/.

12

The Scripture and Disabled People

The heart of God can be clearly seen in both the Old and New Testaments when it comes to His nature. God made us in His image, and that image is to be reflected on Earth for the purpose of bringing glory to Him. God, who is Love, created us out of love, and we are to reflect that love. That love is to be shown to one another unconditionally, regardless of whether individuals lack intellectual or physical abilities. God created all of us to reflect His image.

> God said, Let Us [Father, Son, and Holy Spirit] make mankind in Our image, after Our likeness, and let them have complete authority over the fish of the sea, the birds of the air, the[tame] beasts, and over all of the earth, and over everything that creeps upon the earth So God created man in His own image, in the image and likeness of God He created him; male and female He created them. And God blessed them and said to them, Be fruitful, multiply, and fill the earth, and subdue it [using all its vast resources in the service of God and man]; and have dominion over the fish of the sea, the birds of the air, and over every living creature that moves upon the earth. (Genesis 1:26–28 AMP)

This text indicates that, as God's creations, we are to have dominion over everything on Earth. There is no delineation as to whether God's image in man and woman is expressed any less if there is a disability present in the object of our love. Persons with disabilities, whether mental or physical, are not disqualified by God as not being made in His image or as anything less than human. God Himself said that everything that He made is good. Within the realm of good lie those whom God made who have disabilities. God does not see them as being inferior to those who believe that they are whole!

Throughout scripture we witness individuals with disabilities being used by God in various ways, even if they did not do anything that was earth shaking. The mere fact that they are mentioned in the scriptures by the Holy Spirit, who is the author, makes them of great importance. We have already mentioned Moses and his disability as well as Mephibosheth with his physical disability. Let us look at some others starting in the Old Testament. There are four men mentioned in 2 Kings who have physical disabilities. They are all together and have things in common because of the ailment they possess.

> Now four men who were lepers were at the entrance of the city's gate; and they said to one another, "Why do we sit here until we die? If we say, 'We will enter the city'—then the famine is in the city, and we shall die there; and if we sit still here, we die also. So now come, let us go over to the army of the Syrians. If they spare us alive, we shall live; and if they kill us, we shall but die." So they arose in the twilight and went to the Syrian camp. But when they came to the edge of the camp, no man was there. For the Lord had made the Syrian army hear a noise of chariots and horses, the noise of a great army. They had said to one another, "The king of Israel has hired the Hittite and Egyptian kings to come upon us." So the Syrians arose and fled in the twilight and left their tents, horses, donkeys, even the camp as it was, and fled for their lives. And when these lepers came to the edge of the camp, they went into one tent and ate and drank, and carried away silver, gold, and clothing, and went and hid them [in the

> darkness]. Then they entered another tent and carried from there also and went and hid it. Then they said one to another, "We are not doing right. This is a day of [glad] good news and we are silent and do not speak up! If we wait until daylight, some punishment will come upon us [for not reporting at once]. So now come, let us go and tell the king's household." So they went and called to the gatekeepers of the city. They told them, "We came to the camp of the Syrians, and behold, there was neither sight nor sound of man there - only the horses and donkeys tied, and the tents as they were." Then the gatekeepers called out, and it was told to the king's household within. And the king rose in the night and said to his servants, "I will tell you what the Syrians have done to us. They know that we are hungry; therefore they have gone out of the camp to hide themselves in the open country, thinking, 'When they come out of the city, we shall take them alive and get into the city.' One of his servants said, "Let some men take five of the remaining horses; [if they are caught and killed] they will be no worse off than all the multitude of Israel left in the city to be consumed. Let us send and see." So they took two chariot horses, and the king sent them after the Syrian army, saying, "Go and see." They went after them to the Jordan. All the way was strewn with clothing and equipment which the Syrians had cast away in their flight. And the messengers returned and told the king. Then the people went out and plundered the tents of the Syrians. So, a measure of fine flour was sold for a shekel, and two measures of barley for a shekel, as the Lord had spoken [through Elisha]. (2 Kings 7:3–16 AMP)

Four men who had a skin disorder considered to be leprosy were apparently restricted to a house outside the city. According to the Old Testament law, anyone who had leprosy was unclean and had to be isolated from the community. These men, because of their circumstances that pertained to their survival, decided there was nothing to lose in going to the Syrian camp. They discovered the abandoned camp, for the Syrians had fled when God miraculously caused them to hear the noise of what sounded like a great army. It sounded like the approach of reinforcements for Samaria. The lepers reported back to the gatekeepers of Samaria; they had news too good to keep. The king believed it was a ruse of the Syrians, but his returning messengers proved his suspicions were falsely grounded.

From the story of these four men, we can discern that, despite their disabilities, they were able to do something significant that aided in the survival of their people. The facts that they were in the right place at the right time and that they knew that they should not keep the plunder just for themselves indicate that they had a concern for others despite not being part of the community and being isolated. Some mentally and physically challenged children may be extremely limited in their ability to do much of anything, but there is something tangible that they can contribute to our lives that can be recognized by all who have the eyes to see from their hearts. We are to do our best as parents to discover what abilities they have that can contribute to the family as well as to the lives of others.

In the following scripture we read about a man who suffers physical disability taking part in a wrestling match.

> And Jacob was left alone, and a Man wrestled with him until daybreak. And when [the Man] saw that He did not prevail against [Jacob], He touched the hollow of his thigh; and Jacob's thigh was put out of joint as he wrestled with Him. Then He said, "Let Me go, for day is breaking." But [Jacob] said, "I will not let You go unless You declare a blessing upon me." [The Man] asked him, "What is your name?" And [in shock of realization, whispering] he said, "Jacob [supplanter, schemer, trickster, swindler!]" And He said, "Your name shall be called no more Jacob [supplanter], but Israel [contender with God]; for you have contended and have power with God and with men and have prevailed." Then Jacob asked Him, "Tell me, I pray You, what [in contrast] is Your name?" But He said, "Why is it that you ask My name?" And [the Angel of God declared] a blessing on [Jacob] there. And Jacob called the

> name of the place Peniel [the face of God], saying, "For I have seen God face to face, and my life is spared and not snatched away."And as he passed Penuel [Peniel], the sun rose upon him, and he was limping because of his thigh. That is why to this day the Israelites do not eat the sinew of the hip which is on the hollow of the thigh, because [the Angel of the Lord] touched the hollow of Jacob's thigh on the sinew of the hip. (Genesis 32:24–32 AMP)

> We know from a previous verse in the same text that Jacob had sent everyone who had been with him to the south bank of the river and had spent the night alone. While in the darkness a man, who is identified as God in verse 30, wrestled with his soul. During the struggle Jacob suffered a dislocated hip but continued to fight until he got what he wanted which was a blessing from Him. Jacob desperately needed help, but before he gained it, he had to confess the sin which was symbolized by his name, "heel-catcher," or "deceitful one." God changed his name to Israel, "one who strives, or prevails with God." The change of name, as with Abraham and with Sarah, indicated a change in status as well as a changed inner being. Jacob was not quite sure who was struggling with him until the end of the match. He then arose and testified to his new understanding by calling the place Peniel (30), or Penuel (31), meaning "face-to-face with God." His own new physical disability was to be a constant witness to him that the battle had indeed been real. His descendants were also to memorialize the event by abstaining from eating the thigh (32), or sciatic muscle, of animals which they used for food."[1]

From this account, we can recognize that Jacob had acquired a disability at some point during his life and had to live with a dislocated hip for the remainder of it. The hip served as a reminder for him. But at the beginning, it is not Jacob who seeks God to wrestle with him; rather, it is God who comes to wrestle with Jacob to bring him to a point of both physical and spiritual submission. God has a reason for giving him a physical disability; it is to remind him that he had wrestled with God and had an experience that changed his life. Jacob was known as a deceiver who used God to cover his actions, but then his name was changed by God to Israel, and he would become a blessing to his brother and other relatives. Bible teacher Arthur W. Pink writes,

> Jacob was not wrestling with this Man to obtain a blessing [;] instead, the Man was wrestling with Jacob to gain something from him. The best of the commentators all agreed—it was to reduce Jacob to a sense of his nothingness; to cause him to see what a poor, helpless and worthless creature he was; it was to teach us through him the all-important lesson that in recognized weakness lies our strength.[2]

In July 1967, a women named Joni Eareckson Tada was in a diving accident. She became a paraplegic, confined to a wheelchair for the rest of her life. After going through a terrible time adjusting to life without the ability to walk or to use her hands, she decided to allow God to do whatever He wanted to do with her. She became an author, an artist, and a speaker/lecturer. She has been a blessing to the body of Christ for years. God even brought her a husband in 1987 who has been by her side ever since. Her disability was used by God to have an impact for the kingdom of God. She was not born with a disability but suffered an accident as a teenager that left her with it. If we really think about it, most of us will understand that we will have some sort of disability before we close our eyes for the final time on this earth. As we age, our bodies are subject not only to mental disabilities such as dementia and Alzheimer's but to a host of physical disabilities such as arthritis, deterioration of soft tissue, inflammation, hyper-tension, and even macular degeneration. Whether we are born with disabilities or become hindered by them along our journey in life, one thing is for sure—God wants to get the glory from our lives either way.

As I have already stated, some kind of disability eventually will be experienced by most of us. There are examples of people who, by reason of old age, have lost their physical faculties, but for whom that has been no barrier to them playing an essential part in God's plans. Isaac, by the end of his life, was too blind and too confused to be able to distinguish between his sons, or to discern that a trick was being played on him. And yet the blessing which he pronounced on his younger son, Jacob, had lost none of its spiritual power, and the things which Isaac foresaw for his sons did indeed come to pass.

Similarly, Jacob, renamed Israel, who by the end of his life was too frail to get out of bed, quite deliberately switched his hands over and placed his right hand, the blessing of the firstborn, on the head of the younger of his two grandsons. Joseph, the boys' father, scolded him, but he made it clear that this was no mistake. Despite his physical frailty he had seen that God had plans for the younger boy, and like his father Isaac, the words he spoke in his weakness at the end of his life came to pass.

A few more examples of people who had disabilities and yet were vital to the purposes of God, include Gideon, who appeared to have had an anxiety disorder; Leah, who may have had a squint; Jabez, who was labeled negatively by others but refused to be defined by that label; and Samson, who, despite being blinded, destroyed the temple of the idolatrous god *Dagon*.

There are those individuals in the New Testament as well who had disabilities. Many of these folks, Jesus encountered and healed. Let us look at a few.

> And as they were going out of Jericho, a great throng accompanied Him. And behold, two blind men were sitting by the roadside, and when they heard that Jesus was passing by, they cried out, Lord, have pity and mercy on us, [You] Son of David! The crowds reproved them and told them to keep still; but they cried out all the more, "Lord, have pity and mercy on us, [You] Son of David!" And Jesus stopped and called them, and asked, "What do you want me to do for you?" They answered Him, "Lord, we want our eyes to be opened!" And Jesus, in pity,

> touched their eyes; and instantly they received their sight and followed Him. (Matthew 20:29–34 AMP)

There are three immediate principles that are clearly expressed in this scripture:

1. Jesus had compassion. As soon as those seeking his healing asked, Jesus's compassion was immediately aroused. He cared and felt for them.
2. Jesus touched their eyes. He did more than express compassion and feelings; He reached out to them and touched them. He let them feel His touch and care. He reached out and gave Himself to them. What a lesson for ministry!
3. Jesus healed them. They *immediately* experienced the love and power of God. The men cried out for mercy and were able to receive their sight. They were not able to know if Jesus would ever take notice of them. There is no indication that they were crying out for their sight before Jesus asked them what they wanted. They were longing for something greater than sight that they knew they needed, and that was Jesus Himself, the One who can give mercy. As a result of Jesus hearing them and asking them what they wanted, Jesus gave them sight. They had spiritual eyes to see Jesus before Jesus saw them and gave them physical sight.

Mercy is compassion or forgiveness shown toward someone who has power to punish or harm them instead. They were shouting over the crowd so that Jesus could hear them. They had to have known that Jesus was going to be coming by at a certain time, and they made sure that they had their spot picked out. As a result of crying out for mercy they were able to receive their sight from the One who was capable and willing to give it to them. I cannot promise that, like these men, people who have disabilities will be healed of them, but I can say that Jesus will hear them and give them mercy. Isn't it interesting that the crowd was telling them to be quiet and wanted them to go somewhere else? The crowd was bothered by their continued outcry and loudness. The men, however, through there persistence, were able to get Jesus's attention, and He responded with love and compassion.

There is another insight present within this story. The blind men were not focusing on their disabilities; however, their disabilities exposed the *crowd's* disability. The crowd was not able to see who Jesus was through eyes of faith, and they were blind of heart. Yet, the blind men could see Jesus through the eyes of faith, which enabled them to see Jesus despite their physical disabilities. To God, disabilities do not take away from the way He sees people; it affords Him the opportunity to work through them. This represents the beauty of God and clearly shows how God's thinking is totally different than ours.

This is an important lesson for the church. Often the poor and most needful are pushed back, ignored, neglected, rebuked, and not wanted by the church. They are thought to be lazy or lacking in initiative or unable to contribute much. The church rationalizes that the poor and needy would feel uncomfortable and would not want to be a part of the fellowship anyway.

God's thinking is so different than ours when it comes to all things in life. We are the ones who have an improper way of thinking when approaching life. God accepts and receives those who come to Him the way He desires them to come. He does not reject anyone who desires Him and choses to come to Him. So why do so many look at life through a distorted lens? It is because we are born in a sinful state and our perspective emanates out of that state. We call it a sinful nature. That is why many view lives from classism and believe that it is important. From God's perspective, it does not matter how much money people make, where they live, what kind of car they drive, what type of clothes they wear, what kind of house they live in, etc. However, many think contrary to God. It is foolish to think in such a way! The world needs love; people must experience God in a real way. The world, though it may not see it, calls out for that love and for something different. God wants us to see and think like Him and to be the hands and feet on His behalf. He is calling on all of those who belong to Him to stand in the gap and to help the needy of the world.

The apostle Paul in 2 Corinthians 12 shares his encounter with God.

> True, there is nothing to be gained by it, but [as I am obliged] to boast, I will go on to visions and revelations of the Lord. I know a man in Christ who fourteen years ago - whether in the body or out of the body I do not know, God knows - was caught up to the third heaven. And I know that this man - whether in the body or away from the body I do not know, God knows, Was caught up into paradise, and he heard utterances beyond the power of man to put into words, which man is not permitted to utter. Of this same [man's experiences] I will boast, but of myself (personally) I will not boast, except as regards my infirmities (my weaknesses). Should I desire to boast, I shall not be a witless braggart, for I shall be speaking the truth. But I abstain [from it] so that no one may form a higher estimate of me than [is justified by] what he sees in me or hears from me. And to keep me from being puffed up and too much elated by the exceeding greatness (preeminence) of these revelations, there was given me a thorn (a splinter) in the flesh, a messenger of Satan, to rack and buffet and harass me, to keep me from being excessively exalted. Three times I called upon the Lord and besought [Him] about this and begged that it might depart from me; But He said to me, My grace (My favor and loving-kindness and mercy) is enough for you [sufficient against any danger and enables you to bear the trouble manfully]; for My strength and power are made perfect (fulfilled and completed) and show themselves most effective in [your] weakness. Therefore, I will all the more gladly glory in my weaknesses and infirmities, that the strength and power of Christ (the Messiah) may rest (yes, may pitch a tent over and dwell) upon me! So for the sake of Christ, I am well pleased and take pleasure in infirmities, insults, hardships, persecutions, perplexities and distresses; for when I am weak [in human strength], then am I [truly] strong (able, powerful in divine strength). (2 Corinthians 12:1–10 AMP)

There are three possible reasons for why God refused to remove the thorn from Paul's flesh:

1. God wanted to guard against Paul being puffed up.
2. God wanted to reveal His power in Paul. The weaker the vessel, the more God is glorified when the vessel really serves Christ. Note God's answer to Paul:

    "My grace is sufficient for thee." The presence, love, favor, and blessings of God are sufficient to help the believer walk through any suffering. The word *sufficient* means the power or strength to withstand any danger. God's grace within the believer can carry the believer through anything.

    "My strength is made perfect in weakness." The weaker the believer, the more God can demonstrate His strength. If a man is self-sufficient, he does not need God; but if he is weak, he needs God: the help, provision, and sufficiency of God.

    "Most gladly therefore will I rather glory in my infirmities that the power of Christ may rest upon me." Note the point of this statement: infirmities or weaknesses are purposeful. The believer suffers for a reason: that the power of Christ may be demonstrated and clearly seen in his life.

3. God wanted to teach Paul to live "for Christ's sake." When Paul suffered some infirmity or weakness, it gave Christ the chance to infuse power into Paul and to overcome the weakness for Paul. Paul's infirmity gave Christ an opportunity to prove Himself. Therefore, Paul says that he took pleasure "in infirmities." This is a general term meaning all kinds of sufferings and weaknesses, whether moral or physical. The power of Christ can overcome any weakness or temptation for the believer.

"in reproaches": whether ridicule, insult, slander, rumor

> "in necessities": hardships, needs, deprivations, hunger, thirst, lack of shelter or clothing,
>
> "in persecutions": verbal or physical attack, abuse, or injury.
>
> "in distresses": tight situations, perplexities, disturbances, anxious moments, inescapable problems, and difficulties."[3]

When the believer is weak, he is strongest. How? By the power of Christ. And the power of Christ is much stronger than all the combined forces of humankind. Consider this scripture as well.

> And [Jesus] entered Jericho and was passing through it. And there was a man called Zacchaeus, a chief tax collector, and [he was] rich. And he was trying to see Jesus, which One He was, but he could not on account of the crowd, because he was small in stature. So he ran on ahead and climbed up in a sycamore tree in order to see Him, for He was about to pass that way. And when Jesus reached the place, He looked up and said to him, Zacchaeus, hurry and come down; for I must stay at your house today. So he hurried and came down, and he received and welcomed Him joyfully. And when the people saw it, they all muttered among themselves and indignantly complained, He has gone in to be the guest of and lodge with a man who is devoted to sin and preeminently a sinner. So then Zacchaeus stood up and solemnly declared to the Lord, "See, Lord, the half of my goods I [now] give [by way of restoration] to the poor, and if I have cheated anyone out of anything, I [now] restore four times as much." And Jesus said to him, "Today is [Messianic and spiritual] salvation come to [all the members of] this household, since Zacchaeus too is a [real spiritual] son of Abraham; For the Son of Man came to seek and to save that which was lost." (Luke 19:1–10 AMP)

Zacchaeus seems to have been of abnormally small stature; so much so that he had to climb a tree to see Jesus above the heads of the crowd. It appears that Zacchaeus was what we would call a little person because of his size. He had a history of making himself feel big by defrauding people when he collected their taxes. Jesus noticed him, valued him, and sat and ate a meal with him in his home. Being loved by Jesus enabled him to change and become generous. We read this in Luke:

> In that same hour He rejoiced and gloried in the Holy Spirit and said, I thank You, Father, Lord of heaven and earth, that You have concealed these things [relating to salvation] from the wise and understanding and learned, and revealed them to babes (the childish, unskilled, and untaught). Yes, Father, for such was Your gracious will and choice and good pleasure. (Luke 10:21 AMP)

This verse lets us know that God can give wisdom to anyone. Since God is Sovereign and can do anything, He chooses to do, He has the capability to give insight to those who are intellectually challenged. They can teach us things if we listen and observe. Those who work with people with intellectual disabilities observe that they are frequently quicker to hear from God than the rest of us. They are often seen as foolish in the eyes of this world but are wise toward God. Paul tells us in 1 Corinthians 1:25 that "the foolishness of God is wiser than human wisdom, and the weakness of God is stronger than human strength" (NIV). So, we can see God's special purpose for those with learning disabilities:

In John, we witness many people at a pool which is in front of the temple:

> Sometime later, Jesus went up to Jerusalem for a feast of the Jews. Now there is in Jerusalem near the Sheep Gate a pool, which in Aramaic is called Bethesda and which is surrounded by five covered colonnades. Here a great number of disabled people used to lie: the blind, the lame, the paralyzed. One who was there had been an invalid for thirty-eight years. When Jesus saw him lying there and

> learned that he had been in this condition for a long time, he asked him, "Do you want to get well?" "Sir," the invalid replied, "I have no one to help me into the pool when the water is stirred. While I am trying to get in, someone else goes down ahead of me." Then Jesus said to him, "Get up! Pick up your mat and walk." At once the man was cured; he picked up his mat and walked. The day on which this took place was a Sabbath. (John 5:1–9 NIV)

This text shows that there were numerous individuals with all types of disabilities lying and sitting in front of the temple on a regular basis. One day Jesus gave His attention to one particular man. He asked him, "Do you want to get well?" The man expressed an attitude that depicts what can happen to a person who is in a condition for a long period of time—he was hopeless. "There is no one to put me into the pool," the man replied. To be in such condition and not be able to get into a position where you believe you can receive healing is not a good place to be. The condition speaks for you, and your mind has tossed all hope aside and has settled into a place of resignation and immobility of thought. Most individuals who are intellectually and physically disabled realize that they will be that way all their lives. Their parents realize it also. There are some exceptions; God can heal if He chooses to do so. If it is not part of His plan, He will not. If He doesn't, then He wants to use the one with the disability in other ways. We can know from this text that Jesus is personal, that He will be with us and that He knows us. His grace is sufficient, and His power is present regardless of our condition.

What about this passage that we find in 1 Corinthians?

> For [simply] consider your own call, brethren; not many [of you were considered to be] wise according to human estimates and standards, not many influential and powerful, not many of high and noble birth. [No] for God selected (deliberately chose) what in the world is foolish to put the wise to shame, and what the world calls weak to put the strong to shame. And God also selected (deliberately chose) what in the world is lowborn and

> insignificant and branded and treated with contempt, even the things that are nothing, that He might depose and bring to nothing the things that are, So that no mortal man should [have pretense for glorying and] boast in the presence of God. (1 Corinthians 1:26–29 AMP)

Theologian Amos Yong sums it up like this:

> If people with intellectual disabilities represent the foolishness of the world, what hinders our viewing them as embodying the wisdom of God? This suggests that when we look at individuals with disabilities from an eternal perspective we should alter or revise our whole view of disability. We who consider ourselves to be the ones with the advantages and the upper hand in life – the strong, the clever, the successful, the so called perfect, the ones the world regards as 'gifted' – find that on a spiritual level we can be severely disabled compared to our brothers and sisters who lack those intellectual giftings, but whose spiritual life can be marked by abilities and giftings we never suspected.[4]

NOTES

1 Albert Barnes, Robert Frew (ed), "Genesis," *Barnes' Notes on the Old Testament*, WORDsearch CROSS e-book

2 James Montgomery Boice, *Genesis, Vol. 2: A New Beginning*. Grand Rapids, MI: Baker Books, 2006.

3 *The Preacher's Outline & Sermon Bible* – 1 & 2 Corinthians (Chattanooga: Leadership Ministries Worldwide, 1991).

4 Ros Bayes, "A Biblical View of Disability," Be Thinking, accessed May 2020, www.bethinking.org/human-life/a-biblical-view-of-disability

13

Hope for Their Future

Throughout my life, when it has come to talking about death, I have heard many people immediately want to change the subject or say very forcefully, "I don't want to talk about it." Some find it easier to talk about sex or abortion than to talk about planning a living will. I guess, in their minds, they do not consider abortion death; but while death of an unborn child is often avoidable, for all others on Earth, death is an inevitable part of the life cycle. Every person who has ever been born since the beginning of time has gone back to the ground from which they came, whether through burial or cremation. Similarly, there are individuals who do not like to talk about their personal finances for some unknown reason. They seem to think that it is not anyone else's business when it comes to their money and what they do with it. Could it be that this way of thinking has led a great number of families into poverty?

As someone who knows how to manage money well, I will offer a suggestion to those who think it is not important to learn how to handle it properly. If you do not, you will find yourself, as well as your family, struggling at the end of your life. The way you plan your finances in the early stages of your work career will determine how well off you will be at the end of your life. It will also determine the financial legacy that is left for your children. Financial legacy ties into the spiritual legacy, which is the primary one that you want to create for them. If you decide to plan close to the end or at the end of your life, it will be too late for you to do anything substantive. Estate planning, as well as handling the business around death issues for the entire family, is quite necessary and will prove to be of great value should anything happen during your years of employment.

For example, let us look at life insurance, which is a necessity if you have a family. There seems to be a misunderstanding around life insurance for many people with whom I have spoken over the years. Many do not want to pay life insurance premiums because they see it as just another bill they must pay. They consider it to be a rip-off, particularly if it is never used. However, life insurance should be viewed in the same way as car insurance. It is a *must* that every individual should have. Life insurance is necessary for a surviving spouse should anything happen to the other spouse. It exists to replace the income of that person who may, unfortunately, no longer be present on Earth. How would the income otherwise be replaced for the family? The proper amount of life insurance to cover the loss of the income as well as the amount of money to be needed for the children, whether for educational or medical purposes, should be part of the calculation when obtaining the insurance. Having the proper insurance will afford the same lifestyle without interruption should it be needed by the surviving spouse.

Issues around death are part of the financial business of the family just like purchasing groceries or paying the rent or mortgage. There is a verse in Proverbs that tells us how important it is to have a financial plan:

> Be diligent to know the state of your flocks and look well to your herds [those under your care.] (Proverbs 27:23 AMP)
>
> Be sure you know the condition of your flocks, give careful attention to your herds [those under your care.] (Proverbs 27:23 NIV)

Consider these words. I included two different versions just to give a little clarity. Let us dive into this rich verse. We know that a shepherd is the one who takes care of the sheep and sees to it that their daily needs are met. The shepherd has a great awareness as to what is always happening with the sheep and what is needed for each one. He knows them by name and knows them intimately as well. The word *intimately* describes how personally he knows each sheep. He knows the best environment in which they should graze and the areas where they will be protected. He constantly watches over his flock to make sure that they are safe and secure from predators such as wolves and foxes. There is nothing that gets by the shepherd because of his consistent concern and care for the sheep.

Like the shepherd, the husband, biblically given the position as manager in the home, should always know the condition of his family and should make provisions for their protection, including efficiently preparing for end-of-life issues. This means that everything pertaining to the end-of-life business issues such as wills, living wills, powers of attorney, trusts, etc., are arranged as soon as the marriage begins, even before the first child is born. It is crucial that things be in place as soon as possible long before anything happens to anyone in the family unit. This responsibility is part of the careful attention that is necessary for his flock. Let me help you by suggesting that, in this context, we view death as the wolf that comes to attack your sheep (family). The wolf can show up at any time to snatch a sheep, but the shepherd is always prepared. I do realize that there are families without a husband present and some without a wife. I would suggest the same approach be used by the head of the household depending upon the condition of the family. The same paperwork needs to be legally arranged.

Over the years, I have seen many families who have had to suffer because their houses were not in order when a loved one was lost. I have personal experience with such a circumstance. My dad passed away suddenly of a heart attack at the age of fifty-six. That is quite young, is it not? My mother was a homemaker and had not worked in many years. All that my mother received was $25,000 from a life insurance policy and one-half of his pension. I heard her say subsequently that there was something else he had in place, but it was never confirmed. If he did have something else, he never told her where it was located. The amount of life insurance was not enough for a woman who was not working and would not be able to help her sustain her accustomed lifestyle. If people would begin to carefully plan early in their lives when it comes to finances, hopefully by the time they are close to retirement they would have accumulated enough wealth to provide their own life insurance. They could have enough money to be able to cover all the death and burial expenses. I use this example from my own family experience to indicate to you how fragile life is and how a loved one can leave Earth at any time. What happened with my mom happens every day—a loved one is lost, and the family then struggles. This scenario could have played out differently if my dad had devised a plan at an earlier stage of life. Planning for such situations should begin before couples get married. It should start by a single person getting a life insurance policy and planning how to start saving for retirement.

The family into which I was born was considered normal in the sense that none of us children had any physical or mental disabilities. The family into which my children were born is not the same as my family of origin. Being the head of a family with children with disabilities, I investigate how I can ensure that they are taken care of in future. This is an issue that sits in the front of our minds and remains an issue of complexity to this day. Of all the troublesome things in life with which I deal, the main one that invades my thoughts on a regular basis is how to position my children to be protected after my wife and I are no longer here or no longer able to care for them. This isn't an easy issue for us and hasn't been for a number of years due to the fact that we do not have any extended family members who are in a position to take on the responsibility of our children. I must let you know, however, despite not having family to take on our children when they were young, we had a will on record that expressed our wishes for them should anything happen to us. Though many people most likely do not consciously think about it, the probability for Bev and me to be in an accident together was and still is quite high. Bev and I are often together in a car, in a store or parking lot, or somewhere else together without the children. Then there are the date nights, vacations, conferences, and other events that we attend without them.

You might ask who agreed to take on responsibility for our children. That is a great question! Since I know there are probably many families who find themselves in the same predicament as we are, I will share what we were able to arrange.

At the time, when the children were under five years of age, my wife and I agreed that we would talk to a few good friends who no longer had young children. Please hear what I am about to say, because I feel that this part is particularly important. We talked with a married couple who agreed to take on the responsibility of our children. This couple, however, would not have the responsibility of managing the money. We worked with a financial adviser who would manage the money that would be coming from the estate. This design is necessary so that the boundaries between care and finances are clear. We then had a secondary (backup) person who agreed to take on the responsibility of the children if, for some reason, the first couple could not. Deciding to go outside of family was difficult, but necessary. After examining and evaluating each of our family members, we could see that age, inability, maturity level, values, addictions, and health issues were all factors that needed to be considered. The friends whom we had in place for this task were willing to take on the responsibility of our children, and they exhibited and believed in the same values as we did. Values and beliefs should also be considered when choosing those outside of family to care for your children.

We have had a wonderful financial adviser for over twenty years. He has provided great advice and has helped to educate us about many aspects of the financial world with which we were totally unfamiliar. By the way, he is part of the Brinker Organization. I would highly recommend them if you do not have an adviser. Having a qualified financial adviser is a critical priority for a family with children who have disabilities. The advice and help that such a professional can provide is priceless. Our adviser has helped us in many ways and has been there for most of our children's lives. Many individuals whom I have known in the past, as well as some I know presently, mainly those who are in the lower to middle income level, feel that they do not need a financial adviser because they don't have a great deal of money. Financial advisers or consultants aren't just for people with large amounts of money. They are for people who need advice about managing their money. They also help people plan for their future goals because adequate money will be needed to reach those goals. People should not wait until five to ten years before their retirement to begin to plan for it. They need to start planning for that retirement prior to marriage, and then upon their marriage, they must make the necessary adjustments that would include retirement for both. An adviser helps you reach your financial goals and helps you with the overall planning for the present as well as the future for the family. The financial adviser should be part of the family's personal community to help them whether they have children and whether those children have disabilities or not.

Planning for children with disabilities is quite complicated. We found that there are a lot of services in place to help families like ours, but families must ask for them because there is no one standard system that enables them to find out every resource available. In addition, many of the entities that provide services do not tell families what they offer unless the families ask. Many parents stay isolated and do not put what they believe is their private business "out there" to people. They especially don't let their needs be known. By holding back and staying in a shell like a turtle, they can miss many opportunities and blessings. Help, mostly through people who might be able to relate to their situation, can come about in some remarkably interesting ways. Let me give you some examples.

One day in church a few years back, my wife was talking to someone who was visiting our church for the first time. She had come with the former pastor of the church who was visiting that Sunday as well. My wife had been introduced to this visitor along with our daughter, Danielle, who was twenty-one years old at the time. Danielle, in her usual way, greeted the visitor by showing her the jewelry that she was wearing around her neck and on her arms. The lady immediately realized that Danielle was "different." She mentioned that she had a special needs child who was like our child. She began to talk about her child and transitioned the conversation by asking Bev if we were Danielle's legal guardians. The lady told us that legal guardianship was necessary if children do not have the capacity to make decisions on their own. Without legal guardianship, we would not be able to make decisions for Danielle. To get legal guardianship, we would have to go through the court system. Danielle was already considered an adult at age eighteen by the system. Thus far, we had never had any legal problem; however, we were three years behind schedule. We had no idea that we needed to have guardianship over our daughter to be able to conduct business on her behalf; for example, talk with the doctor about things that were confidential. Medical personnel would need legal permission to talk to us even though we are her parents. Shortly after hearing this information, we proceeded to investigate procuring that legal guardianship. I talked to a lawyer at church who was able to recommend another lawyer who could help us with this situation. Some six months later and $5,000 out of our pocket, we obtained legal guardianship. We later needed this status to get some of the services that we now have for Danielle. This was God speaking to us through a stranger about something that was necessary for us. Just as a side note, guardianship paperwork must be filled out every year with the court system. It can be handled by the guardian or by an attorney. Attorneys charge for their services.

Here is another example. I was getting ready to retire from my job with the City of Philadelphia in August 2016. I had been to several retirement seminars and I was prepared to enter a different phase of my life. I had given Fairmount Park and what became Parks and Recreation thirty years of my life. As I listened to the person who was conducting my preretirement interview, I brought up the fact that I had two children who had disabilities and that one was worse off than the other. She said, "You know that your pension can be extended to your child if she isn't able to work." I could not believe what I had just heard. This was huge! I had attended two retirement seminars, and I had never heard this information. This lady had just blessed me. She proceeded to tell me who to call to get things set up. When I followed her instructions, I learned that the paperwork should have been processed prior to my retirement date. I was told that the transfer would not go through. I talked once again to the person who had informed me about this apparent blessing for my daughter, and she informed me that I could appeal the decision and request a reversal by writing to the Board of Pensions Commissioner. I immediately did just that. About a month later, I received a letter informing me that I had won the appeal. Next, I needed an affidavit drawn up by a lawyer for my file. I also needed to have an irrevocable trust in Danielle's name so that it could go into my file at the pension board. Why was this decision of such great significance? Danielle will continue to get my pension should anything happen to Beverly after I am gone. Normally, the pension would stop when the spouse who was receiving the benefit dies. To know that there is money there for my daughter for the rest of her life after her mom dies is truly a blessing and affords a tremendous amount of comfort. Had I not mentioned the children at the interview, I would have missed out on this benefit and added blessing. How many people who worked for the city were unaware of this benefit and have missed having it in place for their children with severe disabilities?

How about one more! One day I asked my niece, who works in a doctor's office, about which care agency was best among the agencies that hire family members to take care of a loved one. We were considering whether my wife should care for her mother or not. Beverly had finished homeschooling the children, and it was time for her to move on to something else in life. She hadn't worked in over twenty years and was behind with all the technological advances that were being used in the workplace. In addition to talking about Bev's mother, my niece mentioned that care is handled the same way for any family member if the criteria are met. That meant that my daughter would fit into the category to be cared for as well. I had no idea that a person could take care of someone who was incapacitated mentally. I was under the impression that home care was just for older individuals with physical conditions.

We found out that another family member was interested in caring for Bev's mom. After hearing this, we turned our attention to our daughter and began going through the process with an independent enrollment broker. I had heard about them through my cousin who was taking care of her brother. We got to the final stage when a question arose on their end. They asked if we had power of attorney over Danielle, to which I replied, "We are her legal guardians." They, in turn, said that it was the same as being power of attorney and that Bev was not eligible as the caregiver due to a conflict of interest. This meant that Bev could not care for Danielle, but someone else could. This was still a good situation because it meant that Bev could work, and someone else could care for Danielle.

It had been determined that we were eligible to receive help in caring for Danielle, but now we had to figure out, since Bev would not be permitted to be Danielle's caregiver, who could fill that role. We started brainstorming to come up with names of individuals we knew who would be sensitive to Danielle's condition. One day I was on the phone talking to a cousin and I asked if she knew of anyone who was a caregiver in the family who might be interested. She mentioned another cousin who had been caring for her mother who had recently passed away. After a few days, I contacted her and asked if she was interested. She was, and she has been with us ever since. Because I mentioned a need, someone was able to connect us with the person who was a perfect fit for our daughter. That is nothing but God at work!

These accounts are long, but necessary to demonstrate how God works to fill our needs. In every situation I mentioned, God provided just the right person to give us vital information that we needed to locate resources that would help us to secure present and future care for our children. We can agree that some financial things are in place for Danielle, but we still have to change some things for her as well as for David. It is an ongoing fluid situation that requires constant change as we go through different phases of our lives. Currently, we need to update our wills to arrange for someone to be responsible for seeing to it that our adult children are taken care of. The individuals (friends) I mentioned earlier are much older than we are and are no longer able to assume the responsibility of our adult children with disabilities. We have been talking about our options because we need this business to be handled. We are grateful for having had something arranged for all these years, but we must make changes as we move into the future. We need to find someone younger who will be willing to take on the responsibility of our adult children. This can be an arduous task, but once it is completed, we will feel peace and satisfaction knowing that all possible contingencies are covered.

We need not consider more than a few verses from the Word to determine that the wisdom of financial planning is found among its pages. I want you to reflect on the following Scriptures:

[Put first things first.] Prepare your work outside and get it ready for yourself in the field; and afterward build your house and establish a home. (Proverbs 24:27 AMP)

> For which of you, wishing to build a farm building, does not first sit down and calculate the cost [to see] whether he has sufficient means to finish it? Otherwise, when he has laid the foundation and is unable to complete [the building], all who see it will begin to mock and jeer at him. (Luke 14:28–29 AMP)

> Let Pharaoh do this; then let him select and appoint officers over the land and take one-fifth [of the produce] of the [whole] land of Egypt in the seven plenteous years [year by year]. And let them gather all the food of these good years that are coming and lay up grain under the direction and authority of Pharaoh and let them retain food [in fortified granaries] in the cities. And that food

> shall be put in store for the country against the seven years of hunger and famine that are to come upon the land of Egypt, so that the land may not be ruined and cut off by the famine. (Genesis 41:34–36 AMP)

> The rich rule over the poor, and the borrower is servant to the lender. (Proverbs 22:7 AMP)

> Give a portion to seven, yes, even [divide it] to eight, for you know not what evil may come upon the earth. (Ecclesiastes 11:2 AMP)

> There is a serious and severe evil which I have seen under the sun: riches were kept by their owner to his hurt. But those riches are lost in a bad venture; and he becomes the father of a son, and there is nothing in his hand [with which to support the child]. (Ecclesiastes 5:13–14 AMP)

> The thoughts of the [steadily] diligent tend only to plenteousness, but everyone who is impatient and hasty hastens only to want. (Proverbs 21:5 AMP)

We can glean from these scriptures the building blocks and principles that make up the financial planning concept which can be presented to people from a biblical perspective. These principles follow in same order of the scriptures as I presented them:

1. Establish priorities.
2. Create a budget.
3. Build an emergency fund.
4. Avoid debt.
5. Diversify your investments.
6. Reduce risk as you age.
7. Create a financial plan.

These principles can be applied to any family situation. That is why it is so important to begin as early as possible so that when unexpected circumstances arise, such as our current COVID-19 pandemic, we are prepared for it. The size of the family and the amount of income will, without a doubt, determine how much is available for various portions of your financial plan. Having a plan, however, is still of upmost importance no matter the size of the family or the income level. Having an adviser to help determine what is available to you and how to navigate the myriad of scenarios that exist can be quite helpful.

Understanding the importance of a financial plan for a family that has a child with a disability is the first step to prepare the family for the future. The following steps are necessary to prepare or to change the direction as you plan for the care of your child after you are gone.

1. Identify the goals.
2. Evaluate your current condition.
3. Establish the steps you need to take.
4. Implement the steps.
5. Have measures in place to establish your progress.

I had wanted to make a change with my employment for years prior to my retirement from my job with the City of Philadelphia, but I had to determine if I was in a financial position to do so. I had expressed these thoughts to my financial adviser, Joe Brinker. Throughout the years, we met once a year so that he would be abreast with any changes in our lives. Over a period of twenty years, there were a lot of changes involving relationships, property, death, etc. The common denominator of many of the changes concerned finances. As we discussed these changes, he guided us, provided wise counsel, and was able to give us information on several issues we would have had no other way of knowing. He kept us from getting into situations that would have brought harm to our family and to our finances. To be honest, I made some decisions that cost us financially. Why? I did not seek his counsel before moving forward with them. I knew he would question what I was doing, and I did not want him to tell me I should not do it. Isn't that what we do when it comes to the things we want to do that we know God would not want us to do? We all know how to avoid accountability if we genuinely want to get our own way. Once again,

I would suggest that you to invite a financial adviser or coach to ride with you on your journey. His or her guidance can be priceless.

I believe that it is essential for me to be honest and open about our journey to help you with yours. We have gone through a lot of pain in many areas of our lives, and I have come to understand that God has been there the entire time, providing comfort and peace during times of difficulties. The people He has brought into our lives to guide us truly have proved that He is present with us and will provide us with everything that we need.

After David graduated from school (his graduation took place in Harrisburg at a commencement held for homeschoolers), we began to pray and ask the Lord to provide a full-time job for David. The benefits available with full time employment were necessary for our family. David's condition is not as severe as Danielle's, so he is able to do some types of work as long as he is under close supervision. Danielle has been covered totally by Medicaid after coming off my coverage at age twenty-six. She had Medicaid coverage as a secondary coverage most of her life while she was covered under my insurance as her primary insurance while I was working full time with the City of Philadelphia. My insurance will be coming to an end next year, and David will no longer have coverage, not because of his age, but because my five years of coverage after retirement will be over. David required coverage, and a part-time job would not provide that for him. We tried to work through an agency located in Philadelphia that helps to find jobs and to advocate for those who have disabilities, but they dropped the ball on us twice.

David had worked with Parks and Recreation for a few summers. He had worked at a recreation center as a junior counselor and then worked at another center the following year. To make a long story short, David qualified to participate in a federally funded program known as the Community Apprenticeship Program (CAP). It was a twenty-four-month development work experience that offered two career pathways. The first was community engagement, and the second was park environmental services. CAP included a four-day work experience, one day of which entailed professional development, workplace mentorship, and exposure to careers within the parks and recreation industry. The program was designed to provide permanent positions to those who completed it. David was offered a position at one of the recreation centers. God had answered our prayer. David is now a permanent employee with benefits. He has his own health coverage and all the perks that come with having a full-time position. David completed his probationary period December of 2019. COVID-19 shut down Philadelphia in March. Because David was a permanent employee, he was left in a somewhat secure position.

At least half of our concerns about our adult children with disabilities have been alleviated. A great number of our financial concerns have been resolved, but there are other issues that are still pending. We need to amend our wills because, as I mentioned earlier, the individuals who were to take care of David and Danielle have grown older now and are no longer able to undertake their care. So, we must decide where they will stay, and we must establish a trust for our son.

Some might ask if it would be easier to just put them into a carefully chosen institution. Institutions are necessary for some people but should be a last resort. We have two children on the spectrum; one is worse off than the other. They are brother and sister and need to remain together as a family should we not be around. Why would I want them to be institutionalized if they could remain in an environment to which they are accustomed and where they are comfortable? With the financial adviser serving as a partner with us, we have found someone whom we trust who will provide accountability. What a comfort to know that there is an organization that can be trusted to handle all the business issues when parents are no longer around!

Some parents, I am sure, can be overwhelmed with all the details that must be taken care of and the things that need to be in place for their children with disabilities. That is why issues should be handled one at a time and coordinated with individuals who can help you plan. What peace of mind knowing that things are fully planned!

I have worked since I was out of college and will be working for several more years. Hopefully, my house will be paid off within five to ten years; this is the next goal once all other debt is paid off. Why is having no debt of great importance, including the house being paid off? If the house is paid off, the adult children can stay there. One of the biggest issues to be considered on the financial side is where the children will stay. If the house were not paid for and the parents were still carrying the mortgage, money would need to be taken from the estate. This is the first requirement if the property were to be kept in the family. The accounts that contain cash would be liquidated in order to handle the matter. If there is not enough money to pay off the house from the estate, it is quite possible that the children could not remain on the property because the house was not totally owned by the parents. Therefore, the mortgage, if possible, should be paid off as soon as possible if the family can afford to do so. It is also necessary to have a caregiver in place and a person who will manage the home. There are two jobs that are being provided with this type of structure. If the disabled child or children are receiving all the benefits that they are entitled to have, it sets up a good situation. Your home now becomes a home for your children. I advise you to check with a financial adviser to evaluate your personal situation to determine your course of action. Another action that can assure that the children may remain in the home is to have their names on the deed. This might be worth checking out. Because Danielle gets my pension, should anything happen to Bev, there is ample income along with her support from the state to pay for her sustainability. As for David, he has a full-time job with benefits. He will have a pension in his later years as well, should he keep his employment with the city. In addition to David's pension with the city, I have established a Roth IRA for him. Establishing an alternate source of income for his retirement years early in his working career sets him up nicely to have a tremendous financial cushion in his later years.

The manager of the house sees to it that the house is maintained properly and handles all related issues. The manager also sees that David is supervised. If the manager is living on the property, she or he will be at the house most of the time. The caregiver comes to the house every day to take care of Danielle. Danielle may be able to receive additional caregiving services if we are no longer around. I am sharing with you that we would like to see with our family situation after Bev and I are home to be with the Lord. We are closer to having heaven be our home with so many years behind us. My prayer is that this scenario will become reality for our children. As you can see, we are doing our best to plan for their future. I pray that all parents in the same situation will do their best to plan as well. For our plan to materialize in their future, there are things we must do now to provide for them later.

Relationships are key components of a well-constructed plan to provide the best possible future for our challenged children. We must be willing to turn over every rock to procure all they are permitted to have. There will be those along the way who will not help, those who will try to discourage, those who will say that we do not deserve what we are asking for, and those who will stand around and criticize. Despite how badly we hurt when people behave with such negativity, we must keep on pressing forward to the mark of the high calling, the calling that we have been given by God to fulfill, which is the care of the gifts (children) He has given to us. We are to manage everything they must have while we are here, and we must manage those things that must be in place for their future when we are no longer here.

In this chapter, I have intentionally presented to you many of the issues that we have faced during our lives and those we are still facing. We just heard that a neighbor recently passed away suddenly at the age of fifty-three. She leaves behind a husband and a son who is fifteen years of age. Who expected her to pass away suddenly after having a heart attack? We never know when our time will be up, and that is why we need to make sure that family business is organized. I would even advise you to have all your plans together, especially with regard to your death. What does that entail? It means having your funeral paid for if possible; having the plot picked out and paid for or cremation preparations made and paid for; having the funeral arrangements made and paid for; and having all your paperwork done and tucked away somewhere where it can be found. In fact, all your paperwork should be in one location, and you should provide copies appropriate people: lawyer, adviser, person power of attorney, and anyone else concerned. Your spouse and at least one friend should know where to find your paperwork.

Just like a batter who hits a homerun and covers all the bases, you should cover all the bases *before* the game is over.

Postscript: Since I wrote this chapter, there have been some new developments regarding our will. We had been praying for many years that God would provide someone younger who would be willing to take on the responsibility of our children after we die. God answered our prayers! I was approached by a casual friend after a morning Bible study one Wednesday. He told me that God had put our family on his heart, and that He had told him that our children would be involved in his life in some way. The message from God had been so strong that he had changed his desire and decided not to move from Philadelphia. When we had a conversation sometime afterwards, I asked if he and his wife would be willing to take on the responsibility of our children after we are gone. They agreed without hesitation! Apparently, he had sensed that was what God was telling him to do. God once again has met our need in an amazing way. We never approached or asked this couple to consider taking on the responsibility before he came to me. God placed it in his heart to do it before we mentioned it. After our conversation, we had our wills updated. We needed, however, to use a lawyer who was familiar with the law pertaining to protecting the social services that pertain to the needs of disabled individuals. A great burden has been lifted from us. I hope that you are able to see God through the way He provided for the needs of both David and Danielle over and over again. We must be willing to recognize that it must be in His timing.

14

A Counseling Perspective of Mental Health

As a counselor, I have encountered individuals over the years who have come for marriage or relationship counseling who shown underlying mental issues. In just about all the instances in which I experienced this; few were receptive to the idea that a many of their relationship problems could be associated with a cognitive disability that could possibly be hindering their ability to think properly. Professionals who are in the people-caring business—pastors, counselors, social workers, psychologists, psychiatrists—all have worked with individuals who have denied that they have any kind of intellectual disability despite the clear indications. It is easy for someone who deals with people every day and is trained to spot certain characteristics associated with various behaviors to easily detect whether a person is exhibiting healthy, normal behavior or thinking patterns or not. Clients who don't receive the advice of the professional, or at the very least consider what they are being told, are doing themselves a disservice as well as bringing unjust hardship to those they love by ignoring the possibility of a disability or being indifferent about it. When a person shows signs of what appears to be unnecessary uncontrolled behavior, obviously there must be something going on psychologically that is driving the behavior. For example, when people who are stuck in addiction accepts that their lives are out of control and unmanageable but continue to deny that they have a psychological or mental disability that is driving their addiction, there is little hope that they can be helped until they do admit that they need help for an underlying illness.

Many people don't want to accept that they have a disability whether physical or intellectual. We can witness disabilities in others, however. As people get older, a doctor may urge them to give up driving because they are unable to be alert; a coach may tell players who used to be the best on the team that they are no longer good enough to make the team. Personally, I finally must come to terms with myself that I no longer can remember a person's name once I walk away from our first meeting. As I mentioned earlier in another chapter: we all will have some kind of disability before leaving this world.

As an example of evaluating cognitive issues, let me use something that is quite relevant to this current time. During the reality of quarantine in 2020 and amid the presidential election, we witnessed something that I consider very strange. We experienced two candidates, both of whom appeared to have some mental issues. Both would deny that there were any issues, but it is quite clear when they talked that something was not right. Senator Joe Biden, at times, was not able to think properly and seemed to have lost the ability to remember things. President Donald Trump seemed to show that he was a narcissist through and through. How does this play out in the public square with each of these men's behaviors? Senator Joe Biden will be the opposite of President Donald Trump. Senator Biden can possibly be vulnerable to being told what to do with no push back. When it comes to surrendering authority, he can allow individuals to do what they want while President Trump will desire to control everything and tend to be a micromanager. He must constantly confirm to everyone around him of his importance and his position as the one who makes the final decision on things.

I used this example merely to indicate how people in such high positions can ignore their disabilities. It is proof that no one is immune to having them even if they refuse to acknowledge that they have them. Let us not forget that individuals with disabilities, no matter what class, sex, ethnic group, religion, or age, at some point, can be taken advantage of by those who claim to be looking out for their best interests. Many times, these people are looking out only for their own interests. Acceptance of disabilities by those who think they do not have them is the beginning of their freedom and can bring them a peace that they haven't experienced until that acceptance came about. It can also have a tremendous impact on changing the environment and dynamics of their relationships.

One day I received a questionnaire about counseling those with mental illness. I filled it out and, for some unknown reason I saved the questions. I inadvertently pulled them up on the computer just a few days ago. I thought that these questions were relevant to our topic, so I decided to include them so that you can see my mindset as a clinician as opposed to a parent. Just so that you know, I am writing this book from three different perspectives: as a pastor/teacher, a pastoral counselor, and a parent.

1. Pastor, how do you feel that your (Christian) faith helps in counseling people that have mental illness?

I just heard a statistic last week: 27 percent of the population has some type of mental problem. That means that there is slightly more than one out of every four people who have some sort of cognitive issue. Some individuals have mental illness that are out of their control such as those who are bi-polar or those who are clinically depressed. Then there are those who have mental illness caused by traumatic events or circumstances that have taken place in their lives. Still others have some sort of mental issue that is causally linked to sin. When I use the term *sin* in this context, I mean holding on to feelings for years such unforgiveness, resentfulness, bitterness, rage, and malice. These have devastating effects on the human psyche. The Bible provides answers for many of the human conditions with which people wrestle on a regular basis. My focus is to help people identify with those in the scripture who had similar issues, and to see how their faith was able to free them. Many people are held in mental prisons due to lies that they have believed from their childhood. If the lies are replaced with truth, they are made free through that truth. Their behavior can be changed, and they can experience freedom.

2. What do you feel your best course of counseling treatment would be for someone who has a diagnosis of moderate anxiety disorder?

Anxious people tend to worry a lot about things. Many of the things that they worry about are out of their control. I would want to talk about their concerns at that level. What are the legitimate issues that they have reason to be concerned about? Once this information is ascertained, we would begin the process of discussing them. What are the options available for them if there are issues that are within their control? I would look at some individuals in the scripture to see how they were able to deal with their anxious moments; it might help if people could see themselves in the text. I then would have them look at other scriptures that address the peace of God and have them focus on what Jesus asks them to do in their lives on a personal level with the text. Then they must be challenged to do it. I would also challenge them to be connected to a few people of the same sex who can hold them accountable to what they need to be doing and support them as they begin to change their mindset on how to look at their situations. Having accountability is quite necessary and plays a big part in their ability to change.

3. In your counseling, what specific tools do you use? Sessions, worksheets, books, etc.?

Clients first go through a consultation. Then we begin having sessions. There is a minimum of six sessions. Counseling usually last more than six sessions because other issues materialize in their relationships. We use temperament analysis profiles to determine clients' temperaments. It takes three to four weeks to interpret client profiles. We assign books for them to read or assign something that they are to do. Homework is a must. If deeper issues present themselves during the journey, we might have them see someone who is experienced in other areas of need.

4. Are you opposed to using medications for treatment? Yes or no. Please explain.

I cannot prescribe medication; however, I am not opposed to treatment with medications when needed. I am against keeping people on medication longer than necessary. Some people can become dependent on medication or even addicted if they are not monitored closely. The key is to get people to see how they can fit into God's plan and purpose despite their disability. We see this in the life of Moses, who was used by God in a great way despite his depression. We also see this with the prophet Elijah when he went into a temporary depression after a great victory of the prophets of Baal.

5. Do you feel that reading scripture and prayer can ease some symptoms of mental illness? Please explain your thoughts on this.

I do believe that reading scripture and having a consistent time of prayer can ease some symptoms, even for those who suffer from some severe cases. We are made up of three components that work in harmony with each other: body, soul, and spirit. The spirit can have an impact on the soul as well as the body and vice versa. Listening to praise music can also influence people, especially within the emotional part of their being. I must add another necessary element that is also important to people: belief. People must believe, and that is where faith comes into play. We must believe that God is who He says He is and that He can do something for us. Are we able to trust Him with our lives? Yes, we can read the scripture! Yes, we can pray! But if people do not believe what they are reading, their perspective will not change. Believing by faith that God can make a difference and acting on what He tells us to do will have an impact on the situation. If it does not impact the situation directly, at least it can impact the perspective, and that can impact individuals.

6. What is your final attempt to help people before you release them into more extensive therapies?

I share with people that, no matter what they are feeling about their situation, they can know that they are in the will of God and that God has a purpose, despite their condition. God wants to use everyone to be vessels of His glory. I ask people to read 2 Corinthians chapter 5 and really allow God to speak to their hearts. They are special to God, and God knows all about their conditions and situations. Even if they can come to only a certain point in their healing, God wants to use them where they are. Only God truly can see where people truly are in their hearts and accept them for who they really are. That does not mean that He wants them to stay where they are: He wants to see change like all parent's desire for their children.

I hope that these questions give you some insight into how I view intellectual disability with a balanced approach that looks at the entire person from a place of wholeness. Consider the following Scripture:

> Therefore, we do not become discouraged (utterly spiritless, exhausted, and wearied out through fear). Though our outer man is [progressively] decaying and wasting away, yet our inner self is being [progressively] renewed day after day. For our light, momentary affliction (this slight distress of the passing hour) is ever more and more abundantly preparing and producing and achieving for us an everlasting weight of glory [beyond all measure, excessively surpassing all comparisons and all calculations, a vast and transcendent glory and blessedness never to cease], Since we consider and look not to the things that are seen but to the things that are unseen; for the things that are visible are temporal (brief and fleeting), but the things that are invisible are deathless and everlasting. (2 Corinthians 4:16–18 AMP)
>
> For we know that if the tent which is our earthly home is destroyed (dissolved), we have from God a building, a house not made with hands, eternal in the heavens. Here indeed, in this [present abode, body], we sigh and groan inwardly, because we yearn to be clothed over [we yearn to put on our celestial body like a garment, to be fitted out] with our heavenly dwelling, So that by putting it on we may not be found naked (without a body). For while we are still in this tent, we groan under the burden and sigh deeply (weighed down, depressed, oppressed)—not that we want to put off the body (the clothing of the spirit), but rather that we would be further clothed, so that what

> is mortal (our dying body) may be swallowed up by life [after the resurrection]. Now He Who has fashioned us [preparing and making us fit] for this very thing is God, Who also has given us the [Holy] Spirit as a guarantee [of the fulfillment of His promise]. So then, we are always full of good and hopeful and confident courage; we know that while we are at home in the body, we are abroad from the home with the Lord [that is promised us]. For we walk by faith [we regulate our lives and conduct ourselves by our conviction or belief respecting man's relationship to God and divine things, with trust and holy fervor; thus we walk] not by sight or appearance. [Yes] we have confident and hopeful courage and are pleased rather to be away from home out of the body and be at home with the Lord. Therefore, whether we are at home [on earth away from Him] or away from home [and with Him], we are constantly ambitious and strive earnestly to be pleasing to Him. For we must all appear and be revealed as we are before the judgment seat of Christ, so that each one may receive [his pay] according to what he has done in the body, whether good or evil [considering what his purpose and motive have been, and what he has achieved, been busy with, and given himself and his attention to accomplishing]. (2 Corinthians 5:1–10 AMP)

We can receive some more encouragement from the Apostle Paul in this text. Paul, despite getting weaker in his mortality in this life, looked forward to what he would have in heaven. His physical body was wasting away and would not be able to enter heaven. People have new bodies because the body we dwell in now cannot enter heaven. Those who struggle with physical or mental disabilities will have new bodies in heaven. Whether people will receive new bodies and whether they will have a different perspective on how to view the bodies they currently have in the flesh depends on people's belief in Jesus. The scripture I quote here clearly indicates that the Holy Spirit (God) is present in those who will receive new bodies. We must be born again. Those who are severely mentally impaired are God's business. We can trust that God is able to know how to handle them. We need to make sure that *we* are where *we* need to be with the Lord and His salvation that He offers to us. God uses suffering as a means to transform and renew our lives. Paul, who suffered and experienced numerous situations, considered them to be momentary. His view of what God had prepared for him in Christ far outweighed the present circumstances. It was this future outlook that sustained him in the midst of his suffering for the gospel. He then says that our present condition is one that is fading. Although we are jars of clay, God chooses to work though us, transforming us until one day we will possess an immortal body that can be in the presence of God in total Christlikeness.

This great insight that we get from 2 Corinthians chapters 4 and 5 provides additional information about the creation perspective that we talked about earlier regarding how we should look at disabilities. Paul followed with another perspective that helps us focus on what we will have in the future as believers. Just imagine viewing the suffering in our lives as something temporary as compared to our future glory with Jesus, which will be eternal. This is nothing. If parents and caregivers can get on the same page with God, I believe that there can be revival through those who are mentally and physically challenged. What makes me say this? God shows Himself through them, particularly those virtues that we seem to always need in our personal lives. These virtues can be found in Galatians 5:22. They are known as the fruits of the spirit: "But the fruit of the [Holy] Spirit [the work which His presence within accomplishes] is love, joy (gladness), peace, patience (an even temper, forbearance), kindness, goodness (benevolence), faithfulness" (Galatians 5:22 AMP).

God wants to instill in us these attributes. When we view Galatians 5:22 together with 1 Corinthians 13, we can see a wonderful picture of Jesus!

When clients have other issues that feed into their relationship problems, it is necessary for them to deal with the underlying issues first. The relationship problems will not go away until the root causes are eliminated. Many of these root problems are unresolved temporary disabilities that become semipermanent through a refusal to accept their existence. I have never forgotten a statement made by Wayne Monbleau, a preacher who hosts a radio call-in show, and he said it over thirty-five years ago: "Acceptance produces change."

15

Helping Siblings to Understand Their Family Life from God's Perspective

We did not ask to be born! Yet, our births were not accidents. Many people find it extremely difficult to understand why bad things happen to those they consider good people. This question is posed by countless people, even some who exhibit faith. By merely thinking and holding a position on an issue, people exhibit belief systems. That means that your neighbor, mailman, schoolteacher, mechanic, plumber, or librarian has a theology. A belief system can be structured around how God feels and thinks, or it can be absent of His feelings and thoughts. Whether God is part of a person's thinking process or not, that person still possesses a theology.

Theology, in its simplest form, is the study of the nature of God. Our beliefs about God and how He operates in our lives determine how we discern and approach the issues that constitute a great deal of our lives. We also must include another psychological aspect to which all people hold, that being philosophy. Philosophy is the study of the fundamental nature of knowledge, reality, and existence. It is easy to fit both "ologies" together to establish one's own position on and approach to life. All people possess a theology and a philosophy that guide their lives and help them to get through it well or can totally mess it up.

With all the theological and philosophical positions that exist, how does one ever come to understand what real truth is and then live according to that truth? Is it safe to say that truth that can be found amid all the confusion and noise? When we begin to narrow the perspective on life down to one book, the Bible, we can conclude that the physical manifestation of God, Jesus Christ, provided for us great insights that help to shape how we are to look at life and how we understand God's genuine feelings and thoughts about us as well. This includes all the issues of life with which we are faced. When we specifically consider Christian theology and its goal, we can see that it is distinguished from every other belief system in existence. The ultimate goal of Christian theology is to learn about God, His nature, and His will, and how they apply to each of us. Therefore, Christian theology also includes the study of man because God deals with humankind, saves humankind: "For it is by grace you have been saved, through faith—and this not from yourselves, it is the gift of God not by works, so that no one can boast.), and loves humankind" (Ephesians 2:8–9 NIV). "For God so loved the world that he gave his one and only Son, that whoever believes in him shall not perish but have eternal life" (John 3:16 NIV).

It is essential to understand God's perspective when it comes to ourselves and how we view family. If we operate from a philosophy involving ourselves and our family that emanates from our human viewpoint, we interpret things through a lens that distorts our view of our lives and the lives of our children. When void of not just a perspective about God, but void of the true God of the Bible, people do not arrive at a genuine perspective of how He (the God of the Bible) truly views their children. People tend to arrive at their own perspectives on how they believe God thinks and operates.

It is necessary that I be completely up front about what I believe is necessary for us to really know how to journey through lives that are centered on intellectually and physically challenged children. It is necessary to have a theology that is illuminated by the scriptures and specifically by Jesus Christ, who is the revelation of God Himself. Jesus is the only human, though also divine, who has seen God and has been with God (John 14). He also *is* God. Understanding God through the person of His Son Jesus Christ, provides a perspective from which we, as parents, learn how God views us, and also enables us to articulate to our children *without* disabilities who dwell in the house how to understand the environment in which they find themselves. Our words and our limited ability to understand our lives without the help of our Creator fall far short and will render us almost helpless, even impotent, to the point of becoming mentally and emotionally spent.

Before proper language can be provided to help siblings understand the unique environment in which they find themselves, we first must examine a portion of Scripture that can be found in John:

> Therefore Jesus said again, "I tell you the truth, I am the gate for the sheep. All who ever came before me were thieves and robbers, but the sheep did not listen to them. I am the gate; whoever enters through me will be saved. He will come in and go out and find pasture. The thief comes only to steal and kill and destroy; I have come that they may have life and have it to the full. (John 10:7–10 NIV)

Jesus claims to be the Gate or Door for the sheep. Jesus is probably referring to the door of a community sheepfold or a community pasture that housed all the flocks of an area. There is, however, another descriptive picture of Jesus as the door. When the sheep were kept out in the hill country overnight, they were kept in ravines surrounded by several rocky walls. Naturally, the opening into these ravines had no door. The shepherd himself literally became the door, for during the night he would simply lie across the opening. The sheep could get out only by going over him, and the enemies of the sheep could get into the sheep only by going through him. Access in or out was only through the shepherd.

By "door" Jesus meant He is the way or entrance into the sheepfold. Jesus Christ is the way:

- Into God's presence
- Into God's acceptance
- Into the Kingdom of God
- Into Heaven

- Into eternal life
- Into salvation

Therefore, if a person wishes to enter where God is, he must enter the Door of Christ. Here are some other Scriptures that support what Jesus was saying about being the Door.

> Jesus saith unto him, I am the way, the truth, and the life: no man cometh unto the Father, but by me." (John 14:6 KJV)
>
> For through him we both have access by one Spirit unto the Father." (Ephesians 2:18 KJV)
>
> For there is one God, and one mediator between God and man, the man Christ Jesus. (1 Timothy 2:5 KJV)
>
> But now hath he obtained a more excellent ministry, by how much also he is the mediator of a better covenant, which was established upon better promises. (Hebrews 8:6 KJV)
>
> And for this cause he is the mediator of the New Testament. (Hebrews 9:15 KJV)
>
> For Christ is not entered into the holy places made with hands, which are the copies of the true things; but into heaven itself, now to appear in the presence of God for us. (Hebrews 9:24 KJV)
>
> [Christ] is a new and living way, which he hath consecrated for us. (Hebrews 10:20 KJV)
>
> My little children, these things write I unto you, that ye sin not. And if any man sin, we have an <u>advocate</u> with the Father, Jesus Christ the righteous. (1 John 2:1 KJV)

Jesus, in using the motifs of the shepherd and sheep, helps us to understand the need for Him to be our Shepherd. We must look at ourselves as helpless sheep in need of a shepherd. When we receive Christ into our lives, we have access into the Father's kingdom. Once we go through the door of salvation, we have everything that God offers. The description of the pasture helps us to understand what we have. We are secure and at peace because of the presence of the Shepherd. We are under His watch and care. Being in a place of tranquility helps to minimize anxiety because we can rest and be secure under the watchful eye of the Shepherd. Jesus is the only door that opens to healthy and lasting nourishment. He is the only door that leads to the true pasture, the pasture that has the living stream flowing through it and the pasture that has the living food in it. The pasture alone can satisfy and restore the soul. The pasture can give life forever and can feed with knowledge and understanding. We have the benefits of having good pasture available because of the Shepherd that we have. Take the time to read Psalm 23, which was written by King David, who was not only a king, but in his earlier years was a shepherd. He gives us a beautiful picture of his relationship with God, as he is shepherded by God Himself. I hope you can realize how being in Christ gives us what we need to navigate life. This is genuine *God life* that available to us through Christ. We now can establish a new grid that is not centered on the human perspective that falls far short of helping us in our situation (specifically, in parenting all the children in an environment where there is a challenged child) but a grid that is tied directly to the divine, which gives us a perspective that is aligned with the Creator Himself.

Let us look at John 10:10. It says that Jesus, who is the Good Shepherd, has come to give us life. This contrasts with the thief who comes to kill, steal, and destroy. It would be extremely easy to look at our environment with our intellectually and physically challenged children and conclude that life has been stolen, lost, destroyed, or is dead. God can reset our perspective if we have one of defeat and gloom. How? By giving to us *true* life. If we, as parents, can find genuine life in our situation, we can help our other children to see life in it as well. It first must begin with us. Here is what Jesus does when He transforms our minds to see how He brings life. We are not talking about biological life, but *spiritual* life. One commentator that I read put it this way:

Life is the quality and essence, the energy and power, the principle of being. Christ *is* life; He is ...

- The very quality of life
- The very power of life
- The very essence of life
- The very principle of life

Without Christ, there would be no life whatsoever. Life is in Him—within His very being. All things exist and have their being (life) in Him: The purpose, meaning, and significance of being.

- The very purpose of life
- The very meaning of life
- The very significance of life

Life in God is perfection. *Life in God* is all that we must be and possess to live perfectly. This is what is meant by life. *Life in God* is completeness of being, absolute satisfaction, the fullness of all good, and the possession of all good things. *Life in God* is perfect love, joy, peace, long-suffering, gentleness, and goodness.[1]

Knowing what life in Christ is lays a foundation that can help us understand how to view the lives of both our child with a disability as well as the child without a disability. How does understanding God as our Shepherd provide us with answers for all the questions and concerns that the other children in the household may have regarding the family environment? It is important for parents to understand that it is not necessary to answer all the questions at once. Parents might not know all the answers yet or may not have come to a point of seeing everything through God's eyes. This involves a continual learning process as well as an unfolding of understanding and clarity as time passes. God does surgery on our thinking process a little at a time. We can invite our children into our process as He gives us answers or understanding. Knowing who we are in Christ will help us in understanding ourselves as well as our children. Helping them to see their identity in Him is a great first step. Helping them to see that having a child with disabilities does not mean that the family is being punished and is not under the judgment of God is extremely important. Many may believe that they have done something to deserve what has happened to them. Some believe that generational sins could be part of why they are experiencing what they are by having a child with a disability. Please understand that God does not bring about an individual's disability for the purpose of punishment. If our lives are under the care of the Shepherd, we are to be dependent on the Shepherd to provide for all the needs. As you bring things to your children's attention and begin to ask God openly with your children to provide what you need for your child with a disability, as God answers your prayers over time, they will be able to recognize that you are not alone, and that God truly cares.

It is critical that parents pay attention to the other children as well, getting to know them and recognizing how they can help with, as well as understand, the disabled child. Overburdening a sibling can bring about resentment and anger in a big way in the child without the disability. It must be remembered that the other children are not caregivers or servants. It must be recognized that they have lives outside of the family. In fact, it is necessary that they have time for themselves. Parents must also consider what is age appropriate and know how much to share with the other children when necessary.

As parents learn how God thinks and feels about the issues of life, the way God thinks should become of paramount significance. Parents who know that their thinking is shaped by God's thinking will dramatically alter their view of life and their life issues. That means their thinking becomes aligned with His. For example, instead of my feelings being in control of what I think, I now can understand my situation from God's perspective. My perspective now becomes aligned with God's purpose and will. I begin to understand His sovereignty and that He can do whatever He chooses to do when He wants to. He is the superintendent over my life, and I must trust Him despite my feelings. When we as parents can come to this perspective, we then can help other family members begin to understand our position. We might not be able to change their minds or get them to believe what we believe, but we can help them understand where we are mentally and spiritually, and how the peace of God can envelop our hearts and minds in Christ. Understanding may not translate into agreement in some cases, but understanding is pivotal in the communication process.

Helping to communicate with your other children can minimize a lot of the tension that might be present in the environment and helps to create a setting where they feel comfortable in sharing their feelings and concerns.

It is also important for parents to understand that teenage children are dealing with their own issues in addition to whatever their involvement is with the disabled child. The added stress of the other children's concerns can become overwhelming to parents who may be overwhelmed already. The dynamics that may be occurring within the family unit, if not constantly evaluated, can bring about dysfunction. If there is not another parent present to help with the situation, it is necessary that the single parent has someone else with whom to talk as well as a way of getting respite. There will be a temptation to have the other children be pulled into being parents. Other siblings should not be used all the time for babysitting duty unless they enjoy it and do not see it as babysitting but as time spent with their disabled sibling.

How does relationship with God through Christ help with shaping how to answer your children? The Bible provides answers for everything in life. As we become familiar with it, we can give answers that come straight from the Lord through the understanding and application of the Scripture. The Bible gives us understanding on the following:

- We can understand that God has a perspective on everything in life.
- Nothing escapes God's presence or His notice.
- Jesus is the revelation of God and provides us entrance into His Kingdom.
- We can access and use all the tools in God's Kingdom.
- We can understand God's purpose and plan for our family.
- Our disabled children are in the will of God.
- We can understand His will for our family.
- We can understand How God is able to use our disabled child to impact others.
- Our disabled children are not mistakes.
- We can learn how to exercise the fruit of the Spirit in our lives.
- We can learn how to be dependent on God.
- We can learn how to genuinely love.

Biblical understanding is directly tied to having a walk with God. As we get to know Him intimately, we begin to understand the above aspects of God's will. Being able to help our children understand these dynamics will go a long way in giving them some understanding about God even if they cannot fully comprehend it all. We are told in scripture to instruct our children and to teach them in the way that they should go. Is that not what we are doing when we show them how God interacts and intersects our lives as well as theirs?

God uses circumstances in our lives to change us. We must help our children to understand that our lives as believers in Christ belong to Him. We are to submit to Him. He wants us to have love, empathy, and compassion for others. Our willingness to come alongside those who need love is showing them Jesus when we reach out to meet their need, whether it is in our home or not. Every household is unique, but the goal is the same, to be used by God to positively impact others. It would be great for any family whether they have children with intellectual or physical disabilities or not, to have such a mission and a vision statement. This will help the family to have a guide as to what they could be doing together as a family to impact the kingdom. Guess what! Their mission may only be to take care of that child with the disability. If that is the case, then that family has an impact on God's kingdom, whether they believe it or not. Knowing God's purpose can make a big difference in how families view their environments as well as how they move forward in life. No matter how demanding the task presumably will be, the family will understand from God's perspective that what they are doing springs from their calling from God.

We receive insight about ourselves from the Bible as we get to know Christ. The list of characteristics in the Bible can also aid in helping parents know how to respond to those who are insensitive to them or their children who are physically and intellectually challenged. Some people are just ignorant or obnoxious when it comes to interacting with individuals who are different than they are. Some intentionally are just unkind, and some are just fools. We need to develop different responses for different situations. For example, if my daughter, who is twenty-eight years of age, tries to show another adult her jewelry and that person just walks away, that tells me that the adult is not very perceptive in understanding someone who has an intellectual disability. I would not get upset with that person. I would perceive that he or she was simply not very astute or observant. If the adult said, "What is wrong with you? I am not interested in your jewelry," I then would need to say something in a very calm way: "Excuse me. My daughter is on the spectrum, and this is how she communicates." Depending on what the person says next, I would respond accordingly. It is necessary to stay cool in front people who have offended our children or us. Getting upset will most likely cause us to say something that we should not say and that we would possibly regret later. Being under the control of the Lord will help in a great way to help us manage our emotions in what might be considered a time of conflict. We might have to say a quick prayer before we respond if necessary. God will give us the words to say in the situation. We just need to call on Him and trust His leading.

Unfortunately, parents with physically and intellectually challenged children must always be prepared to handle unforeseen situations with people who are insensitive. Some have thick skins while others do not. Maintaining control of our emotions is necessary to prevent situations from escalating. Parents should never get into shouting matches or arguments with those who have offended them or their children. Children themselves can be quite mean when it comes to children who are not like them. When we witness our child with a disability being verbally abused, we should say something to the offender or to their parents or authority figure if they are younger. In many instances, people say things out of ignorance and may need some understanding about the person with the disability. We need to watch the tone in which we say things and make sure we do not completely "lose it" despite their actions. At least trying to address our concern can get that child to think about what they have done. We must also be prepared to get some negative feedback from them if they happen to be disrespectful. We must remind ourselves that words, though hurtful, might bother us more than they bother our challenged child.

I would love to share a final scripture with you that I hope will bring you encouragement:

> If you have any encouragement from being united with Christ, if any comfort from his love, if any fellowship with the Spirit, if any tenderness and compassion, then make

> my joy complete by being like-minded, having the same love, being one in spirit and purpose. Do nothing out of selfish ambition or vain conceit, but in humility consider others better than yourselves. Each of you should look not only to your own interests, but also to the interests of others. Your attitude should be the same as that of Christ Jesus. (Philippians 2:1–5 NIV)

If we allow these words to sink into our minds, we can find great comfort in them. Being united with Christ takes away what we might consider to be meaninglessness in our situation with our children with disabilities. As I stated earlier, we can have a different perspective that is born through being united with Christ. Being united with Christ means that Christ is with us in our situation, regardless of our feelings or thoughts. Being united with Christ aligns us to be of the same mindset as Christ. Remember that Christ was not only a man, but God. God is with us and provides divine encouragement for us no matter in what circumstance we find ourselves. God helps to have a different attitude, one that pleases Him, because His attitude becomes infused into ours. A friend of mind made a great statement! He said that we desire to be right over desiring righteousness. Think about that for a minute. Ask yourself a question as a parent of a challenged child: Am I able to perceive the righteousness of Christ in how I care for my child or am I allowing my mind to accept what it tells me, believing that everything it says is right? Being united with Christ brings comfort to our troubled souls. Being united with Christ helps us to be *other* people minded. In this case, the other people are our challenged children. These verses alone can impact our thinking if we accept their truths. Our natural inclination begs us to focus on ourselves. The encouragement that we get from theses verses with regard to tenderness and compassion should move us to act out of the tenderness and compassion that Jesus had for us. Compassion is the trait that stirred Christ to reach out for us. Compassion is the force that drives Him to keep after us time and again—even if we are in rebellion and stand opposed to Him. We may be bad tempered or irritable; we may even curse Him and totally ignore Him. But His compassion drives Him to stay after us as long as we live.

We are to let the compassion of Christ flow both in and through us. His compassion will comfort us when we differ and are disturbed; it will stir us to reach out in compassion when others differ and become disturbed. As parents, we can share these precious truths with all our children as well as apply them with those we meet who rub us the wrong way. What an encouragement! Where do we get this encouragement? From the Bible!

As we keep our eyes on the prize that is ahead of us, we must remember that God is for us and knows everything that we are dealing with. We must rely on Him for strength and patience. He will fight our battles for us. Our mantra must be Romans 8:28 "And we know that in all things God works for the good of those who love him; who have been *called according to his purpose*" (NIV, italic emphasis mine):

NOTES

1 *The Preacher's Outline & Sermon Bible – John*. Chattanooga: Leadership Ministries Worldwide, 1991. WORD*search* CROSS e-book.

16

Introduction to the Story of Theodore DeShields

We have shared with you our story. I hope that those who have children with physical or psychological disabilities were able to identify with what was laid out in the first part of this book. Our struggle was real, and I have attempted to be very candid with you concerning everything we have had to deal with both internally and externally as parents of two children with disabilities. If you would have asked me a few years ago to articulate what was described in our family, I do not believe that I would have been able to go into details as I did in this book. I must be honest and say that God enabled me to look back and to see how His hand was graciously guiding our steps.

My purpose for writing such a book was to be able to help those who have disabled children to know what to do and how to see their lives through the lens of scripture. Our God is loving and gracious, and He can help us at every juncture of life. Having a perspective that comes from our Creator can change how we view our situation and ultimately have an impact on the lives of virtually everyone in our circle. I believe that our story can also help those who do not understand what parents with children with special needs experience daily. I hope that, with greater understanding, there will be a greater sensitivity. It was my endeavor to be able to have an influence on people's thinking, to have their minds aligned with God's. I pray that the majority of those who read this book will experience a change of mindset, or at least begin to think how they may enter the lives of their friends, neighbors, church members, or anyone who is part of an environment that includes children with disabilities. I pray that all who have engaged with our story have received something that they can use to change their attitudes and actions toward those who have children with disabilities. My desire is that you will see that all people who know Jesus can know that those with disabilities are called according to His purpose.

I now would like to make a slight detour toward the second part of this book. It is the story of a friend of mine whom I had the opportunity to meet while attending Penn State University in the early eighties. His name was Theodore A. DeShields. He died after only being on Earth for twenty-eight years. At the time of his death, he was headed toward a wonderful life when, out of nowhere, it was cut short. The story is written by his mother Jewel DeShields, who penned it some ten years after his unexpected death. The story is written as it was told by her to me. You might ask why I would want to place this biography into a book that has to do with parenting children with disabilities. How would her story of her son be relevant to the topic that we were talking about in Part 1?

The story has to do with a man who never was supposed to be born. Mrs. DeShields, in an incredibly open and honest way, shares her struggles with this child and is generous in sharing her feelings with her own personal issues, including depression and isolation. Her story is one of hope and promise, one that shows her dependence on God to help her make decisions that helped to keep her child alive while she parented him properly. Her story ties into our story with our children. Her son, who should never have been able to endure birth, had to face many physical problems as a child. She had to face many of the issues with her son while her husband appeared to be just a spectator at times on the sidelines. The type of environment that existed in our family dynamic existed in Mrs. DeShields's world.

Despite being on Earth for only twenty-eight years, Theo was placed here for a certain period of time because God had a purpose for his life. When Theo had completed his assignment, one that God Himself understood, it was time for him to go be with the One whom he loved and desired to please. Mrs. DeShields's story contains nuggets of wisdom throughout as well as a record of her up-and-down struggles with her relationship with God and how God used her son to bring her back to where she needed to be with Him. She shares the pain that she experienced before he was born and the pain she experienced after his death. She also shares her victories and her joys.

I believe that all families, whether or not there are children with disabilities, will be encouraged and strengthened by her story. When both stories are put together, they provide a powerful picture of God's purpose for our lives. Every person whom God allows to come into existence has a purpose and can bring glory to Him. God is the One who desires to get glory out of lives. His glory can come from someone who has a disability and who is a member of a family or from someone who has been born of a woman who was never thought she would be able to have another child due to her physical problems. As you read her story, I pray that God will show you how you as well as any of your family members can fulfill God's purpose for your life as well as theirs. I hope that you will enjoy the story of Theodore (gift of God) and will be blessed by it.

PART 2

THE STORY OF THEODORE DESHIELDS AS TOLD BY HIS MOTHER, JEWEL DESHIELDS

17

My Son Is Dead

I hesitated to write this story. My reasoning was not what you might think. It's just very personal. Our lives were so intertwined that his death left me shattered and broken. The raw edges of my heart are still bleeding; but I am gathering the places of my life, endeavoring to smile through my tears, and leaning heavily on the Lord Jesus Christ.

Thursday, September 24, 1987, was a routine day until I arrived home in the early afternoon and found two naval officers who had brought the news that our only son, HM 2 Theodore Deshields Jr. was dead. His father, recently retired, had been cutting the front lawn when, accompanied by the local police, the navy car had arrived. We live in a small community, and the neighbors were wondering at the excitement as they peered through windows and doors.

My husband had wisely forbidden the police from coming to get me and had insisted that they leave, but he had asked the chaplain and naval legal adviser to wait with him until I returned home.

Although I had noticed the officer's car when I had passed it earlier, I had not associated it with my home. I drove up the driveway, shut off the ignition, stepped out of the car, and walked into the most devastating shock of my life. My husband, Ted, met me in the driveway and tried valiantly but unsuccessfully to control himself as he told me to leave the groceries in the car and come into the house. I looked beyond my husband and saw through the windows of the back porch the white summer uniforms of the naval officers. I noticed that one was a chaplain. (My father had been a chaplain.) His presence along with the unforgettable expression of grief on my husband's face left me no doubt that our son—our only son, our beloved son—was dead!

I was guided to a sofa where my tears finally gave way to questions: What had happened? Was it an automobile accident? When did he die? Are you sure there is no mistake? The incomplete information available left many of my questions unanswered. He was definitely dead, they assured me, but the circumstances surrounding his death would be unavailable until later that night. In the meantime, we notified friends and family members, and our little home was filled with people, each one totally shocked at the awful news.

The navy finally received the coroner's report, and they notified us that Theo had died of a myocardial infarction—a heart attack at age twenty-eight! He had been assigned to the Groton, Connecticut, submarine base and worked as a preventative medicine technician. However, since he was attending Hartford Graduate School, completing requirements for a second master's degree in business administration, he was living off base in a private home in Ledyard, Connecticut. One of his roommates had found him dead in bed after he noticed his car still in front of the house long after he should have gone to work. The rescue squad was called, and the coroner had invaded his beautiful body to determine the cause of death. When we later received the report, we noted, not unexpectedly, that no drugs or alcohol were involved. We were told he had popcorn and Kool-Aid with his roommates at eleven o'clock the night before and then had gone up to bed for the last time.

One of his roommates had made a call to the naval base with the disheartening news and was told, "That's impossible. Stop joking! Tell Theo to get in here!" After his death was verified, a shockwave swept through the base where officers, corpsmen, civilians, and patients were stunned into solemn belief. Although Theo had been stationed there only eighteen months, his many friendships crossed all social and racial barriers as he enveloped everyone he met with his bright, contagious smile and obvious love for people. His body was sent home, and a personal friend, another hospital corpsman, chose to escort him and remain with him until after the funeral.

On Saturday, a memorial service was held at the Groton Naval Base. It was originally scheduled for the chapel, but it was soon obvious the chapel could not contain all who wanted to attend. The service was moved to the dining hall. We received the following letter from the chaplain of the base:

> Dear Mr. and Mrs. DeShields,
>
> I have been very saddened in the passing away of your son. I extend to you my sincerest sympathy in these hard times. In knowing your son, however, I feel that he would say, "Let life go on." If anyone should be placed in the Lord's Kingdom, it would be him. He endeavored feverishly to do His work. Theo was always cheerful and helpful in extending his time to others and going the additional step. He worked hard at all times trying to better himself. Some of the good times that I recall are seeing him play basketball or his involvement with the hospital recreation committee.
>
> Your son actually talked me into being Santa Claus for the Christmas party. It was funny in that I was the last to know. When I asked why he didn't volunteer; it was "Awe come on, Chief, a black Santa!" In knowing as many people as I do, I told him I'm sure it wouldn't matter at all. But he still got me. It was fun, but harder than I thought.
>
> In closing, your son represented the Navy, his church, and race in a truly commendable fashion. It wasn't hard to see the excellent job that you had done in the raising of your son. As a father, I only hope that I can do as good of a job with my sons. I only hope this note may help in your moment of sorrow. I am sure that you have received many because many people were disheartened.

> It was a pleasure in knowing your son and being able to call him my friend.
>
> Thank you.
>
> Sincerely
>
> Henry Kelp, Chaplain

It was Theo's habit, no matter where he was living, to affiliate himself with a local church. He would meet with the pastor and ask to be placed under "watch care" explaining that he had a permanent membership at his home church but just wanted to be considered a member temporarily while he was in the area. He was attending Shiloh Baptist Church in Groton, Connecticut, where his good friend, Reverend Benjamin Watts, was the pastor. Reverend Watts was asked and readily agreed to participate in the memorial service.

When Reverend Watts called to offer condolences, we requested an audio tape of the memorial service, which he was kind enough to send. This tape has been a real blessing to us as we listened to his friends describe their relationships with Theo.

Our pastor, Reverend Calvin R. Woods, and several other members of our church were sitting in the living room on Friday, September 25, 1987, when the mail was delivered. My husband, Ted, brought it in and, with tears glistening on his cheeks, handed me a letter from our son. It was postmarked September 23 and had been written the day before, just two days before his death. As I reached out to receive the letter from Ted's trembling hand, I glanced at the faces around me; some were horrified, while others were already crying, and they didn't know what to expect from me. I mentally thanked God for this final word from our beloved son as I slowly opened and read aloud his last letter:

> Dear Folks:
>
> Hi! Just a note. Received the shoes; they're very nice—thank you again. Please sell the two pictures with calligraphy for $12.50 each. Thanks. I'm very grateful

for the sale. I have been busy with school, research, and reading the Word. Ezekiel is so intense. It can't be read quickly! I'm also praying and asking God for strength because I truly need it. God has been good to me, and I'm discovering this more and more.

I am planning a party for my little brother and my first anniversary. It will be on the 30th of September '87. I might be home the second weekend in October. It's a three-day weekend, and I have it off. I will let you know when the date gets closer. It all depends on schoolwork.

One of my research papers is on AIDS and insurance. It's a very interesting topic. I am grateful to God who has been the guide for my life, and am so sorry for those who experience this debilitating disease. I am learning how the insurance industry views this disease and what they are planning to do with reference to claims.

Well, I must close. I will write again soon. I promised myself I'd write a letter a day and see how my mail flow will go. Take care … see you soon.

Love always,

Theo

Jeremiah 33:3 and Philippians 4:4–9

We had sent him a new pair of boots, and he had given us two pictures to sell for him. He often photographed flowers, enlarged the pictures, and wrote or copied appropriate poems in calligraphy in the background. He was an excellent photographer and specialized in flowers. He framed the pictures and sold them or gave them to his friends as gifts.

He had informed us earlier in the year that he was reading the Bible for the fifth time and had finally reached the book of Ezekiel.

Being a Big Brother was another one of his loves, and we had met his little brother, Lincoln, and his family on our last visit a few weeks earlier. Lincoln was eleven years old and really liked Chinese food, so Theo had planned to take him out for a special Chinese dinner on the thirtieth.

For many years, Theo had put significant scripture references at the close of all his correspondence. Each card or letter contained that final message from the Bible. He knew the Word of God very well and could readily choose appropriate scripture. In this case, we were in awe of his choices. Jeremiah 33:3 was the theme verse of the Odosagih Bible Conference in Lime Lake, New York, from which we had just returned. It is printed on all their brochures and also on a large poster on the wall in the dining hall. Before each meal it is their custom to repeat in unison, "Call upon me and I will answer thee, and shew thee great and mighty things which thou knowest not" (KJV).

We both realized we had not told Theo about this. Then Reverend Woods, our pastor, turned to Philippians 4:4–9 which he read aloud with great emotion:

> Rejoice in the Lord always: *and* again I say, Rejoice. Let your moderation be known unto all men. The Lord *is* at hand. Be careful for nothing; but in everything by prayer and supplication with thanksgiving let your requests be made known unto God. And the peace of God, which passeth all understanding, shall keep your hearts and minds through Christ Jesus. Finally, brethren, whatsoever things are true, whatsoever things *are* honest, whatsoever things *are* just, whatsoever things *are* pure, whatsoever things *are* lovely, whatsoever things *are* of good report; if *there be* any virtue, and if *there be* any praise, think on these things. Those things, which ye have both learned, and received, and heard, and seen in me, do: and the God of peace shall be with you. (KJV)

We sat in stunned silence. The effect of that scripture in conjunction with the circumstances was almost too much for us. It was truly awesome. I cannot speak for the others, but those verses have become my recipe for peace; and as the words penetrated and permeated my mind and heart, blessed peace replaced the painful panic I was experiencing.

On Monday morning, my husband and I, accompanied by Jennifer Milton, Theo's sister, stood looking at a scene I could never have imagined: Theo DeShields, Jr., age twenty-eight, six feet, five and a half inches tall, 195 pounds of perfectly formed, beautiful brown body in a white navy uniform, lying forever motionless in a silver casket. The explosion of emotion was intense. In retrospect, I can remember the pain of my heart breaking into multiple pieces and each piece swelling and breaking, swelling, and breaking over and over again. The rolling waves of agony nearly inundated me that day. My only rational thought was a question: "Will this pain ever cease?"

I removed the glasses from his face. He didn't look natural in them because he had been wearing contact lenses recently. I wanted to tell him to give me a hug. I wanted to hear his voice; but I could not have what I wanted. It was so bitterly impossible.

Later we returned home where everyone was attempting to comfort us. From early morning until late each evening, they came to offer their love and presence to alleviate our sorrow. Food was provided and assistance in arranging the numerous details for the funeral service was freely given. A reporter from our local paper, *The Courier Post*, called us regarding the brief obituary which they had received from the mortician. He asked for more details and indicated that he wanted to write a feature obituary and include a picture. We provided the requested information, and on Tuesday, September 29, the following obituary was published.

> Somerdale—Services will be tomorrow for Petty Officer 3rd Class Theodore DeShields Jr., who died of a heart attack Thursday at the Groton, Conn., Naval Hospital where he worked as a preventive medicine technician in the medical corps. He was 28.
>
> A committed Christian, Mr. DeShields had attended the Martin Luther Christian Day School in Pennsauken and in 1977 graduated from Baptist High School in Haddon Heights. He then enrolled in Cedarville College, a

Christian Liberal Arts school in Cedarville, Ohio, from which he earned a Bachelor of Arts degree.

In the summer of 1976, between his junior and senior years, Mr. DeShields—who was 6 feet, 5 1/2 inches tall and a good athlete—went abroad with Athletes for Christ, playing basketball in the Philippines and in Hong Kong. He had intended to enter the field of preventive medicine, but the trip influenced him to study drug and alcohol abuse counseling instead. He enrolled in Penn State University where he earned a master's degree in that field. He then worked as a counselor for Al-Assist, an alcohol and drug counseling agency in Philadelphia.

In January 1985, he joined the navy, intending to stay in the service for six years. He took basic training in hospital corps school at the Great Lakes Naval School in Illinois and then went to Oakland, California, where he was trained as a preventive medicine technician. While stationed at the Groton Naval Hospital, he attended Hartford Graduate School, a division of Rensselaer Polytechnic Institute, where he would have completed the requirements for a master's of business administration degree in 1988.

In Connecticut, Mr. DeShields was active in the Big Brother organization that provides male role models for children who lack them in their lives. The first anniversary of Mr. DeShields' meeting his Little Brother will be Wednesday, the day he will be buried.

Mr. DeShields had been in good health, and his unexpected death was a shock to his family and coworkers.

"The naval hospital in Groton had a memorial service for him, and the place was packed," said his mother, Jewel DeShields. He was a young man whose smile was known by everybody. He was very friendly. He played basketball

> and other sports. He was very outgoing. He cooked, did calligraphy, and took beautiful photographs. He had a million friends … His religious convictions profoundly influenced his life and were reflected in a letter he wrote his parents …"

Melvin East, my sister's husband, turned the facts of Theo's life into an imaginary flight of a meteor, ablaze briefly and just as suddenly extinguished … The obituary concluded with:

> On Thursday, September 24, 1987, the light of the "meteor" ceased, but the trail of brilliance will always remain as a role model for all. In twenty-eight short years, Theodore DeShields Jr. has achieved more goals, been more places, done more things, wasted less time, and found more fulfillment than most who have lived much longer.

My youngest sister gave us a poem which she had clipped from a paper or magazine a few days earlier and had been saving for a reason suddenly made clear. We all agreed that the unknown author somehow had Theo in mind when "In Celebration of You" was composed. The section of the poem that captured my heart is found in the following words by James Kavanaugh.

> But most of all, I could never replace
>
> Your smile, your eyes,
>
> Your gentleness and giving, your loyalty and caring,
>
> The memories we've shared,
>
> The love that is forever; there despite time or distance.
>
> So, today I celebrate your very existence,

Thank all of life for your life, ...

That my world would never be the same, without you.

The service at Parkside United Methodist Church was simple and beautiful. Relatives and friends filled every available space. Our hands were held; our trembling, exhausted bodies were embraced; our tears were mingled with those of the stunned and sorrowful mourners of our son who had so briefly blessed our lives. A former pastor of our church, Reverend Charles Bender, told of his love for "Teddy" as a boy and "Theo" as a man. He had shared a similar experience with Theo because he also had traveled to the Philippines and had consulted with Theo in preparation for his trip. Cedarville College was represented by Pastor Harold Green who spoke of the lasting impression Theo's presence made upon the faculty and students during the four years he attended. Baptist High School in Haddon Heights was well represented by many fellow students and basketball teammates. Even parents of his teammates came to show their respect for the young man whom they had cheered on the basketball court as co-captain of the team. The next morning, October 1, 1987, with full military honors, Theodore DeShields Jr. was buried a few steps from a winding road at Lakeview Cemetery in Cinnaminson, New Jersey. A brief graveside service was conducted by our pastor, and the men and women of the military participated with polished precision. I was still in deep shock, as evidenced by the expression on my face in the pictures taken by friends and later given to us. When we arrived at the cemetery, almost everyone noted the presence of a large flock of birds feeding in the grass a short distance away. I must admit I paid no further attention to them and certainly associated no spiritual significance to their presence. The sound of "Taps" echoed in the silence and the twenty-one-gun salute boomed across the heavens. A folded flag was placed in my empty arms. Individual flowers were carefully laid on the top of the silver casket. Then, with the folded symbol of our bereavement clutched to my heart, I was led away to the waiting car.

The Willing Workers organization of our church had prepared a delicious luncheon for our family members and friends. It was during this time of fellowship that the first person asked me the question: "Did you see the birds at the cemetery?" I replied that I had, but I wondered at the strange expression that accompanied the question. Various other comments soon required an explanation: "It was the strangest thing I've ever seen." "I still can't believe …"

"What are you talking about?" I asked. "What happened with the birds?" Several people joined in telling the following story of something so bizarre that it defies a logical explanation: Because of the size of the flock, the feeding birds in the field were observed by many people at the cemetery that day. And most imagined they certainly would fly away with the arrival of the carloads of people. They did not. Then people thought that surely the birds would take to the air when the twenty-one-gun salute was be fired. They did not! But when the ceremony was complete, just before we left the cemetery, they flew off in perfect formation. The words of the first stanza of "In Celebration of You" were surely inspired by God and prompted all observers to sense His presence.

We were grateful that some of the navy personnel stayed to fellowship with the family and out-of-town guests. Theo's roommates from Connecticut; his girlfriend, Annischa Reid, and her mother, Elizabeth, from the Bahamas; and of course, many others blessed us with their presence. Our family realized that the next day, October 1, was our sister Patricia's birthday, so our eldest brother, Gerald Hayden from Michigan stood to make the announcement. He asked our guests to join the family in wishing his "baby sister" a happy birthday by singing the familiar tune. Later, I overheard a comment to the effect that our family was unbelievable because, in the midst of sorrow, we thought of others. That's no marvel—life goes on!

Annischa, or "Nish," is a lovely young woman who was almost engaged to Theo. They had known each other for eight years. She lives in Nassau, and it was my terribly unpleasant duty to telephone her regarding Theo's death. I had called her with this news late Thursday night, and on Friday, she advised when she and her mother would arrive.

Theo had many girlfriends, but there was something special about his relationship with Annischa. I've always believed it was the manner of their meeting that added a spiritual dimension. Theo was a senior at Cedarville College the year he went to the Philippines to play basketball. The Collingswood United Methodist Church and many friends and family members had provided his "support." He was eager to go as a short-term missionary; and even though he was the only black student to consider it, he forged ahead with his plans to tour the Philippine Islands with Athletes for Christ. At the same time, Annischa Reid was a student at Liberty Baptist College in Virginia. She was very active in sports and had been selected to go to the Philippines with their track team. Nish is tall, brown, and beautiful and was also the only black student traveling with her school.

Yes, you guessed it. These two teams had a layover in the Los Angeles Airport, and friendly teammates made a point of getting these two "stand outs" together. The two exchanged addresses, and although they did not travel together or see one another again for four months, they managed to begin a relationship through correspondence and phone calls. Both felt their meeting was God ordained.

Her first visit to our home was at Thanksgiving the same year. By automobile, she traveled north with some friends from school. We met them at a McDonald's just off the turnpike at Exit 4. Because of Theo's continuous prodding, we were early and watched as he eagerly awaited the arrival of a young woman he had seen only once. Finally, a Volkswagen pulled into the parking lot. It was jammed to the doors with more passengers than the law allows. Somehow a beautiful girl extracted herself and her luggage from that tiny car. That act alone proved her athletic ability.

It was exciting to observe two Christian young people desiring only to please God in their relationship, learning about one another. Nish was shy with us that first visit, but on subsequent visits, we became quite close. During the Christmas Holidays in 1984, Theo visited Nassau to meet her family. He had completed his master's program at Penn State and had worked and lived at home for exactly one year. Since his job did not pay enough to repay student loans, he had decided to enlist in the navy for six years. He planned a few days' vacation in the Bahamas before reporting for duty at Great Lakes in January 1985.

He tucked a little gold charm in the shape of the words *You're Special* in a gift box for "his girl" and departed with such high hopes of finalizing future plans. But something happened. He came home hurt and disappointed. The relationship appeared to have ended on a note of "Let's just be friends—no romance involved." I was grateful for the confidence he placed in my opinion as he asked what he should do. I comforted him as best I could and reminded him of the way God closes and opens doors. Nothing happens in our lives that is not ordained by Him, so he must continue to trust Him to provide all his needs. He finally agreed he should write a letter of thanks to Annischa's family and then discontinue his correspondence with Nish.

Theo departed for the Great Lakes determined to meet all challenges head on. He planned to study hard, get through basic training, travel, meet new people, share his faith, and have some fun. He intended to forget Annischa and indicated to us in his letters that his relationship with her was history.

Within a year, however, when Theo was stationed in Oakland, California, attending Preventive Medicine Technician's School, she began to write and call him. When I visited with him in Oakland in December 1985, he confided that she had finally explained her actions, requested his forgiveness, and wanted to resume their relationship. I was again impressed when this knowledgeable young man sought my opinion concerning this latest development. We had long, lopsided discussions (he did most of the talking), and finally his decision was to resume correspondence with Nish, but not to sever any other close friendships until God made it clear to him who should have that special place in his heart.

While Theo was stationed in Groton, Connecticut, he never allowed Nish to visit him there, but would meet her at our home for a vacation whenever he had leave. After her last visit at Christmas 1986, all the family was awaiting the "announcement." However, there wasn't one. There were other problems. Annischa was a teacher in Nassau and had a contract to complete. Theo was applying for officer's training and would not receive his master's in business administration until August 1988. Many financial problems had to be solved, so they were only "almost engaged" at the time of his death. After the funeral, we received the following letter from this dear sweet girl, Annischa.

> October 1, 1987
>
> Hi, Mom and Dad,
>
> Before I say anything else, let me tell you how much I appreciate all that you did for my mom and me while we

were there with you. It means so much because, in all your grief, you took time out to make sure we were taken care of and provided for. You see, words will never be able to express the thanks I feel because you not only opened your home to us, but you opened your hearts and just reached out and enveloped us in your love and tender care. Thank you so much, not only for your love, but also for the privilege and honor that you allowed me in getting to know and love such a fine gentleman as the son you raised.

We have both loved and lost, but it is so much better "to have loved and lost, than to not have loved at all." Theo and I have shared many good and bad times. We've shared love and hurt, but the good times and the love we shared were strong enough to enable us to recover from the hurt and pain. I know that there were times when I've caused Theo a lot of hurt, but I thank God that he died knowing that I loved him. And I know without a doubt that he loved me. I'll never forget him, and I will cherish the love that he had for me. As far as I'm concerned, I'll always be "Someone Special" because of Theo and the love that he had for me. Through his love he has taught me to be less selfish, more patient, and he showed me that it is possible to have an unconditional love for others here on this Earth. The many other little things I have learned from him I'll never be able to put down on paper or express in words. Mom, it hurts so much. Sometimes, like now, I wonder how I'm gonna make it without Theo in my corner to encourage and cheer me on. Knowing him and loving him has been a great source of strength and self-confidence. He was always one to tell me and make me believe that I could achieve anything I wanted to in this life. He always knew what to say and what to do in any given situation. He knew when I needed words of comfort, he knew when I needed to hear a good joke, he was interested in me and what I was doing, but most of all, he knew when all I needed was for someone to listen to me. Theo was my All in All in a very special way.

Mom, I feel so alone right now. God had a reason for taking away the most important person in my life right now and turning all my life and plans into shambles. There is a lesson to be learned in all of this because, with God, there is always a reason for everything He does. When I get home, I have to sit still and listen and get into His Word to find out what it is I'm supposed to do or where I'm supposed to be headed. I'm lost right now, and the only one I have to call on to lead and direct me now is Him. Mom, Dad, I'm really gonna need your prayers just as I know you're gonna need my prayers, not to get over the hurt of this loss, but for the strength and ability to learn to live with it day by day.

You know we were all very blessed to have had one such as Theo to have walked among us. I hope and pray that, in my time left, I will become half the person he was. He lived his life for Christ first and foremost. His love for God was exemplified in all that he said and did. He was indeed an angel in our midst. He's gone now, but the love and joy he shared with all of us will linger on forever and never be forgotten.

I can go on and on, but I must get up early in the morning to catch a plane home. I'm really gonna miss you guys. I guess by now you realize how much I love and appreciate you and your love and even more so how much I loved and appreciated Theo and the difference he has made in my life.

With lots of love, your adopted daughter, Nish. Psalms 27:1.

> P.S. Please express our thanks and appreciation to everyone who helped us in one way or the other while we were there. I would never remember all their names, but the kindness will not be forgotten. Remember I love you both. Today is the first day of the rest of your lives. God loves you!

In early October, we realized the house was no longer filled with people. Instead, it was filled with stacks of cards and letters, flowers, plants, and the heaviest, darkest, most sickening and shockingly empty feeling imaginable. One night I sat up in my bed and listened to loud, uncontrolled screams and sobbing. It eventually dawned upon me that the explosion of pent-up emotion was my own reaction to the inconsolable horror and hurt of my grief. With wisdom from God, my husband encircled me in his arms and said, "Let it all out! Go ahead and cry! You have to! Don't even try to keep it in!" I seemed to be observing the scene from elsewhere in the room as a strange woman, so distraught, was being comforted. My consciousness finally re-entered my mind, and I was again aware of a precious scripture, long ago committed to memory, and my attention was focused on Joshua 1:9: "Have I not commanded thee? Be strong and of good courage; be not afraid, neither by thou dismayed; for the Lord thy God is with thee wherever thou goest" (KJV). "I lay down and slept: I awaked; for the Lord sustained me" (Psalm 3:5 KJV).

The cards and letters continued to arrive. Each mail delivery brought letters and notes with comments such as "You don't know me, but your son did this or that ..." "He was a great guy, and I just wanted you to know that he led me to the Lord." "He helped me through a difficult time." "He saved my life when I was contemplating suicide."

One day we realized that many of Theo's friends and acquaintances in other parts of the country probably did not know of his death. So upon receipt of his personal effects, which the navy had packed up and sent down to us in a moving van, we used his address book to notify them. Since there were numerous names, we prepared the following note:

> We regret to advise you of the sudden death of our son, "Theo," on September 24, 1987. He died of a heart attack and was found in his bed at his residence in Connecticut.

A memorial service was held a Groton Naval Hospital where he worked, and his funeral was in Camden, New Jersey. It was over two weeks before we had access to his personal belongings and are just now able to notify his many friends in other areas.

Sorrowfully,

Theodore and Jewel H. DeShields

We mailed this along with a copy of the obituary and the program from the funeral service. It was a formidable task and kept us busy for several weeks, as we also were in the process of acknowledging the gifts and condolences which we received daily. We had probably used a couple of rolls of stamps, and then the responses began to come in from this group of Theo's friends who were equally shocked and distressed at the news. Many thanked us for taking the time to find and notify them.

Our days were continually filled with activity. Good friends visited and called. However, the quiet times were especially difficult. I had determined in my heart from the beginning of my grief that I would not ask God why this had happened. I very frequently consoled myself with the words of Job "And said, Naked came I out of my mother's womb, and naked shall I return thither: the Lord gave, and the Lord hath taken away; blessed be the name of the Lord. (Job 1:21 KJV).

But my mind was confused by Job's comment in Job 3:25 (KJV) "For the thing which I greatly feared is come upon me, and that which I was afraid of is come unto me." Determining why this verse was appropriate to my feelings was rather confusing until I acknowledged to myself that I had lived with a foreboding fear for many years. The acknowledgment of the fear took the form of the thought—He's too good to be true. Something will surely happen to him."

18

The Child Who Wasn't Supposed to Be

As I sat at my desk, the tears began to roll down my cheeks. Quickly brushing them away, I glanced up and around the room. The shock was beginning to penetrate, and all I could remember clearly was "You need an immediate operation!" Having just returned to work after an eleven o'clock appointment with a gynecologist, I had skipped lunch, and now my head began to throb. How would I make it through the long afternoon with this burden of bewilderment and dread? *I must get back to my work*, I told myself repeatedly, but my mind kept hearing the words *complete hysterectomy*, and again I tasted salty tears. How will I explain this to my husband? We've only been married two months, and of course we want to have children. My daughter by a previous marriage was eight years old, and we didn't want to wait to start a family because I was thirty years old. How could this be true? Here I was married to a strong, healthy man who had never been married before and had no children, and I had to tell him I needed a hysterectomy. I wanted to put my head down on my desk and sob, but I couldn't. I would have to wait to do that until I arrived at home.

By five o'clock, I was a complete wreck. My head ached and my throat was tight and painful from holding back the sobs of fear and frustration that continually welled up only to be forced back down again. I finally finished that awful day, and I got home and went up to the bedroom to talk to my husband. He worked at night and had just gotten up. By this time, I was glad to have a listening ear and a shoulder to cry on. We had promised to always tell each other the truth, the whole truth, and nothing but the truth, so I just blurted it out—all of it, how I had fibroid tumors in my uterus, and I needed to have an operation. At first, I couldn't tell how he was reacting to this news, but I finally realized he was concerned about me rather than my inability to have his child. And, as we consoled one another, I thanked God repeatedly that I had married a loving Christian man.

The next day at work, my dear friend, Lois, noticed the sadness I was experiencing. We both were employed by the government department in the same section and often had lunch together. She asked what was troubling me, and since she had been the matron of honor at our wedding and was pregnant with her first child, I shared with her the results of my visit to the doctor. I had known that Lois had been married for twelve years and was four months pregnant when she stood with me at my wedding. However, I had assumed it was the way she and her husband had planned it. But she told me something that day that drastically changed my life. Lois had wanted children from the very beginning of her marriage, and following extensive testing, it had been discovered that she had the problem that prevented conception. She was referred to a woman doctor who had treated her very successfully, and now she was expecting their first child. Eagerly she told me the details of her medical treatment and wrote the doctor's name on a card, insisting I call for an appointment, as she was certain this doctor could help me also.

I called that very day, and early on Saturday morning was being ushered into the office of Dr. May Agnes Gowdey of Riverton, New Jersey. After taking my medical history, she gave me a complete examination. As I sat beside her desk, she patted Mr. Chips, her cocker spaniel, looked me in the eye and stated, "You've been told you need a hysterectomy, haven't you?" Surprised, I admitted that was exactly the case, and I was terribly unhappy about the prospect. I told her it was a detestable thought, but I supposed it was necessary.

She took paper and a pen and drew a diagram and pointed out the location and size of the fibroid tumors in my uterus. In the course of the conversation, she asked two important questions. First, "How badly do you want a child?" Second, "What are you willing to endure in order to become a mother?" It didn't take me a long time to decide if it was possible. I'd be willing to go through whatever was necessary. But she hastened to explain that, since it would not be easy and had many risks, I should speak with my husband, give it plenty of thought, and come back the following week if I wanted to begin treatment. She could not guarantee success, but for the first time, a glowing hope warmed my heart.

She did ask if it had been a male doctor who was so eager to operate. When I said yes, she just shook her head and said that some men do not understand what some women are willing to endure in order to bring children into the world. That's why they often recommend surgery. They believe we should simply remove the problems and make things easy for ourselves.

I went home thinking my mind was already made up. But she was right; if it was going to be a difficult process, I really should discuss it with my husband. Deep within my heart, I knew I wanted at least one more child. My daughter, Jennifer, was a real joy to both of us, but Ted deserved a child of his own. Both of us had come from large families. He had four brothers and five sisters, and I had three brothers and two sisters.

We talked for hours and wished for a simple solution, but there was no other easy way except to adopt. Pursuing our own conception would be the difficult uncertain way, but the child would be our own—the result of our love. And we finally agreed it was worth the risks involved and was what we both wanted. He promised to support me all the way as long as I wanted to try.

In a week, we returned to the doctor's office where we began a program that eventually included mega-doses of vitamins, minor surgery, and basal temperature thermometers. Finally, after two years, I became pregnant. But it was only eight weeks before I suffered a miscarriage.

At this time, our morale reached a very low point. I vacillated between wanting to give up completely and the nagging strong desire to eventually have a child. After a few weeks, we agreed to continue, and Dr. Gowdey offered much encouragement. She was rapidly becoming a dear friend. She told me of her struggle as she pioneered in the medical profession.

Within three months, I was pregnant again, and this time, as soon as it was suspected, I was put to bed for almost two months. After the pregnancy was established, life became a pattern—a few weeks out of bed and then a few weeks of complete bed rest. This was a hard adjustment for my family as I had to direct the household from an upstairs bedroom. This was not bed rest with bathroom privileges! This was complete bed rest with as little movement as possible. I was totally dependent on someone for every need. It was humiliating for me and a real nuisance to Ted and Jennifer. The Lord has subtle ways of teaching humility. However, the worst was the uncertainty and constant dread of what might suddenly happen. Could I carry full term? Would the baby growing within me be healthy and perfectly normal? Would I deliver naturally or by cesarean section? So many concerns kept me awake at night, and the days were long as I wearily lay in bed.

Finally, after about six months, I was able to be up even though there were many restrictions on my activities. Oh, but it was wonderful to be able to sit downstairs in the living room and knit and sew for the baby.

I spent many hours analyzing how I felt about this situation. It was so difficult to be positive that we were doing the right thing in having a child. Maybe God didn't want us to have a baby. Maybe we were just asking for trouble. After all, if my body was not normal, could I have a normal baby? Would he or she be deformed or disabled? I went from those questions to what would happen if Ted and I broke up? I had been unsuccessful in marriage before. What if I was left with two children to raise alone? Women have a tendency to overanalyze every thought, and I desperately needed someone to listen as I voiced these fears. Whenever I tried to speak with Ted about some of these questions, I soon learned from his reactions that it was too much for him to handle. He simply could not offer the encouragement I needed, and his own fears were intensified when I pressed him to talk with me about my concerns. He even said one day, "I can't talk about it!" Other times he'd just say, "I have to go to work." During that time of my life, my relationship with God was rather casual. I didn't bother Him and didn't expect Him to bother me. But I wished for a friend to share my troubles.

Christmas came, and my husband gave me a pearl and diamond ring saying a finger was all he could buy anything to fit. Yes, I was definitely expanding. I was happier and not as fearful. Remaining on the strict diet and restricted activities was not easy, but the goal was now in sight.

Our baby was due at the end of March; however, one snowy day in early February, I woke Ted up with the news that I was in labor. Thank goodness I remained calm because Ted was so nervous he was running around doing unnecessary things. I finally told him to get in the car and take me to the hospital. He even got lost and had to ask directions at a gas station. The week before, he had known exactly where the hospital was located. I had called Dr. Gowdey, who was in her Philadelphia office. It was snowing as we rushed up the highway, and after the labor pains and fear of an accident, I breathed easier when we arrived safely. I had worried about needing a cesarean, but our son was in such a hurry that, within an hour after our arrival at the hospital, he was born into this world lustily proclaiming his independence. The doctor and nurses had no time for the usual medical help for mother, and I learned first-hand about natural childbirth. When Dr. Gowdey rushed into the delivery room out of breath, her first words to me were, "Why didn't you wait for me?"

And so, February 9, 1959, was assigned to Theodore DeShields Jr. as the first day of the rest of his life. We never could have expected the amazing adventures awaiting us. He was healthy, seemed normal in every way, and the doctors released us to go home on the fourteenth of February. I made a big show of giving him to his father for a Valentine present! Our son weighed six pounds and ten ounces at birth, and when held by his huge father appeared tiny indeed. His father would hold him for hours, examining his little hands and feet and waiting for him to open his eyes. He would look at him, look at me, and shake his head; and many times, I saw a tear glistening on his cheek.

My mother came to help with household chores, and we were all so happy that the pain and problems of the past three years were all but forgotten. The name Theodore means "gift of God," and this child truly was that. Mom called him a precious child and spent many hours lovingly caring for him.

His big sister, Jennifer, eleven years his senior, became a willing helper also, even though she had been reluctant to relinquish her position in the family as the "only child." I watched happily as she warmed up to the baby brother who had upset the status quo!

We called him Teddy Junior and marveled how this beautiful, healthy little boy rapidly became the center of attention in the DeShields household. He weighed almost seven pounds for a very short time, and then began to add length and weight so fast that we were usually unable to put the same outfit on him more than twice. He was always hungry and had to be fed every three hours around the clock. Even in the hospital, the nurse had brought him to his mother an hour early to be nursed because he cried so pitifully. It seems that my strict diet during pregnancy had caused him to be underweight. He easily could have weighed eight or nine pounds, but because of the tumors, I had to count calories to keep his and my weight down to a minimum. I actually gained only nineteen pounds. So this boy was hungry, and he lost no time in trying to catch up. We were all exhausted by the end of his first month at home. He finally calmed down when I enlarged the nipple hole in a bottle and put some rice cereal in his milk. What a blessing to get a few hours of peaceful sleep!

When he was less than a month old, I found him in his crib with his little face covered with blood. We rushed him to Dr. Gowdey who discovered there was a membrane closing one nostril. She had no instrument small enough to operate on him, and therefore sent us immediately to an ear, nose, and throat specialist. He was able to perform surgery to open his nostril right in his office as I held my screaming child's head as firmly as possible in trembling hands. This was a rare problem, potentially dangerous, and we were very frightened.

As I stood watching him sleep peacefully later that evening, I contemplated how close we had come to losing him. I whispered a short prayer to God and wondered how this little fellow had managed to increase my awareness of the presence of God in my life.

19

The Early Struggles of Motherhood

We soon settled into a routine. Everything done to care for a family has to be done all over again each day, and sometimes sooner—preparing food, washing dishes, cleaning the home, washing the clothes, diapering the baby, and later going to the PTA meetings, helping with homework. Every mother knows how busy life becomes. However, I became increasingly aware of a sadness and tiredness that just wouldn't go away. After a while, other in the family noticed my periods of silence and lack of enthusiasm. I can remember feeling worthless, unable to make routine decisions, and becoming disinterested in almost everything. To my credit, I never neglected Teddy. I took care of all his physical needs, but by the time he should have walked, he didn't. By the time he should have talked, he didn't. And this lack in development seemed not to concern me in the least.

My mother and sister, Patricia, who is a nurse, insisted I get a check-up. The doctor diagnosed postpartum depression. There were times when I thought I was rapidly losing my mind. Many days became a blur in my fuzzy memory. This was just one more impossible situation for my life and my fun-loving sportsman husband. Ted seemed to me to be retreating into his own hard shell. He would drive me to the doctor's office, but since I didn't talk to him, he didn't talk to me. It was getting expensive, and I was not making much progress.

It wasn't long before Dr. Gowdey referred me to a clinic at Philadelphia

Psychiatric Hospital. I was enrolled in an experimental drug-testing program. It would be much less expensive because the medication was free, and I would receive counseling as long as necessary.

My husband would come home from working all night, put me in the car, and drive approximately one hour to the hospital. He would wait for me, sleeping soundly in the car or in the waiting room. Then he would drive me home. Sometimes we didn't say ten words the entire time. There had been no angry words between us. I just didn't talk, and he didn't know what to do about it.

The doctors at the clinic would prescribe various drugs for me to take for a week. When I returned, I would be examined and asked whether I felt better or worse. I never figured out why they changed the medication regardless of what I said. Neither did they require that I return the left-over drugs that seemed to help and throw away anything else. After several months of these weekly appointments, I soon had accumulated a full drawer of pill bottles, all antidepressants that had made me feel somewhat better. They were marked with control numbers, and I never knew the names of the drugs I took.

For almost eighteen months, I suffered recurring symptoms. The effect of my depression was experienced by the entire family. It slowed Teddy Junior's development of communication skills. I was even silent with him and made no effort to encourage him to talk. He would not ask for a drink of water, but would just get his plastic cup, point it at the kitchen sink, and without comment, I would fill his glass and hand it to him. When someone else would insist that he say "water" or he would not get any, he would go upstairs to the bathroom where he could get it from the bathtub faucets.

When a person is depressed, it is not evident at all times. I appeared normal to most people, but often wild thoughts consumed my waking hours. I felt I might hurt someone by what I said or did, so it was better not to do or say anything. These feelings zigzagged in and out, sort of up and down in my mind. I seemed to be functioning in slow motion to a constantly fluttering heartbeat. I know it makes very little since, but no one could tell me to "pull myself together" or "snap out of it" or "stop being so sad." I really resented such futile efforts to help me. Something deep within me was out of kilter, and I just wanted a way out of my skull to find a place to rest. It was an exhausting effort to do anything, even sleep, and the pills offered my only rescue. What a price to pay just for giving birth!

One day I realized how dependent I was becoming on that prescription medication for depression. I was taking pills all day every day and still did not feel normal. As far as my family knew, the medication was helping. They encouraged me to continue to go to the clinic and would even ask me if I had taken my medicine. But as weeks went by, something within me began to rebel against the artificial stimulants, and I yearned to be free of the dependency on medication.

God must have been speaking to me because the desire to stop taking the drugs became a strong compulsion. I began to take several fewer pills each day, and of course, my body immediately started rebelling. I knew then that it was not a simple act of control but a fight to regain control, and it was not going to be an easy victory. That is why I believe God helped me. Even though I did not at first enlist His help, a faith that I would be strong enough to eventually quit taking the medication inspired me to continue to decrease the dosage and not give in to addiction.

The struggle continued. I would arise determined not to take medication that day unless absolutely necessary. I had no encouragement as no one knew how I felt or what I was trying to do. I stopped going to the clinic but could not bring myself to destroy the pills I had accumulated. Sometimes I would lie on the floor on my back, spread my arms, and just hold on when my nerves were so raw with the desire for that medication. But after a while, I would get up, get dressed, and take Teddy Junior for a walk in the park. There we would sit on a bench and watch the squirrels bury acorns. Sometimes I would take lunch so I could stay away from the house all day. I read stories to Teddy and tried not to think of the war going on within me.

I was afraid to stop taking the medication "cold turkey" because I really didn't know what might happen to me without it. So I tried to take less each week until I could stop altogether. Whenever my body began to feel almost comfortable, it was time to cut down on the quantity again. I did notice that the symptoms of withdrawal were lessening. I must be on the right track, I determined.

When I opened the final bottle of pills, my intention was to make them last indefinitely by using them only once in a while to relieve tension. Can you imagine how wonderful it was when I realized that I had forgotten about taking medicine for over a week? I praise God now that He helped me to wean myself away from addictive medication. Slowly I became a better mother to Jennifer and Teddy, the child we had wanted so desperately.

When Teddy was almost three years old and still not talking, my sister nagged us to have him tested to determine if this beautiful child had been damaged in some way. We began to fear that he might be partially deaf. We took him to Children's Hospital in Philadelphia, where the tests were negative. He was not brain damaged. He could hear, see, and feel. His intelligence was normal, and he was able to speak if he wanted to. The doctor said that Teddy would talk when he had something to say. It was recommended that he be placed in a nursery school environment where he could play with other children his age. Eventually we got him enrolled in a daycare program for half days where the other children had him talking about everything by the time he was four years old.

Teddy was growing fast and was taller than most children his age. He was energetic, inquisitive, and very friendly. With a healthier mother, we were becoming a more normal family, except we did not go to church together. Jennifer and Teddy Sr. were attending the Baptist Church, but Teddy Jr. and I didn't go at all. There was a Methodist Church across the street from our home, and sometimes I would watch the people go in and out, but I was alienated from God and resisted any urge to cross the street and visit His house. It would be a little longer before the healing could begin because I was not yet ready to acknowledge that the separation and divorce of my parents had driven a wedge between the church and me. At the age of fourteen, the world that I knew came to an abrupt halt. My father, a prominent minister, deserted his wife of sixteen years to pursue his love of the organist of his church, leaving his wife to raise five of his six children alone. It is not surprising that I was bitter. Since I was the oldest of the children who lived with our mother, it was my job to help her with the younger ones, as she had to work very hard to support us.

My teenage years were different than what I had envisioned as a youngster when the dream of a college education was paramount. All my dreams were soon dissolved within my daily struggle to go to school, help with the children, and work at a part-time job. My older brother, who stayed with our father, was only fifteen months older than I, and we had grown up almost like twins since all the other children were three years apart. Therefore, when the divorce was final, he was fifteen and I was fourteen years of age. I had lost a father and a brother at a critical stage in my development. We lived on the east coast in Philadelphia, and my brother and father lived in Indiana.

Up until the separation, I had been in church all the time since we lived in a parsonage and our lives revolved around the activities of our church. It was a humiliating experience to have the scandalous activities of a prominent father published in the daily newspaper. I have to admit that I was ashamed of him. Why had God permitted this upheaval in my life?

So, as I watched the people taking their children into the church, my feelings were confused because, deep down, I knew God was faithful, but human beings can and often do let us down. But faith can be shattered when a person professes to be faithful and to live for God and then engages in unprincipled behavior, letting us down. I could not bring myself to cross the street and go to that church. My mother was also disillusioned and stayed away from the organized church for many years. Each of us in the family had to find our way back to a loving heavenly Father who had never deserted us even though we had turned our back on Him.

In September 1964, Teddy Jr. was five and a half years old and entering kindergarten. The daycare center he had attended for a little more than a year had prepared him to get along better with other children to a degree, but he was still hyperactive and needed to be constantly supervised. I wondered how he had gone from a docile, easy-going child to this boisterous, talkative, ever-active boy who wanted to be the center of attention at all times. Once, when he was four and a half, I had to hold both of his hands and ask the proprietor of a card shop to show me the cards I wished to examine. I had to do this to keep him from wrecking the place. He was not trying to be disobedient; he just appeared unable to take it slow enough not to be reckless. Since he was so large for his age, many people assured he was mentally challenged. I could see it in their eyes—the pity they felt for such a handsome little fellow who had a mental or emotional disability. I knew what they thought was not true, but I understood why that impression was being made.

So, when I took him to Parkside Elementary School and left him the first day, I was worried that he would have a problem adjusting to this drastic change in his life. He did not realize at first that the teacher was supposed to be in charge. He wanted to tell everyone what to do and how to do it. One of the first comments the teacher made to me was, "He has to learn who is the boss around here!" His first teacher was a member of Parkside Church and a lovely Christian young woman. Once she was able to convey to him that he was not to give orders, but to follow directions, things went more smoothly.

One day Teddy came home from school dragging a piece of manila drawing paper which he held by one corner. When he came into the house, he showed it to me proudly, but he was not too excited. He just handed it to me and said, "Mom, here's my picture." I picked it up, looked at it, and discerned that it was something he had drawn, but I couldn't figure out exactly what it was because the whole page was completely black. He had colored this entire page with his black crayon. I looked at it and questioned, "This is your picture?" He said, "Yes." So I asked, "What is it?" I was trying not to laugh or show any scorn. He seemed a little annoyed at my ignorance and said, "Well, the teacher told us to draw something, and I decided to draw night." Of course, it amounted to a completely black piece of paper. I have to admit that I was somewhat concerned about him at this time. I thought, *Is this kid all right?* But I said to him, "Well, you certainly drew a good picture of night!"

20

He Is Growing Up Quickly

Teddy Jr. was growing rapidly. His years in the first and second grade were spent enjoying his schooling. He enjoyed the company of other children. He loved to play and to laugh and to learn. He would come home excited about everything that he had learned. He participated in everything. He was always involved, always exuberant, and always careful to explain everything that had happened during the day. He loved to talk about his activities.

The only real problem in the first two or three years of grade school involved constant bouts of asthma. Sometimes he would be unable to attend school more than three weeks every month during the winter. Every cold brought on the dreaded tightening of the chest and horrible wheezing as he struggled to breathe. If it started while he was in school, he would have to lean against trees and fences in his effort to walk the two blocks home. I developed a sixth sense and, if I suspected that he was in trouble, I would meet him at the corner and support him as he walked the last block. Then it would be to bed with the medication and the vaporizer. I spent nights too numerous to count in the rocking chair in his room holding him upright to assist his breathing.

The doctor had warned me not to allow him to see my fear or distress. It would cause him to panic and would certainly aggravate his condition. I was forced to become an expert at hiding my fears. As he struggled for each breath and became fearful, he would look at my face. Having found no fear in my eyes, he would allow his body to relax, and breathing would become less difficult and labored. Oh, what a bond of love and trust was being forged between us! He was just a little boy.

I remember his stiff-upper-lip-approach to the sixteen test pricks of his arm at the hospital clinic to determine his allergies. He didn't cry but asked repeatedly, "Is this the last one?" The nurse replied, "Just a few more, young man. Just a few more." The painful ordeal was finished, but there was more to come as he was treated with shots for several years to lessen his extreme allergies to dust, mold, and animal dander. We were advised by the doctors to air condition his room, get rid of all stuffed toys, carpets, and house plants. I had never realized how much these things harbor dust. The night that I took away his teddy bears and stuffed toys and hid them in the trunk in the basement was a particularly painful time for the both of us. The next morning, when he missed his favorite, I had to tell him that they were gone and that he couldn't have them any longer. It was difficult to make up an excuse that was acceptable to him, and all I saw was the hurt and pain in his face. I gave him other things to occupy his time. He had an ant farm, and that gave him a lot of pleasure. He learned to play games by himself and to read books. He had a membership in Doctor Seuss's book-of-the-month club, and for many years he enjoyed *Green Eggs and Ham*, *The Cat and the Hat, How the Grinch Stole Christmas*, and then every one of the published Doctor Seuss books. He read over and over again and enjoyed them tremendously. He had a great time even though he was often ill.

His father loved him dearly, but he couldn't deal with the illness. It was very hard for him to sit and watch his son suffer. It made him feel so helpless, and most of the time he would get up and go out of the room because his face mirrored our boy's feelings, and I couldn't teach him how to hide the fear that he had. Oftentimes, he would leave me to do all the nursing when Teddy Jr. was sick. During this time, his sister Jenifer was a big help because she played with him and spent time with him although she was eleven years older. She enjoyed his company also. We began to coalesce together as a family.

Teddy was very tall for his age. A neighbor boy came up to me when I was walking on the sidewalk in front of our house and said, "I don't understand, Mrs. DeShields. Teddy is so much taller than I am!" So, I looked at him, and I figured that this question deserved an answer. This young man was very concerned, and he just couldn't figure it out. I said, "How tall is your father?" He told me. I then asked, "How tall is your mother?" He told me. I then asked, "Have you seen Teddy's father?" He said "Yeah, and he is a big man." I asked, "Am I taller than your mother?" He answered, "Yeah." I said, "Well, there is your answer. Tall people usually have tall children. Shorter people usually have shorter children. Don't worry about it. It is no big deal." He said "Okay. I just couldn't figure out how he could grow so big in such a short time."

When a child has physical problems, it is the easiest thing in the world to spoil them. Teddy, being the only boy in the family, and having an older sister, was practically an only child because she was occupied in an entirely different way. Since she was out of the home more often than in the home, he had to find entertainment on his own. The problem was that he wanted to spend a great deal of time with me. I wanted to spend time with him because I enjoyed his company, but I couldn't allow him to do what he wanted to do all the time. It was a process that I was involved in—weaning him away from me and yet enjoying his company. Sometimes at night he wanted to come and stay in my room, lie on my bed, and watch TV before he had to go to sleep. Since his father was working at night, I was in my room alone. It would have been the easiest thing in the world to allow him to spend a great deal of time with me like that, but I realized that it would not have been a good thing to do.

Teddy wanted to join the scout group that was active at the church, but he had trouble with his asthma and allergies. The doctor suggested that it might not be a good idea for him to go away on sleepovers where he would be away from home at night. I had to talk him out of his desire to go. We would offer him some sort of incentive so that he would stay out of the scouts for a while until he was able to do the things. When the day finally came when he was sufficiently immune because he had been taking shots for his allergies, he was able to go away on an overnight or two and did pretty well. He looked forward to going to camp in the summertime. His sister had gone away to camp called Merrowvista in Ossipee, New Hampshire, for a month at a time when she was his age. He wanted to do this also. She had told him so much about Merrowvista that he really wanted to go. So, when he was old enough to go, he began to get ready. He had his list of all the things that he had to have in order to go. We were able to gather up all the necessary equipment—mosquito netting, boots, umbrella, and clothing. I told him to get the footlocker out and that he would do his own packing. He replied, "Okay, Mom! That's no problem."

He consulted the list and brought out some of the stuff. I suggested that he lay out everything on the bed and then we would pack, because he was endeavoring to just throw it all into the trunk. It was almost filled to the top with things he had just thrown in. I said, "Lay everything out on the bed, and we will check the list after you get everything together." Two or three times he called me upstairs to check how he was getting along. I said, "Check the list to make sure you have gathered everything and *then* call me." Finally, we went through the list. He had everything on the bed including the correct number of each item he was to have. I said, "All right, now that you have everything together, let's pack it into the footlocker." And then I stepped aside. He said, "You want me to do it?" I said, "Yes, of course." He started picking up things and stacking them into the footlocker. Long before he had finished, the footlocker was full. I said, "It doesn't look like it is going to fit." He said, "Mom, I'm going to have to have another footlocker." I said, "No, no, no! You must get your stuff into *this* footlocker. It will fit." I knew that he needed to roll the things up and pack them tightly in order to make them fit. I said, "Take everything out, and I will show you how to do it." We removed everything from the footlocker, and we started to roll the underwear and pack it tightly. We packed the bottom layer very, very tightly so that it would fit. Then we put the second layer in, and finally everything was in, and it fit very well. I had learned how to do this myself when I had sent Jenny off to camp, and I had packed suitcases for my brothers.

I had learned a lot from my brothers because they were in the service and had learned how to pack duffle bags. I had watched them. After we got everything packed, my son said, "That's great mom! Now I'm all ready." I said, "Wait, where are you going?" "I'm going out to play." I said, "No you aren't." I took everything out of the footlocker and put it on the bed. I said, "You pack it now." Well, he wasn't too pleased with me at that moment. I said, "You must do it yourself." In fact, I believe he was angry with me. He said, "Why did you do that? Why did you take it all out?" I sat him down and I said, "Listen, if I pack it for you, how will you get your clothes back home? You will be up there, and you will need to know how to put your things in this trunk to bring them home. Learn how to pack them, and then you will be able to pack them when you come home." He realized that made sense, so he kept at it until he got it the way that I had demonstrated. It wasn't easy for him. He had to repack two or three times to make everything fit. He knew that it *would* fit because I had done it in his presence. When he finally had done it himself, he called me up and was proud. "Mom, I did it! I know that I can pack to come home." "Good! I replied." Interestingly enough, when he did come home from his first month in camp, he told me that he had to help three or four guys pack their trunks because they hadn't been forced to pack themselves before they came to camp.

The first year that Teddy went away to camp, he had begun in January to read through the Bible with one of the printed schedules that are often given out in church. He had decided that he was going to follow that schedule faithfully, and at the end of the year he would have read the King James Version of the Bible all the way through. I admit that I was skeptical because he was so young, and I really did not think he would finish. We often make New Year's resolutions, and we start out gung ho, but we fall and falter along the way. He insisted that he was going to do it. Several times I had asked him how he was doing with his Bible reading He would always respond, "I am up to date, Mom."

When the time came for him to go away to camp for a month, I thought, *Well, that will probably be the end of the Bible reading.* I mentioned it to him and asked him, "How are you going to keep up with the Bible reading this summer when you go away to camp?" He said, "Don't worry. I'm fine." I said, "I hope so. You said that you would be pretty busy, and there are going to be a lot of people around. There will be a lot of youngsters, so how are you going to find the time to read several chapters in the Bible every day?" He insisted that he would be able to do it, and he definitely planned to keep up with his Bible reading.

When he came home from camp that year, I asked him point blank, "How did you do with your Bible reading?" He said, "Mom, I am up to date." I asked, "How did you find time?" He said, "At first the guys kidded me when we were eating at the picnic table. I learned that the best way of doing it was to get up real early in the morning and go out by myself and read my Bible. I would go to the woods where I could be by myself."

The emotion that I experienced at that moment was a strange blend of pride, awe, and foreboding. As the ominous feeling of "he is too good to be true" again resounded in my heart. I thought, *That's real dedication.* And I had to admit that it made a tremendous impression on me that this youngster could be so committed and dedicated to doing something that was difficult. He would find a way, even on a month-long vacation in the mountains. With all the opposition and all the activities that would pull him away, he managed to get up early and read his Bible.

His father was involved with sports—mainly baseball, basketball, bowling, and golf. When he went to the local games, he often took Teddy with him. Teddy would take his basketball and wander off from the baseball game to find a basketball court and practice with whomever he found that would play with him. As his skills increased, he played with the Cagers, a church team from the Collingswood church. His father would sometimes referee the Cagers basketball game on Saturday mornings at the church.

It was during this time that I learned to bowl, and I would take Teddy and his friends to bowl in the junior bowling league every Saturday. He won a few trophies and was recruited to bowl in a tournament. He was so excited. I shared his joy and enthusiasm and asked the when and where questions. The answer came back, "Eleven o'clock on Sunday mornings." He asked, "What shall I do, Mom?" "It's a matter of priority, son," I stated. "There are hundreds of activities on Sunday mornings. If you choose anything else but church and Sunday school, you will be letting God know what you think is most important. And to your friends, you will be demonstrating displacement of your loyalty." He thought for a moment. I could see the disappointment and desire in his eyes. He shook his head sadly and said, "That is that. No tournament." In the car going home, I listened without comment as his friends told him how much they really needed him and pleaded that they would have a chance to win with him on the team. He was head and shoulders above most boys his age. He remained calm, and he told them how sorry he was that the wrong time had been chosen to play the tournament. He never changed his mind, never mentioned it again, and on Sunday, he went to Sunday school and church as usual. Again, my fleeting thought was, *He's too good to be true.*

Near Christmas that year, he told me that he was reading the book of Revelation and was absolutely certain that he could be finished by the end of the year. He completed his goal: he finished his Bible. He told me, "Mom, I've done it." I made up my mind then that, if this youngster could do it, I could too. I was not going to allow his dedication or his commitment to continue to make me feel ashamed of myself. For many years, I had thought that I should read more of my Bible, but it took a young boy—a determined young boy—to show me that, if I wanted to, I could do it. I just had to want to badly enough. So, I did. The very next year, we celebrated because I had done something that was difficult and required a commitment. I learned that I had stick-to-itiveness that had remained hidden until my son was able to bring it out. Thanks, kid!

21

The Battle to Do Well

When Teddy was in the seventh grade, trouble really erupted. He wanted to study and accomplish things, but the majority of the students in his class did not care for academics. At that time, the teachers appeared to be inept or unqualified to change the atmosphere in the classroom. His school hours were made miserable as the girls constantly tried to entice him to fight. He would come home and sit down and ask very sadly, "What is wrong with me, Mom? I try to treat them like ladies, and they act ridiculous. The girl whose desk faces mind wipes her shoes deliberately on my pants for no reason. She laughs when I don't like it and asks, 'What are you going to do about it? Do you want to fight after school?' I wish I knew why she acts like that." After a long pause, he said, "I suppose no one at home loves her."

We did all what we could to work within the system for three months trying to improve conditions. However, when it appeared hopeless, we transferred him to Martin Luther Christian Day School. He attended through eighth grade, and his school hours again became challenging and rewarding.

In 1971, the city was changing. Downtown where a bridge approach had been widened, many of the homes had been torn down creating a real need for single-family homes in the city. Those who could afford to move to the suburbs did, and those who couldn't move in with family members or crowded into apartments. At once, previously quiet neighborhoods began to overflow with new residents, and the neighborhood schools received an influx of children from different ethnic backgrounds, abilities, and previous home environments. Our daughter had attended the local junior high school, but it was hard to believe the changes that had taken place in only eleven years. Teddy arrived at the junior high school well prepared to study and eager to learn. In fact, he had really loved his science and math classes at the elementary school. He found that students at the junior high school didn't care very much about studying. He was considered "weird" because he wanted to do what was expected by the teacher. Upon investigation, we found that many of the teachers were young recent graduates from college and quite inexperienced at handling discipline problems of the junior high age group. The regular teachers were often absent. I suspected that they were looking for better jobs in the suburbs. However, substitutes, whether young or older, seemed to assume a babysitter role and rarely gave assignments to be completed at home. It was discouraging to our son. He came home from school many days very frustrated with the lack of the progress in the assigned book. He would say things like, "Mom, how will we ever finish the math book? We've only done the first part of the chapter. It's been a whole month." But the problems after class were also confusing to him. He tried to understand why kids always seemed to want to fight after school. There were groups of girls who, it seemed, had a war going on. Someone was always getting hurt or suspended for fighting. It seemed to Teddy that the school was in turmoil, and he was totally helpless to remedy the situation.

At the annual spring concert, Jennifer and I sat in the audience and watched as sloppily dressed students left their seats repeatedly, ran up and down the aisles, talked loudly to each other, and paid little attention to the music being performed on the stage. Previously, I had attended a similar concert when Jenny was in the choir. The audience had been orderly and well dressed. The atmosphere had been entirely different as well-mannered young people enjoyed the evening of music with their family members and friends. The contrast was so profound that I looked at my daughter and said, "We've got to get Teddy out of this school." I made a vow that very night to find a private school that he could attend. I had no idea what the cost would be. I just knew that it was necessary, and no matter what the sacrifice, it had to be done.

Martin Luther Christian Day School was dedicated to providing a Christian education up through eighth grade. Teddy was enrolled when he was in seventh grade. He liked it. It was quite different from the public school system, and we were introduced to the fact that we would still be paying the taxes in the city for the public school system as well as expenses at the private Christian school. When you enroll your child into private school, the tuition must be paid, books must be bought, transportation must be provided, and sometimes even a uniform. Thankfully, we didn't have to buy uniforms, but we had to provide everything else. It was an interesting two years of adjusting to a very different approach to education. For example, if Teddy wanted to go out for soccer, we would have to provide transportation. Whenever they had a game, the parents had quite a responsibility. I learned very early that my days were not my own. I had to get him to school very early in the morning, and then I would have to back and pick him up after school every afternoon, leaving my dinner half cooked. However, the benefits far outweighed every inconvenience. He was happy because he was learning life principles from the coach and the teacher who was one in the same. My husband was not able to attend parent-teacher conferences, but I asked if I could tape the teacher's comments so that my husband could hear them. It was interesting to listen to that tape years later and hear what this nice man had to say about our son.

Teddy was able to make some good friends at Martin Luther, and some of them went on to the high school that Teddy eventually attended. So he had some friends in the suburban community around the inner-city where we lived. One of the first things that we became aware of as parents was the fact that all his friends were not in the same telephone zone. So, after he got on the phone chatting with his friends after school, I got horrendous telephone bills. The very first time, of course, we were quite upset. We had to teach him that he could not just chat with his friends on local toll calls.

Of course, he complained that those were his friends and he wanted to talk to them after school. He said that other kids could talk with their friends, so why couldn't he? After we explained about the expense of it, we had to come to a compromise. My husband and I decided that we would pay a certain amount each month for toll calls. Over that, he would have to pay for the rest out of his allowance. He learned to call his friends, briefly get assignments, or say the necessary things, and not chat very long, especially when he had reached the maximum of his allotment. We used to hear him say, "Hey, look, I've got to get off the telephone. It's costing me money." I told him, "These are the facts of life, son. It costs us for you to chat, but when it costs you, you get off the telephone. What does that tell you?"

There was something very important that we were learning about Theo, Theodore, or Teddy, as we called him in those days. We learned that he was extremely motivated to study, to produce, and to do the *right thing*. He was basically an honest person. Many times he would say or do things, and I realized that he really felt the necessity of always telling the truth, doing the right things, and sharing his love and compassion with those younger than he was or those helpless in any way. I will never forget the time he admonished me for stepping on ants. We were walking down the street, and I made it a point to step on every ant I saw, especially those big black ones. I had learned that they were carpenter ants and that they ate wood in houses; they were just as destructive as termites. Every ant I saw, I trampled, but not Teddy. He would say, "Mom, why did you step on him? He wasn't doing you any harm. He didn't do anything to you." I used to look at him and wonder. I learned that, if I had to step on ants, I didn't let him see me do it.

I came across a baby bird out in the yard one day. It couldn't fly. It had fallen out of its nest, and of course, the cats and the dogs would have made short work of him. Teddy took charge of him and put him in a box. He put the bird in the garage every night. He pulled the door down just enough so that the mother bird could get in there. Believe it or not, that mother bird came in there, fed her baby, and flew out when Teddy went into the garage. He kept the bird safe and allowed the mother bird to take care of her baby. I was amazed. He knew that the baby bird was being fed. The baby bird was growing and chirping all over the place sitting on the box whenever Teddy played with him out in the yard. Then, Teddy would put him back into the garage to protect him. Finally, one day, the bird was strong enough to fly away. I have pictures in my photo album of this boy and a little sparrow that was perched on the side of a box. It was just a sparrow, but Teddy felt that he wanted to protect that bird so that it would not lose its life unnecessarily.

My doctor had given Teddy an old microscope. Teddy enjoyed playing with it. Many times when people asked him what he wanted to be when he grew up, he would remark that he was going to be a doctor. Well, all I ever did was discourage him. I felt that, if he was going to be a doctor, he would have to do it over many obstacles. I told him how hard it was going to be to get the funding, and how long it would take. Someone asked me, "Why are you discouraging him?" "Well," I said, "If he is going to be a doctor, I really cannot discourage him. It will be something that is within him, and he will fight for it." I didn't tell him that he could not be a doctor; I just explained to how difficult it would be. At any rate, he used that microscope so often, examining all kinds of things on slides. One day he had a very bad cold and had to stay home from church. When I came home from church, he was up in his room with the vaporizer going so that he could get some relief from his coughing. As soon as I came in, he called down to me, "Mother, come here quick. I've got something important to show you." I went upstairs into his room. He gestured to a slide under the microscope. "Look at this." I sat, and I looked. He was using quite high magnification, and I could see little things were moving around. I said, "What is this?" I asked him. He said, "Mom, they have to be germs." I said, "Where did you get it?" He said, "It just dripped out of my nose and fell onto the slide! So I decided to look at it under the microscope." He said, "You really should wash your hands after you blow your nose." I remarked that I had been telling him that for years. "Now you know why," I said.

22

The Necessity of Discipline

During Teddy's sixth, seventh, and eighth years, I tried hard to establish a discipline routine even though it was very difficult. A child who must endure pain and disappointment in being unable to go outside and play with his friends touches a soft spot in the heart of his parents, and it becomes easy not to insist on obedience. I really can't say I know how I learned, and I really can't remember actually studying books on child rearing, but I remember how my mother raised her children. She never permitted us to get away with very much, and I was determined that this young man would know who was in charge. My mother believed very strongly in "Train up a child in the way that he should go and he will not depart from it" (Proverbs 22:6 KJV). When I was looking that up in the Bible, I also discovered Proverbs 22:15: "Foolishness is bound up in the heart of a child but the rod of correction shall drive it far from him" (KJV). One day I read Psalm 29:15: "The rod and reproof give wisdom, but a child left to himself bringeth his mother to shame" (KJV). Proverbs 29:17 says, "Correct thy son and he shall give thee rest, yea, he shall be a delight unto thy soul" (KJV). I considered this my aim and mandate from God. So, whenever Teddy disobeyed, I felt that it was my duty to give him a spanking. It was expected that he would be taller than me at a young age, and I felt I must establish a pattern of obedience long before that day arrived.

His father and I agreed for the most part about how discipline should be administered, but since he was away very often, most of the discipline was left to me. One time when his father was at home and Teddy was disobedient, my husband gave him a spanking. Teddy was four or five at the time, and Ted had never spanked him before. As Teddy was sobbing in his room, I looked in on Ted, who was sitting on the side of his bed with his head in his hands. When I saw that he too had tears in his eyes, I couldn't believe it. He said he would never hit him again because he felt he was too big and heavy handed, and he might hurt him. I knew he had not lost his temper or hit him anywhere but on his "seat of understanding," and only two or three licks. So I couldn't understand his attitude. We agreed that physical discipline would be my job, and he would back me up verbally.

One day when I was spanking him, Teddy cried out, "You're going to kill me, Mom! Mom! You're going to kill me!" Of course that wasn't true. I was spanking him in the padded place that God provided, and I knew that I was not going to kill him because I was in total control of myself. I was amused at his effort to keep me from delivering one more blow. I laughed and I said "No, no, no son, I am not going to kill you. Don't even worry about it." Later on, when I was reading my Bible, I came across a verse that was appropriate to read to this child. The verse is in Proverbs 23: 13–14. It says, "Withhold not correction from the child: for *if* thou beatest him with the rod, he shall not die.Thou shalt beat him with the rod, and shalt deliver his soul from hell." (KJV).

Teddy was old enough to read and understand. I took him to the Bible, and I showed him each of these verses. After I had read them to him, with him reading along with me, he looked at me and said, "I guess that means I'd better straighten up or you are going to keep on beating me." I said, "You got that right." You know, I think I had delivered my last spanking. He rose to the occasion and realized that I meant business, so he obeyed. I do want to say that, every time I gave him a spanking, while his tears were fresh, I would hold him in my arms, kiss him, and tell him how much I loved him. I would tell him that the only reason I spanked him was because of his disobedience, not because I didn't love him. He seemed to understand that, and it wasn't long before he felt that it was better—much better—to be an obedient son. Thank you, Lord, for the provision that you have made in your Word for raising children; that they will rise up and call their mother, their father, the disciplinarians, *blessed.*

The church across the street began to beckon even more. Teddy's kindergarten teacher was also a Sunday school teacher at the church. She had invited him to come to Sunday school many times, and he began to nag me to go. At first, I would take him to Sunday school, leave him, and go back to pick him up later. Then I was approached by the members to attend service, and occasionally I would.

Ted Sr. had been taking Jennifer with him to his church, and she had been baptized there, but I had never attended with them. So there I was going to the Methodist Church across the street. I was only going occasionally, but when I went, it was almost impossible to get my rambunctious little boy to sit still during the services. I was experiencing my own problem just being in God's house, and I did not need the aggravation of this child crawling on the floor to pick up whatever he could drop and making a lot of noise. I felt embarrassed when I could not control him. I told him that, if he didn't behave in church, I would certainly spank him when we got home. He promptly forgot what I had said the next Sunday that we attended.

At the conclusion of the service, I would take him by his hand so firmly that he would "get the message" as we walked up the street toward the house. He would look up at me with those big brown eyes full of apprehension and with panic in his voice, would ask, "Am I going to get it?" As soon as we walked across the threshold, I would put his head in the chair and spank his bottom because I had promised him that he would "get it" if he didn't behave in church. I never punished him for making a childish mistake or having an accident and breaking something. If he was told to do or not to do something and he deliberately disobeyed, he could expect and would surely receive just punishment. We talked about his behavior, and he soon began to try much harder to do what he knew to be the right thing. I was truly amazed at how quickly the message was getting through to him and how eager he was to please his parents and his teachers.

Teddy liked to play games. We played Candy Land and old maid and soon graduated to Chinese checkers, regular checkers, Monopoly, and then Scrabble, which rapidly became his favorite. He challenged everyone to a game of some sort. We all were intrigued by his competitive spirit. He loved to win whenever he played. More than likely, he won when he played with his friends; but when the adults accepted his challenge and then speedily won the game, he would come to me with tears in his eyes because his sister or father had beat him so badly. He hated to let them see him cry, but he would bring his disappointment to his mom. At first, I didn't address the issues. I just consoled my son and tried to change the subject. But eventually, as he played games more often and with others, I noticed he always managed to cry when he was not a winner. The question plagued me. How was I going to teach him to be a good loser as well as a humble and considerate winner? I didn't want to squelch his motivation to do his best, but I certainly needed to emphasize to him that he would not win all the time, and that others want to win also. He had to learn to accept that fact.

It was my mother who helped him gain a healthy perspective about winning and losing. He would meet her at the door when she came to visit, issuing a challenge to her for a game of Scrabble, which was her favorite game also. She was an expert player and proud of her ability to win even when matched with college graduates. So, a second or third grader had virtually no chance of winning. After dinner, the game would be set up, and we'd watch as she wiped him out. He'd go off to bed with those tears glistening in his eyes, trying unsuccessfully to hide his disappointment.

The next day, he would come to me and ask why his grandmother would never let him win. Suddenly I knew what she would say. I remembered the many lessons I had learned from her as I grew up. So I suggested that, the next time he saw her, he should have a little talk with her and ask point blank why she didn't let him win. And so, during her next visit, Teddy took his grandmother aside to talk in private. It seemed he had planned what he would say and felt he had a case against her because she should let him win at least once in a while. She asked him why he thought she should let him win. He said, "I'm your grandson, and I'm just a kid, and it wouldn't hurt you to let me win once in a while." They were sitting on the sofa, and she put her arm around him and said, "That's exactly why I don't let you win—because you are my grandson. I love you, and I want you to learn how to win and how to lose." She said, "I win because I have studied and practiced this game. I win because I'm much older than you. I win because I have more education than you do. So, therefore, I deserve to win. But there was a time when I lost. I lost because I hadn't practiced. I didn't know the game as well as I do now. I lost because I played with people who knew the game better than I did. So, I lost to them until I learned how to win. I don't win every time I play, but I win most of the time. Now, while I was a loser, I determined that I would learn how to play the game and how to win when I played; so I play to win, and that's what you can do. Study, and every time you lose, learn something from your opponent and continue to try. Oh, it may be a long time before you can beat me, but sometimes you will be able to win against others. However, don't expect to win all the time, but learn from a winner, and pretty soon you will win more often. If I allowed you to win when you had not earned it, that would be deceitful on my part, and I can't do that. If you beat me fair and square, I'll be the first one to congratulate you, but I'll never allow you to win without earning it. I challenge you to learn spelling, to learn as many words as you can, to watch how the game is played, learn the strategy, and one day you're going to beat me because you have a good mind, and you have a good chance of being a better player than I'll ever be. Every time we play and I win, I want you to be able to tell me what you learned from me that day. Every time you play and lose, learn something that will help you win the next time."

Mother and I shared a good laugh about that conversation. I noticed, however, that he gave what she had said a very serious thought because his attitudes about winning and losing began to change. He began to accept his losses and made a conscientious effort to learn from his mistakes. It was surprising and gratifying to notice how he incorporated this new character trait as he faced other challenges as well.

The local bowling lanes called me one day to recruit new bowlers for a ladies' league. It was to include free lessons for six weeks, complete with coffee and donuts. Since it would be an opportunity for me to get out of the house and learn something new, I jumped at the chance. My husband bowled regularly with his teams from work, but I had not enjoyed any sport recently and got very excited about receiving some expert instruction. My hope was that, when I progressed to a point where Ted would not be ashamed of me, he might join a league with me, and we could finally do something fun together. I completed the course of instruction and joined the league. It was the beginning of a life-long interest that has provided our house with many days of pleasure. As soon as I learned, I found out that there was a junior bowling league that Teddy Jr. could join. Instructors would teach the youngsters how to bowl the correct way, and I enrolled him immediately.

Since I had to drive him to the lanes every Saturday and I had my league time next during the week, I found that at least two days a week were "bowling days" and that now we had scores to compare and strategies to discuss. As Teddy talked about the fun he had bowling, I soon found myself taking a car full of boys every Saturday morning to the bowling lanes. He would have invited the whole neighborhood to go with him if I had driven a van. I had said that two or three boys were enough. He made some good friends during those years, earned quite a few trophies, developed a love for competitive sports, and learned that he was a "natural" athlete in some sports, like his father.

But now that he was bowling and getting out more, he came to us with a very serious problem. He had decided that we did not give him enough allowance. We had been giving him "spending money" to teach the value of [loose] change since he was quite young but had progressed to an allowance as he grew older. He was required to do chores around the house to earn the allowance, but now it was not enough. We agreed that his allowance might need to be increased and asked him to write out his budget. After we explained what a budget was, he went to his room to figure it out. But, at age five, he had not considered anything but Sunday school contribution and snacks. So, we asked the question, "How about your bowling fees? How about saving for Christmas and birthday presents?" He ran back upstairs to revise the budget. This time it was more realistic, and we increased his allowance to cover almost all his "expenses." When he noticed the deficit even after the increase he said, "Even though I'll be getting more money each week, I still won't have enough because now I have to pay for my bowling and save some." He looked at us and asked, "What can I do?" I used this opportunity to suggest, "Have you thought about getting a job?" He just stared at me, but I plunged on with, "You could earn money here in the neighborhood by doing small jobs for people. You could rake leaves, sweep sidewalks, and when it gets colder and snows, you could shovel the snow." I even suggested that he ask the ladies who did not have husbands or children of their own if he could do some chores around the home.

He received these ideas with enthusiasm and went to the garage to get the broom and a rake. He ran down to the corner and rang the doorbell of a friendly widowed lady who had been talking to him whenever he passed her house. She was happy to give him a job cleaning the leaves from around the bushes in her backyard and putting out the trash. He came home that very day with $20, his first earnings from yard work, and from that day on, we gave him a minimum allowance and he earned the rest. After his father taught him how to trim the hedges and cut the grass, he added that ability to his endeavors.

Teddy was growing very fast. His feet were getting larger, his legs were getting longer, and his arms and hands seemed to change overnight. He was clumsy because of this, but was always in a hurry to get something done. He seemed to fall on the stairs so often that we had a ritual we followed whenever I heard the crash. I would ask, "Did you fall downstairs?" He would reply, "No, up." If I said, "Did you fall up the stairs?" Then he would say, "No, down!" Thank God he never broke any bones.

We had a step-on garbage can in the kitchen with an inner pail that had to be emptied and washed with disinfectant every day. The garbage and trash can were his assigned task even though it wasn't his favorite job. Periodically when I saw him rush to step on the pedal of the garbage can, reach in and grab that inner pail by the handle, and rush out the kitchen door and down the back steps, I'd call out, "Ted, take it easy! You'll have an accident with that pail one of these days." He'd give me the "Oh, Mother!" look and slam out the back door with the garbage can swinging in his hand. One day when his buddies were waiting for him in the back alley to join them with his basketball, he raced into the kitchen, grabbed a full pail of garbage, stepped on an untied shoestring, and fell down the back steps. How that garbage landed upside down on him, I'll never know. Well, there he was sprawled on the steps covered with fresh garbage. Before I could even ask if he was alright, he yelled "Why didn't you tell me to take it easy?" After a long pause during which the futility of that question seeped into his mind, a smile and then a giggle erupted. And then, finally, we both joined in at least two minutes of raucous laughter, after which he had to go clean up while the guys waited—for a long time. Another lesson learned.

23

God Begins to Shape Teddy's Life

In 1968, when Teddy Jr. was nine years old, he accepted Christ as his personal Savior. He had been attending church and Sunday school regularly for several years, and one day the message from the pulpit caused the realization that he was lost and in need of salvation. He went forward to the altar and gave his life to the Lord Jesus Christ. He was baptized on December 15, 1968, in the Methodist tradition of sprinkling. It was a decision that he made completely on his own, and we were pleasantly surprised when he joined the Parkside United Methodist Church.

The years that Teddy attended the Parkside Elementary School were exciting for him. He was in fifth and sixth grade, tall for his age, very active, getting good marks in school, and getting along better with everyone. His illnesses seemed to be almost behind him. Life was fun. While he was attending Parkside Elementary, Teddy was found to be extremely near-sighted and began to wear thick glasses. He also began to get serious about his Lego building blocks and entered the Lego Model contest. He had high hopes of winning first place, which was a trip to Denmark. Everyone began to give him Lego blocks for his birthday and Christmas, and soon he could build anything he wanted with the snap-together blue, red, yellow, and white blocks.

For one year only, Teddy attended Hatch Junior High School. The year was 1971, and the city was changing. Previously our daughter had attended that school, and we could hardly believe the changes that had come about in eleven years. Teddy had gone there well prepared to study. In fact, he loved his science class and math classes. Then he found that many of the students didn't care about studying. They got away with everything they could. Often the teacher was not there, and the substitute did not discipline the class.

The need of a Christian High School for Teddy became an urgent concern for us. God was well aware of the need and had already established a Christian school in Haddon Heights, New Jersey. It was an outgrowth of the Haddon Heights Baptist Church, and it opened its doors for students in 1973. Teddy began classes in September 1974, thereby becoming the very first black boy to attend. His friendly manner, devotion to his studies, and athletic ability created an atmosphere of congeniality among the students and faculty, but it was often difficult to be cast in the role of a (racial) "pioneer." Many long talks at the kitchen table were necessary to stabilize his values. He was an "inner city" kid attending an all-white suburban school. Even though it was a Christian school, the "learning about" and "acceptance of" each other had to flow both ways. High school is normally a time for getting to know the opposite sex by socializing and even dating your classmates. Teddy's relationship with his female classmates, however, was expected to be entirely different. He was out there in no man's land, trusting, loving, and vulnerable. Those who loved him most had to take him to the door marked *prejudice*, open it inch by inch, and escort him into the real world. It was done delicately and did not damage or even mar his Christian love. As the facts of life penetrated, he revealed his unanimous desire when he came to us and said, "Mom and Dad, I just want to have friends." And he set about turning that desire into a beautiful reality. He was a member of the basketball team and was elected cocaptain. He graduated with a 3.6 grade point average, third highest in his class, surpassed by two girls with 4.0 GPAs. While he was in high school, he worked during the summer at various jobs. However, the groundwork for his work ethic had been laid by his desire to earn extra money several years before.

While he was in high school, it was my daily challenge to keep him fed. The boy could eat more food more quickly than anybody I had ever seen in my life. His father, who was also a six foot five and a-half inches tall, could also put away quite a bit of food. So I was constantly required to cook large pots of food. This teenager could gulp it down so quickly, I was amazed. I would just sit back and watch sometimes as he would get two plates of spaghetti and meatballs, baked beans, and hot dogs or practically anything I would cook up. He would just devour it. In self-defense, I taught him how to cook, and I said, "You can make your own pancakes, and you can fry your own bacon and sausage when you're in a hurry to get out to school." I learned some secrets to keep him from wrecking the entire kitchen. I would boil the bacon and have it available. All he had to do was put it in the pan for a few minutes. This was before microwaving. I would parboil the sausage as well. He only had to put it in the pan and brown it quickly. He'd put the eggs on top and then make three pieces of toast. He then would drink a half a pint or a pint of milk, eat some fruit, drink some juice, and he was out of there in fifteen minutes. I really think that I got in his way when he was trying to get finished in the kitchen so he could leave early. I was glad that he could cook.

One day after eating a couple plates of dinner—whatever it was—he was cleaning up the dishes in the kitchen while I sat in the living room relaxing for a moment. He appeared in the doorway and said, "Mother, would you believe I am still hungry?" "You must be kidding," I said. "You just finished eating, and you haven't even washed the dishes. You are still hungry? You ate two plates of food and then some." He said, "Mom, "I am not kidding, I'm still hungry." I remembered the popcorn popper that I had recently bought. I said, "How about making some popcorn?" That seemed like a good idea to him, and he dashed off into the kitchen. I could hear him taking the popcorn popper out of the box and plugging it in. I heard him pouring the popcorn into the popper. In a few minutes, it was popping. He came back and stood in the doorway and asked the question that I will never forget. "Mom, what can I eat while the popcorn is popping?"

My mother and her sister, my three sisters, and their husbands would sometimes plan big family dinners. We would try to determine how much food to prepare. We had the family broken up into four categories. There were the Hs, the Ps, the Gs, and the BPs. They were the hogs, the pigs, the gluttons, and the bottomless pits. Those teenage boys were in the category of BPs. They couldn't be filled up. They would just eat until the food ran out. We all had a good time. I had to remind Teddy when he went out to eat at someone's house not to eat so much. He needed to save some for others. He didn't realize how much food I prepared for him during his growing years, and he expected other people to have as much prepared when he was there. Sometimes he needed to be reminded.

One evening when we all were out for dinner, I was gently reminded why we had sent Teddy Jr. to Christian school. We were seated at a table directly opposite another man and his wife. Everyone began talking about Christian schools and how some children flourish well when in a Christian school. I mentioned the fact that my son was in Christian school. Most of the people at the table could hear us and were in agreement with our decision. One man waited until all the others had had their say, and then he came out with the fact that he disagreed thoroughly with the idea of Christian schools. He felt that they did not prepare students for the outside world and that, when they graduated from the sheltered environment of a Christian school, kids would go out ill prepared to deal with the "real world." This was the first time that I had ever been exposed to a difference of opinion like that. Most people agreed that, if you could afford it, Christian schools were a good choice because they provided a better environment for young people. This man, in all sincerity, expressed his opinion and was waiting for my response. I believe that I appealed to God. I can't remember exactly how long it took me to formulate an answer, but I felt that he was wrong. I was searching my heart for a good example or something that would convince him of the way I felt. Something said to me to ask him. "Do you have a garden, or do you plant flowers around your house?" He said, "Yes." "When you buy bedding plants, where have they been raised before you bring them to place in your garden?" He replied, "A hot house I guess." So, I asked, "Does the hot house–controlled environment prepare them to thrive in the ground or does it hinder them from being successfully transplanted?" He looked at me and said, "How can you apply that to children? I know where you are going with this." I said, "Well, think about it. If they are in a protected controlled environment until they are ready to be transplanted into the world, they have a foundation. They have been protected so that they can cope with the quote *real world* as you see it. So there are two ways of looking at it. Some people thrive better when they have been protected when they are young from too much outside influence of the world. Maybe there are exceptions, but I prefer to protect my child until he is ready. Knowing him and his personality, I think he needs that kind of protection." The other people at the table were either nodding or still thinking, but the man who disagreed with me was looking at me with a puzzled expression and he said, "Where did you get that illustration?" I said, "He knows all things." It was an interesting evening.

24

Spiritual Development

Teddy gave me a *Strong's Exhaustive Concordance* and wrote the following on the inside cover:

> Mom, happy birthday. May God continue your endeavors to understand the Book of Books. I hope that this book will be invaluable in this quest. Thanks for being my mother for nineteen years. The value of your friendship and your being will always be cherished above all material things and intangibles. Thanks also for your priceless example of a Christian mother and her role in the home. God bless you continually for many more birthdays. Sincerely with love, Theodore DeShields Jr., August 26, 1978.
>
> PS. Study well and share it with others. The strength of what we do today may be felt in future days, so continue to be strong, for we will always be revealed and revered.

Teddy was well aware of the fact that his dad and I were going our separate ways in that we were very busy people. His father and I spent very little time together. He thought his dad and I were not spending enough time having fun. He bought a scrapbook and presented it to us for our twenty-second anniversary with this accompanying note:

> To my parents on their twenty-second anniversary:

> Well, another year has passed, never to be relived. I'm sure that you have fond memories of the events in your lives together. As your son, I want you to preserve those moments. This gift is a specific, special way to preserve the times of your lives. I pray that you will place several items of interest to you both in this book. I would love to see you two parents working on this. I pray that you see the ultimate benefit, the profitable experiences, the excitement and fun as you relive these cherished memories of yesterday. Life is full of memories, easy come easy go, but they never can be stolen from you. Precious memories, deserved and thoughtful, looked at to see the value in them. A memory cannot be bought, purchased, or spent, but it can be bad or good. As you see the white pages of this book, see them as a birth of a life and the growth and maturing years of that life. I prayerfully considered this gift before I bought it. Please, this is for you two, both of you, Dad and Mom. United you can stand, divided you might fall. A house cannot stand if the two parties, husband and wife, are at arms' length. Love is built on precious time together. Realize the emphasis.

Then he wrote a prayer:

> God, I pray for my parents. Spare them for many years of happiness together. Please help my parents, both of them, to see the importance of togetherness. Love can be shown in so many other ways. Please help them see that and then act upon it. God, I thank you for my parents, the time, the patience, the understanding when I goof up or fall flat on my face, the love they give me. Please bless them. Give them continual wisdom and never leave them or forsake them, In Jesus' precious name. Amen.
>
> Sincerely with your best interest and affectionately caring and lovingly,

Your son, Theodore Jr.

Then he added a little insert on the side that said:

> Time, a precious thing, a tool, a device we live by; yet when it is all gone, what's left? Memories of the time, the times past, precious memories stored here.

He told us that he wanted us to go places, do things together, and record our experiences in this little red book. We were touched by what he said. We agreed to what he said, but the status quo remained unchanged. It was amazing to me that this young man had perceived a need that I had never expressed to him. How much I had wanted to be closer to his father but had realized years before that it probably would never be fulfilled and had learned to live in the perimeters of our marriage. As he grew older, he sensed it and did all he could to bring into my life what he knew I really wanted. Unfortunately, too many people, after twenty years of marriage or more, are content with the status quo.

While Teddy was attending Baptist High School and enjoying playing basketball with the team, many times, the team would have an away game. They would arrive back at the school in the late evening. Since we had only one car and his father worked at night, he would have no means of transportation after he got back to the school. Most of the young people lived in the Haddon Heights area and could walk home. For others, their parents would be waiting there in cars to take them home. Teddy was at a disadvantage. Usually, he would have to ask someone to give a ride home. Of course, coaches, parents, and sometimes the pastor of the church gave him rides to Camden. He felt bad asking for rides all the time. Even though I knew that he was embarrassed sometimes about it, it never had been a point of great concern because he would arrive home all excited about the game. He wouldn't say too much about who had brought him home except that he was grateful that whoever it was had been nice enough to do it. I just accepted this as something that I could not do anything about, so I joined him in gratitude. But eventually this became a problem for him, and one day at the dinner table, he began to talk about how nice it would be to live in Haddon Heights. This way, he would not have to ask anybody for a ride home. He could use his bicycle or walk home with other friends. It seemed to us as though he had given it quite a bit of thought. We did not comment. We were eating dinner, and neither my husband nor I said too much about it until we realized that he was quite serious. He was sort of asking us if we could possibly move out of the city into Haddon Heights. My husband looked at him and said, "Teddy, we cannot afford to move right now. We're going to stay here for a while yet." Teddy looked at me and said, "But, Mom, if you got a job, we would have enough money to move. Lots of mother's work, and if you had a job, we could move." My husband calmly put his fork down, looked at his son, and said, "I'm going to tell you something, boy: there is no one who puts my wife out to work but me." Teddy realized what he was saying, and he never mentioned it again. We laughed about it later, but he had been quite serious in suggesting that his mother should get a job.

Many years later, I can recall hearing Teddy say that it was such a blessing to come home and find his mother at home, preparing meals, having snacks with him, talking over the day's activities, and being able to attend his games and the activities that he was engaged in, taking trips, and doing all the things that he would want his mother to be able to do with him. He considered it a blessing that his mother had not gone out to work while he was growing up. We looked back on the time that he had suggested that I get a job, and we laughed about it.

Many mothers work. Some of them have to, and others do so because they want to. I was content staying at home. I wanted to be the mother that he and Jennifer needed. Therefore, I never really felt pressured to get a job. I praise God that He provided for our physical and financial needs. It was not necessary for me to work, and my husband was willing to pay the bills and keep me at home to be with the family. I am very grateful for that. I know that it could have been otherwise, but when I look back in retrospect, I am so thankful that I was able to spend that time with my family.

In those days, there were so many other problems because Teddy was attending school out of his neighborhood. Sometimes boys in the neighborhood would want to pick fights because they felt that Teddy thought he was better than they were because he didn't go to the local school. He would come into the house wondering why people acted the way they did. Jealousy wasn't something that he had been acquainted with, and he didn't realize or understand what was going on in their minds. He had no animosity against anyone. He wanted to play with or talk with anybody he met. We spent many hours over a year or so just talking about jealousy and prejudices and the necessity of understanding other people and how they feel, and how we can relate to them even if they don't always agree with us or see our point of view. It was a time of spiritual development also. Since Teddy was a Christian, we could go to the Bible and study the Psalms and the Proverbs and the stories of the great characters in the scripture. Teddy could relate to them, and it is by far the best way for young people to learn to develop Christian values. He also learned to expect and accept the fact that there are Christians who are jealous and those who are prejudiced.

Baptist High School at 3rd and Station Avenues in Haddon Heights, New Jersey, is a ministry of Haddon Heights Baptist Church. It is located in a white suburban community. Teddy was obliged to walk several blocks to a main street and take a bus to get to school every morning. He liked the school immediately, but he found that he was the only black boy attending. We asked him how he felt about that. He informed us that it didn't matter to him at all. People were people, and he was going to have a good high school experience. He liked the school, and he was going to study and love the opportunity he had to play basketball. When Teddy brought home his first report card from Baptist High School, I read with interest the open letter to the parents on the front of the card:

> The Bible teaches [that] the fear of the Lord is the beginning of wisdom. As a Christian School, we begin here and then a much greater understanding in academic areas is possible. Our Christian schoolteachers wish to serve you well. You as parents are urged to consult with them at any time. Close cooperation of home and school are needed if both are to succeed in the education of our youth. We appreciate your confidence in placing your child in our school and will welcome your comments as you sign and return this report. There was a Scripture at the end:

> Isaiah 54: 13 KJV: "And all thy children shall be taught of the Lord."

In his freshman year, the Bible was taught as a major subject. He carried the Bible, mathematics, history, science, foreign language, physical education, and health classes. The Bible course dealt with doctrine and religious cults. I can recall typing a paper for him on cults. I learned a great deal that I had never known before about various religious cults in the United States and all over the world. Theodore was an above-average student and always put forth a great deal of effort. He was commended by his teachers for that. The California Achievement Test was administered in the spring of 1977. His cumulative grade point average was a 3.45. His rank in the class was third out of twenty-eight students.

Teddy enjoyed playing on the basketball team and had reasonable success as a center. We made it a point to attend as many games as we could. In the 1975–76 season, Teddy scored the most points for varsity basketball: thirty-five points. He had a 17.6 point game average. He had the most rebounds that year as well with 382. He had the most in one game with twenty-six. He had the best rebound average for the season with 14.8. He really did enjoy playing basketball. That wasn't his only sport, however. That year he enjoyed receiving a special merit award from the American bowling conference. He bowled in a junior scratch league, and country musician and guitarist Velma Smith was his league coach.

On our twentieth wedding anniversary, Teddy gave us a handwritten note that read:

> Happy twentieth anniversary to the greatest, fantastic, stupendous beyond belief, incredibly neat, groovy, etc. parents. From your silly son sometimes.
>
> Love always, Theodore the Griz
>
> June 30, 1976, in the year of our Lord
>
> May God give you twenty more years.

Now this business about "the Griz" came about because one day Teddy said, "I don't want to be called a teddy bear anymore." I said, "What would you like for me to call you?" He said, "Well, I am a pretty bad bear these days; how about Grizzly?" So, every now and then from that time on, when he felt that it was merited, he would call himself the Griz. It would give us a great laugh, especially as he was a gentle giant with nothing grizzly about him. In April 1977, the Baptist High School presented a drama and music presentation, *The Apostle*. He volunteered to take care of the lighting for the choir. Every time something was going on, he would try to get involved with it in one way or another. Also, in April 1977, we received the following letter:

> It is always a joy to write to parents when there is good news to share. This is one of those joyful occasions. Yesterday, prior to our chapel program, the new members of the Baptist High School Honors Society were announced and recognized. I am pleased to inform you that Ted was one of those who received this honor. Honor Society members must have maintained a high school average of 3.3:(B+) and be nominated on the basis of character, leadership ability, and Christian service by the faculty. Ten students were announced yesterday. There are now twelve members in the honor society. As you can see by the limited number, it is quite an honor to be nominated for membership in the honor society. Ted is to be congratulated for this accomplishment. We are planning an induction service followed by a reception. We hope that you will reserve the evening of April 25 at 7:30 p.m. for this occasion.

What a blessing! We really enjoyed that evening.

During his four years at Baptist High School, Teddy received two attendance awards for perfect attendance and four athletic awards (one for soccer and three for basketball). He also received three scholarship awards and an honor's award for first place in the science fair.

While Teddy was attending Baptist High School and going to Days of Decision Bible Conference at Swan Lake, New York, on summer vacation, he was always trying to work and earn money and to learn as much as he could. The year that he worked at Days of Decision as a freshman, he worked on the grounds, and I recall telling him that he should try to learn something from every opportunity that was afforded to him. As learned to cut the grass with the power mowers, he would also stand around and watch when someone was repairing a mower. He was very interested in everything that went on around him, whereas the other boys sometimes would run off to play or to jump in the pool or whatever when they had a break. Instead, Teddy would often learn how to do something. So, he came home with the knowledge of how to repair lawn mowers. The next year, when he was a junior, he worked in the snack shops where he learned how to make banana splits, milkshakes, and sandwiches on the grill and other sorts of short order cooking. He enjoyed it and enjoyed being with the people.

I sometimes went there on weekends during the summer. He was very proud of his banana splits, milkshakes, and ice cream sundaes. Then, his very last year, he was the head bus boy in the dining hall. That was during his senior year at Baptist High. He took charge of the bus boys, the younger ones coming up later. He seemed to know everything about running the dining room. I thought about how good this was for him. Not only was he learning spiritual things from the people who were there to speak or to teach, but he was also learning some practical things that would help him later in life when he joined the workforce. When he was home, he would find a job. He worked at Jefferson Ward where he learned how to operate the computer cash register, McDonald's, Roy Rogers, and the Salad Boy in Pennsauken. He was always able to find a job. Then, when he was in college, he was able to use the skills that he had learned in landscaping to get a good job with PATCO, which is the public transport speed line in that area, where he worked as a caretaker who helped maintain the grounds along the speed line. PATCO hired only college students. He had developed a good work ethic while he was in high school, working after school and during the summer.

Teddy made many friends at Baptist High School. He enjoyed his four years there and had a good relationship with his fellow students and the faculty. He played basketball and was elected cocaptain of the team. He kept in touch with his high school friends. With Teddy, once a friend, always a friend.

He would come home from school or from the service and call or write to friends. During these high school years, he matured spiritually and grew physically. By the time he graduated from Baptist High School in June 1977, he was six foot five and a half inches tall, wore a size 14 D shoe, and had a smile that would light up a room.

25

A Divine Appointment

While Teddy was at Martin Luther King Christian Day School, he was challenged to study the Bible. The Bible was taught as a major subject. He had to prepare papers as well as lectures. He also had to study the books of the Bible in depth. He often asked me to type up his notes. As I did this, I learned a great deal. In fact, I was intrigued at the depth of the Bible study he was getting. I can truthfully say that he was a great influence on me in my effort to live according to the precepts of the Bible. I started to become active in the Women's Society of Christian Service. I was teaching a Bible study and attending a Bible study at a local church. I was also teaching Sunday school.

For some reason, I remember a specific prayer I prayed at a prayer service for the Women's Society. I went to the altar, and I prayed that God would make me the woman that He wanted me to be, the wife that He wanted me to be, the mother that He wanted me to be, the sister that He wanted me to be, and the friend that He wanted me to be. I was learning that what I wanted for my life might not be the same as what He wanted. I was willing to relinquish my desires for my life in favor of His. Perhaps that was the real turning point in my relationship with my Savior. The closer I was drawn to my Savior, the more precious was His gift to me of my children, both Jennifer and Theodore Jr.

After we sent Teddy to camp for a month for several summers, we learned about Days of Decision Bible Conference at Swan Lake, New York. We had been looking for a vacation spot and heard about DOD (as it was called) on the Family Radio station. We made our reservation for one week, and the entire family enjoyed our stay in the Catskill Mountains. Teddy was particularly impressed with the staff of young people—all high school and college age. He asked numerous questions and made friends with both boys and girls from all parts of the country who were working there for the summer. All the way home after our first visit, he talked of getting a job there as soon as he was old enough. A young man from Florida Bible College witnessed to Teddy and gave him a new Bible with the stipulation that he read the book of John and encircle or underline the word *believe.* He completed the book during the ride home and that Bible became one of his first to be worn out by constant use. He was determined to work at Days of Decision Bible Conference and set about making this goal a reality. His application was submitted, and he was accepted on staff in 1975 to work with the ground maintenance crew. In 1976, he worked in many snack shops. That's when he learned to make banana splits and ice cream sundaes for which he became famous. The last summer there, he worked as head bus boy in the huge dining hall. That year a van load of friends from our church went to the conference for the Saturday night smorgasbord and staff concert. It was a surprise for Teddy, and he was so happy to see everyone. After their work was completed, the staff was allowed to enjoy the basketball and tennis courts, use the swimming pool, play ball, and so forth. They were also encouraged to mingle with the young guests, witness for the Lord (all staff were believers), and talk with the speakers and missionaries. The speakers were pastors, missionaries, professors, and deans of Bible colleges and were usually there for a week at a time.

Teddy considered it a gold mine for gathering friends. He asked the speaker to sign his Bible flyleaf. One of his first purchases was a new *Scofield Reference Bible.* The staff was given a discount at the bookstore on the grounds, so he bought two Bibles that year, one for himself and one for my birthday in August. I have his worn one before me and I'm looking at names such as:

William A. Mierop—John 3:30

Lew Steward—Philippians 2:16

Bob Palmer—Philippians 3:10

Lehman Strauss—1 Corinthians 10:31

Pastor Andy Telford—John 5:24

David D. Allen—Psalms 119:11

Dick Grueger—Romans 10:9–10

John Cawood—2 Corinthians 5:21

Mal Johnson—Psalms 91:1

And this is only a partial list of the great men of God who influenced his Christian development during his summer at Days of Decision. Teddy rarely missed the Bible lessons. He marked the Bible and always kept a notebook to record the exciting truths he was learning about the Lord. During this period, he developed the habit of furnishing a scripture reference at the close of all correspondence. He did not just write one favorite verse, but he chose the scripture carefully, as an additional message to his letter.

Teddy made friends with another staff member, Gail Gromaki, and when her father, Dr. Robert Gromaki, arrived as one of the speakers, Teddy was introduced to the dean of New Testament studies of Cedarville College, a Baptist liberal arts college just south of Springfield, Ohio. Dr. Gromaki watched Teddy play basketball and approached him one day to ask him where he planned to attend college. Teddy, not having made a decision yet, was interested in his favorable comments regarding Cedarville College. It was obvious to Teddy that Dr. G. really wanted him to come to his school and play on the basketball team. I suppose it was the nearest thing to being recruited he had ever felt. Dr. G. gave Teddy the course catalog and asked him to seriously consider applying. He did read the catalog and was impressed with what was offered, but soon forgot all about it when he returned home in September to begin his junior year at Baptist High School. Nevertheless, it was obviously God's intention that he would attend Cedarville College, and the encounter with Dr. Gromaki during the summer was only the beginning of a chain of interesting events.

Since Haddon Heights Baptist Church was encouraging their young members to attend Christian college, they provided the young people of high school age the opportunity to visit several different Christian liberal arts colleges for weekend tours. The youth would sign up until the van was filled, and away they would go for a campus visit. If there were not enough interested in going from the church, the offer would be extended. That's what happened when a trip was planned to Cedarville College in Cedarville Ohio. Teddy was happy to sign up for a weekend trip to visit the College Dr. Gromaki wanted him to attend.

He was very excited about the prospect but did not tell any of his fellow students of his contacts at the college. Upon their arrival, they were looking around before dinner in the student dining hall. Teddy slipped off to find Dr. Gromaki's classroom. He stood outside the glass door until he caught his eye and enjoyed the surprise on the professor's face as he hurried out to the hall to greet him warmly. He insisted on taking Teddy to his home for dinner so he could see Gail again. When the other students from Baptist High learned that Teddy would be eating at the professor's home while they ate in the school dining hall, they were amazed. One wondered aloud, "How did he pull that off? He knows more people!" Teddy was impressed with the college and later decided he would apply to only that one college—Cedarville. He was convinced he would be accepted, and he eventually was.

However, the year at Baptist High School was exciting for the young boy who was becoming an over-six-foot-tall basketball player. He was respected and loved, and he retained numerous class friendships from his high school days. During his junior year, he came home from Sunday school one day and announced that he would not be going back to his Sunday school class at our church. In answer to my question why, he stated, "Because I know more about the Bible than my teacher, so it's a waste of time for me." At first, I didn't know how to respond to that statement, since he probably did have more in depth Bible training than his teacher. So, I withheld my comments and awaited instruction from our Lord. Later, when I brought up the subject for discussion, an idea was formulating in my mind which appeared to be an excellent solution to this problem. I stated bluntly, "If you know more than your teacher, then you should be teaching those who know less than you." I waited for the idea to take root and noted the twinkling of the smile of acceptance as he answered, "You're right, Mom. I could teach some eight-, nine-, and ten-year-old boys." We agreed that I would approach the superintendent of the Sunday school to see what could be arranged.

Shortly thereafter, Teddy was introduced to a small class of energetic youngsters who dared him to attempt to teach them. Teddy tried to use the regular Sunday school material, but soon realized he needed unusually exciting material and an interesting approach to capture and sustain their attention. The complete set of the *Chronicles of Narnia* by C. S. Lewis had been given to him for Christmas several years before, and he had read all seven books more than once. He found them entertaining and somehow adapted the stories and characters into a gospel message that provided the excitement to hold the interest of his students. The boys enjoyed the class almost as much as he enjoyed teaching it. I enjoyed observing our Lord doing a mighty work in young men's lives. Teddy had to give up the class when he went away to school and was probably unaware of the "good work" he had been planted that would "bring forth fruit, some one hundred-fold, some sixty, and some thirty" (Matthew 13:23 KJV).

Christmas shopping was a real challenge for Teddy. His funds were very limited but that didn't prevent him from compiling a long list. One year I looked at it and shook my head in amazement "How do you expect to buy gifts for so many?" I asked. "I don't know, but I'll think of something," he said. Then with much thought and great care he would select an inexpensive but useful item, wrap it carefully and present it along with his famous smile to a surprised recipient. I remember a small Christmas flower arrangement he gave my sister's family, and I am delighted to see it still in use Christmas after Christmas. She even remembers that he gave it to them. His cousins hang special Christmas balls on their tree each year that remind them of Teddy. He also gave many books that he chose to meet specific needs in friends' lives. When his money was exhausted, he learned to make gifts. Most of the inexpensive gifts so lovingly given by Teddy are still in use by their recipients. They often say, "Teddy gave me this, and I will keep it in memory of him." I found out that he would watch his father and I for months to ascertain what to give for our birthdays. He noticed I needed a sport watch, and ten years later I'm still wearing the little timepiece he gave me. He gave me a *Strong's Exhaustive Concordance* and wrote a special message on the inside cover. He thought that his dad and I were not spending enough time together having fun, so he bought a scrapbook and presented it for our anniversary.

After attending a funeral one day, I remarked that I would rather have flowers given to me while I am living than to pile them all over my casket after my death. While in his teens, he would occasionally bring me a silk rose as a complete surprise. Upon reaching manhood, he faithfully remembered special days and would send flowers and plants from wherever he happened to be. Would you marvel at the character of this young man? I did and wondered why we were blessed with his presence. I was confronted with the mystery of a young man in this day and age who was seemingly too good to be true.

As an elementary school student, Teddy was fitted for glasses. It usually took at least two weeks to get new lenses every time we had them changed. The problems this presented were magnified by the fact that he could not see without them and if they were knocked off while he was participating in sports, and he would be sure to step on them trying to find them. He wore size thirteen shoes at the time, so stepping on his glasses was usually fatal for the frames. Sometimes a lens would be crushed. Often, he had to tape, clip, glue, sew, or tie his glasses together in order to make it home. And then the problem was mine because it still took at least two weeks to get new glasses. It seemed to us it always happened just before the class pictures were to be taken, and there he was in his lopsided glasses recorded forever. One time he had been wearing these patched glasses for over a week and some friends made a lopsided plaque in woodshop and presented it to him with great fanfare. On it was written "Ted—you need new glasses." I had saved several of these battered specimens, planning to show them to him when and if he complained about how often his own children might break their glasses. We soon became wise enough to invest in an additional pair of glasses especially designed for active sports. The heavy rubber frame and special hinges on the side pieces were designed to take the physical abuse of an all-out basketball game. It was late August, and Teddy had two new pairs of glasses to begin the fall term—at great expense. His "sport frames," as he called them, were in a little brown case, which he carried in his gym bag. I had formed the necessary habit of sewing name tags into all his clothes and writing his name on all his possessions. Thankfully, the little brown case that contained the sport frames was no exception. So began an incident that will be forever engraved in my memory.

Teddy received permission to ride his bike to the park to play basketball. He was anxious to stay in shape and be ready for the fall season at Baptist High School. He had his new sport frames with him when he left the park to return home. But somewhere along the road, the case with the glasses must have fallen from his pocket and was lost. When I returned home, he was waiting on the porch with the sad news. Tears were in his eyes as he expressed his sorrow and wondered what his father's reaction would be. I told him he could be sure his father would be angry, and I gave him some useless admonition regarding his carelessness. We discussed his route from the park to our home and realized that he had traveled around a traffic circle and along a busy highway, which certainly lessened the possibility of even finding the glasses, much less finding them intact. Then, suddenly, it seemed that God spoke to me, and I was moved to suggest that we unite our hearts in fervent prayer. I took his hands in mine, and we stood there on the porch and bowed our heads. I asked him to pray first, and even now I enjoy the memory of hearing him tell his Heavenly Father how sorry he was for being careless and losing his glasses. He asked God to help him find them, and if that was not to be, he asked God to keep his daddy from being too mad at him. He then waited for my prayer. It was a very specific prayer. I praised God that He knew the exact location of Teddy's glasses. I asked Him to protect them until they could be found. Then, to my complete surprise, I was led to request specifically that a Christian would find the glasses and return them to our home. When I opened my eyes and looked at Teddy, I realized he was shocked at my straightforward request to Almighty God. I didn't discuss it with him, but I told him I would be back soon as I had to go out again.

When I parked the car in front of the house a short time later, I could see Teddy jumping up and down on the porch. He was so extremely excited. "Well, what happened?" I asked. He began to speak so rapidly, I finally told him to sit down, slow down, and start at the beginning.

Shortly after my departure, a man had rung the doorbell. Teddy didn't know him, so he asked his name. But the man asked, "Are you Teddy

DeShields?" When Teddy answered in the affirmative, the man gave him the sport frames, unharmed in the case, and asked if Teddy's father was at home. Since he was not, he began talking with Teddy. The man said that he had been driving home from work in his pickup truck around the Airport Circle and spotted the little brown eyeglass case lying beside the road. He'd stopped his truck and gone back to pick it up. He told Teddy that it was a very unusual thing for him to do because the traffic around the circle at that time of the day was very heavy. But something told him to go back and "pick up that case." Then he told our son that he was a friend of his father's, having belonged to the same church years before. He gave Teddy his name and asked him to have his father call him.

Oh, how we rejoiced that God had answered our prayers! However, this episode did not end there. When we told Dad the name of the man who had returned the glasses, he added the finishing touch. He shared that, when he was single living at home with his family and attending Calvary Baptist Church, he had volunteered to take that man's daughter to the Children's Hospital of Philadelphia for her regular allergy shots. His parents were employed during the daytime, and since Teddy's dad was working at night, he was available and willing to do it. That little girl is now a well-known evangelist in the area, and her family has remained strong in the Christian faith. In retrospect, it is quite clear that our Lord was teaching a lesson in faith to the DeShields family. I learned not to be afraid to make specific requests to God. It doesn't put Him on the spot, so to speak, to ask for a definite answer to prayer. Well, you say, "What if He didn't answer in the affirmative and the glasses were never found and returned?" Of course, that possibility existed, but would God have placed upon my heart the prayer if He was not intending to answer? Proverbs 3: 5–6 and Hebrews 11:6 took on new meaning for me.

Although Teddy didn't discuss his deep feelings regarding that incident, from that day until his death, his life was evidence of a faith that could only be compared with the righteous man described in Psalm 1:3 "And he shall be like a tree planted by the rivers of waters, that bringeth forth his fruit in his season; his leaf also shall not wither; and whatsoever he doeth shall prosper" (KJV). His faith in God was unshakable, and the times were numerous when he encouraged friends and family alike to "Trust in God because He answers prayer!"

26

The Start of the College Years

Theo had applied to only one college, Cedarville Liberal Arts College in Cedarville Ohio. He was very certain that he would be accepted. He began to prepare to go away to college and had worked hard to help buy his clothes and his books. We applied for scholarship aid and were granted some help, but thank God who provided the money for him to go away to college. In September 1977, we were able to drive him to college. After we helped him to unload and get settled in his room, he stood on a balcony saying good-bye. He waved to us. He was wearing a cap, and he tipped it as he waved. He looked so happy. He seemed to have a wonderful attitude about starting college. It was very exciting. It was infectious. I knew that I was going to miss him, yet the joy that he was experiencing was contagious. I watched him as we drove away, and I said to my husband, "Well, he is launched! We have done all we can do to give him a firm, solid foundation. Now, it is really up to him." I said a prayer that God would watch over him and protect him. That He would keep him safe and that our son would be able to do well in school. Then, we made the long trip home to an empty house. I say empty because he was the last child to leave. I had heard about the empty nest syndrome but had never experienced it. Here it was, front and center. I had to face it, and I didn't know how I was going to manage. I kept saying in my heart, "With God's help, I can do it. I can do it. I can do all things through Christ who strengthens me." Then I set about getting busy.

While Teddy was attending Baptist High School, the junior-senior banquet was scheduled to be held on May 13, 1977, at the Tavistock Country Club. The theme was "The Way We Were," and the guest speaker was Dr. John Cawood of the Philadelphia College of Bible. This was not a prom that was usually held by non-Christian schools. It was a sit-down banquet. Students and their dates would be seated at separate tables from their parents, who were also invited. Teddy needed a date, so he asked several girls, one at a time, in his church family to go with him to the banquet, but each girl found an excuse for not going. Finally, he came to me and asked me what the problem could be; he could not understand why the young ladies didn't want to go with him at such an important occasion at his high school. He had to explain to each girl that there would not be any dancing and that it was a banquet during which there would be a speaker and musical entertainment. She was to wear a gown, and it would be just like a prom—without dancing. One girl actually promised him that she would go and then changed her mind. So, he was left a few weeks before the banquet with no date. Of course, he was pretty upset. We sat down and talked about it, and I endeavored to find out why he thought that the girls were refusing to go or finding excuses not to go. He said he believed that they were afraid to be around so many people of the other race. He felt that they were going to be uncomfortable in the setting. He really was on the horns of a dilemma because he could have asked the girls from his school to go with him, but he felt that Baptist High would not be too happy with that arrangement since he was the only black boy at school.

I thought of a young woman who was several years his senior, but who was attending Philadelphia College of Bible and was a very nice Christian girl. He hadn't thought of asking her because he said, "Mom, she's older than I am, and she's in college. She wouldn't want to go to a high school banquet." I had already asked her mother if she thought that her daughter would be willing to go to the banquet with my son and had been assured that she would go with him and would enjoy being in his presence. She especially would like to hear the dean of her college speak. I felt free in advising him to ask her and to see what would happen. The more he thought about it, the more he felt that it would be a feather in his cap if he could ask an older girl to go with him—a nice girl of whom he would feel proud. He called her on the phone, and she accepted. Then he came to me so pleased that he had found someone to go with him. I did not have the heart to tell him that I had paved the way and knew that finally he would be rewarded with acceptance. In looking back on that incident, I think how often we, as parents, pave the way for the experiences of our young people because we want to keep them from having further heartbreak. It was a big deal for him, a minor thing for me. But oh, how important it was to have a date for the junior-senior banquet! Since he was outstanding at school, he would have felt terribly humiliated if he'd not had a date for the banquet.

This young lady was a good friend of his for many years. Her family and my family have always been close. When I look at the pictures we took that night, as she stood beside him on the lawn of the beautiful country club, and I see the happiness in his face and the pride that he felt in being able to escort her, I realize how important these experiences are in the lives of young people. I hadn't said anything when he was asking different girls to go with him. Although they were not the choices that I would have made for him, I felt that he was responsible enough to do these things on his own. I didn't say anything until he actually came to me for advice. Then I'd made a suggestion. And I thank God that he followed through, because it ended up being a special day for him. Of course, we, as his parents, were able to enjoy that evening with them.

Teddy knew that there were two girls in his class who were straight-A students. All through his junior and senior years, he worked very diligently to bring his marks up hoping to do better all the time. He kept trying. Finally, in his senior year, he made the honor roll and earned a grade point average was 3.6. He realized that he still had not surpassed the two girls, each of whom had achieved a GPA of 4.0. Before graduation, he knew that he would not be asked to give the valedictorian address. He lived in hope that there would be two valedictorians, and maybe he would get the salutatory address. It was not to be. At graduation, the two young ladies who had the 4.0 averages got everything. All the awards that were to be given were given to those two young ladies because they had straight-A averages. He was honored, of course, for making the honor roll. I personally was kind of disappointed when no special honor was given to him. The girls had tied for first place, and that was satisfactory to the ones who gave out the awards. Teddy noted my disappointment in a conversation we had one day, and I said, "Personally, I don't think it is fair that you didn't receive special honors for being third place in the class even though actually it was second place because the two girls tied for first. You really had second place." He looked at me and said, "Mother, that doesn't matter. I don't really feel hurt about it. I understand what you are saying. I just want to graduate and realize that I have done the best that I can do." I have to admit that I did not feel that way. I felt that he had been deprived of an honor that he had rightfully earned. He felt proud of what he had done and felt no real pain in not receiving special recognition from the school and faculty. I admired him for simply passing it off as unimportant. Again my heart said to me, "He is too good to be true."

When Teddy went away to college, I knew that he would be eager to talk to us and to tell us everything that was going on. I really wasn't prepared for the great amount of detail that he included in his letters. For some reason, I could not throw his letters away. I still find that difficult to understand. It seemed that I was destined to keep all the things that he wrote. I found in my possession folders and large envelopes filled with all his letters numbered in the proper sequence. I didn't know why I hadn't just thrown them away. I can go back and look through his letters from Cedarville and understand what he was feeling. Even now, years later, I look at his letters, written in his tiny printing. Actually, he never did conquer cursive writing. He found out that his writing was illegible. I asked him to print. He could print faster than most people could write.

I noted some general things about his letters. He always addressed them either "Dear Folks" or "Dear Dad and Mom." He always signed his letters "With love" and gave a scripture at the end. Naturally, I'm not going to include all his letters in this book. I would rather offer excerpts from his letters. That way, I won't change his thoughts, and readers will get a picture of this young man and how he grew in maturity as the four years of his college experience passed by.

Here is something from his very first letter:

> Dear Dad and Mom,
>
> Howdy! How's everything at home? The Bible Conference week was exciting, busy, and eventful. Many students

committed their lives to the Lord. The speakers were fantastic. Al Smith really could sing. Today was my first day at work. It is pretty easy, but it really cuts my Saturday into shreds. Right now, I am doing my laundry—that's right, my laundry. However, I found a girl who is willing to do my laundry when I get too busy. The work will not interfere with my basketball because I can have somebody take my place when I can't work due to basketball games. I am looking forward to starting classes on October 3rd.

Dad and Mom, there was a talk given in one of the chapel services that really made me feel glad that I was able to stick it out in Baptist High School. Dr. Murry Murdock was talking on the subject of dating and marriage and what was right for a person. It was really good, and it strengthened my viewpoint on not going steady. The girls really like me a lot here, and they treat me as a person, which is drastically different [and] I really am surprised and happy. Yes, folks, it's true, Blacks on this campus are treated like everyone else. I've only been here a week, and everybody knows me. It has really been a lot of fun this past week, and I hope that I will be able to do all of the things that I need to do. Well, I sign off now, and I hope that I will be able to keep you posted on my activities and events. I will tell you right now that I can't be home for Thanksgiving. We will be practicing basketball that week, and games will be starting up during that time. Continue to pray for these needs.

1. That I will not get sick
2. That I be able to keep the grades up
3. That I will be able to have consistent devotions
4. That I will be able to have fun and get everything done this quarter

Take care, and God bless you.

Love,

Theo

In a few days, we received another letter. It was actually five pages long. In this letter he said that his classes were starting and that they were okay and that he had a very nice roommate. He was taking general chemistry and cellular biology, and he told us that they had chapel every day. He was also taking Old Testament survey, and he had selected cycling as an elective. He also said that he ran for the office of treasurer of the freshman class. He gave a speech, and it was funny enough to win the office. He said that they had cuts for the basketball team and that he had made it through that. "We have to run one and a half miles, six laps around the track. Then we have to do six quarter-mile sprints, which are very demanding. Thursday and Friday are the last two days of that, then we will probably condition in the gym." He said that his social life was better than anticipated because the people were so nice there. He remarked that high school would have been super if it had been like the situation at Cedarville. One interesting comment was, "Of course, I miss you, but I cannot be thinking of that constantly." He spoke at length about not wanting to work on Saturdays because it cut into his study time. I can't remember whether I encouraged him to keep the job or to give it up. He said his roommate was from Ohio and was six foot five. He also played basketball. He said his older brother was the varsity captain that year. At the end of his letter, he printed "Honesty is beginning to reap bountiful benefits." I never could figure out what he meant by that. On October 24, he wrote again.

Dear Folks:

Things are moving right along. Work, with the studies, is really keeping me busy. It's interesting, though, and I enjoy it. I just completed a book for Old Testament survey, and was I ever happy to get that finished! My financial position is pretty stable, though it could be better, of course. By the way, I want to remind you that the snow is about ready to fall here, and some gloves would be helpful. Basketball news: practices are rough, strenuous, and very demanding, but fun too. The JV is having a scrimmage on Thursday, and I have a good chance of getting action on a team level. Dr. Wendall Hempton, president of the Association of Baptists for World Evangelism, located in Cherry Hill, was here. He was really glad to see me. Dad, maybe you could talk to him about getting involved in talking to the Sixers about Christ. Yes, he informed us ABWE was beginning a witnessing campaign for the NBA. He was at the gym where the Sixers practice, and the doctor got hurt. Dr. Hempton drove him to the hospital and wheeled him around for X-rays. This took three hours. During this time, Dr. Hempton found out that Julius Erving was raised in a Christian home and that he did go to Sunday school as a kid. However, he had not made a profession of faith, but the door is open. Dr. Hempton has also opened his home for a Bible study for professional athletes in baseball, basketball, and professional hockey. Dad, Dr. Hempton would like to hear from you. You could help in this area. I was really excited to hear that. He commented that it would be great to fly home for Christmas. He also commented on the fact that we would be able to sell our house quickly. He said, "I really miss the chats that we used to have, but I am expanding my interest with other persons. I stopped and read that sentence again. "Then I applied the pain killer and realized that that is what he needs to do. I went on with the letter. I wish your parents could hear the lectures in the Bible. They are super."

Well, say goodbye, good night, love you always.

In November he wrote:

Well, only three weeks until I am home. It will be nice. Thank you again for this experience, the benefit, the chance to be on my own. Please pray that the next quarter will be no Cs. My chemistry is so far in the C range, but my downfall is multiple choice. I will, however, not give up the fight. Philippians 4:49 (KJV) says "Rejoice in the Lord always" (not just sometimes either), and again I say rejoice. Continue to pray to the Lord for guidance and direction. I still see in my future a ministry on the mission field with my medicine as a vehicle that the Lord can use. If God wants me to be a doctor, the door will be open. But, if he shuts that door, He will open the other door. I really am not worried about my future because God holds it. I may minor in Bible, to have a good foundation for the field.

In the evening chapels on Sunday, the Christian service department has the summer evangelists, students who do missionary work in foreign countries, give a slide and visual presentation of that country. Some of the countries visited were Ireland, Scotland, Israel, Spain, Africa, and Australia. And the basketball team goes to the Philippines. The girl who went to Africa was a senior, and she went to see how she would fare on the mission field there. She really enjoyed it. The presentation was excellent. She is thinking seriously of going back. When I talked with her, she cited to me the differences between the Black Americans and the Black Africans. Each missionary must depend on God to provide for his or her needs. They are totally, completely dependent upon God for the money necessary to take these trips. I would like to try a summer team, but I have to give it a lot more thought and weigh the pros and the cons. I would like to discuss it with you and to see what you think of all this and all the other details involved.

I can see an honest improvement in my basketball. I can dribble and shoot better and with a little more confidence.

> I really am learning a lot because I ask the seniors or the experienced varsity players questions about how to get in a better position and how to take a better shot or about going up strong. They tell me a few things, and I try them when I am working out by myself before practice. The game with Wilberforce University was interesting because I did a move that my roommate's brother, who's captain of the varsity team, showed me, and it scored eight points. Everybody was surprised, but most of all, I was surprised because, in practice, I was never like that. I never shoot that well, but that game was ridiculously, unusually superb. We played as a team. Everyone contributed. The points that I got were also from some mighty fine passes from the rest of the team. The first game will be one that I will never forget. Pray that we will keep a good attitude on and off the court.
>
> I am really happy about my choice to come to Cedarville College. Goodness, folks, I miss everyone. I'm looking forward to seeing everyone in church. Has anything changed? Have any of the young ladies grown up? This coming summer, I am going to get my license. I am sick of depending on someone else for running around to Xenia or Daton or Springfield, etc. What am I going to do about Christmas shopping? Here is a list of people whom I do not at present have a gift for. [He gave this whole list of family members.] Help me out, folks. Give me some practical advice?"

We sent Theo an airplane ticket, and he came home in about a week or so at Christmas. Oh, we had so much fun getting reacquainted, but much too soon the time was over. We were again receiving letters from him from school. The very first one spoke of how he had arrived back safely and that four guys had been waiting for him at the airport. He had gotten grades. He said that he had gotten a 2.0 average, which was a C. It made him feel sad, but he realized now what he had to do. He had to work much harder. He said that he had received a D in cellular biology. Then in capital letters he said:

> *THAT'S MY LAST D EVER!* I am not happy about that, but I am not going to let it get me down. I know that I can do it. This quarter will either make me or break me. I purchased a book entitled, *How to Take Tests*. It outlines the procedures for taking objective and subjective tests, the types given in college, and many other useful hints included. I hope to do much better this quarter. Practice is going good in basketball. This Monday the second we play Rio Grande. They will be the toughest team yet that we have had to play. I can't waste any time these days Mom. I hope that you had a joyous New Year and that you will continue to accomplish many goals during the winter quarter while I am not at home. Well, I must close. But before I do, I want to tell you about finishing Revelations, which means that I have now completed the New Testament again. Take care. Dad, have fun watching the bowl games. Mom, for New Year's cook some black-eyed peas and ham hocks. Smile, God bless you always."
>
> Love,
>
> Your Son

Later in January 1978, Teddy wrote:

> Howdy! How are things at home? Thanks, Mom, for calling on Saturday. Well, let me tell you all the news around Cedarville College. There's a pastor here, Pastor Greene, the Christian Service Director. He's a real good friend of all the students. He's been preaching fire and brimstone from Ephesians 3 and 4. If you read those two chapters, you will get a picture of how all Christians should live together as a harmonious group, no bad language, no stealing, no cutting or slandering fellow students, etc. We

should be hearers and doers of the Word. The ultimate purpose is to edify the believer. The speakers really share their hearts concerning their Christian service. By the way, for these missionaries it's a lifetime occupation. So many Blacks in the United States have not had the gospel shared with them. It's a shame that a Christian nation like the US has places where the gospel has not been given. Mom, I'm doing very well. I recently had a stomach virus and had to miss a game because of it. The next time we had a game, I played, but I was really tired. We won, and the coach appreciated my effort. *Now* let me tell you about the weather. Ohio is something else. The weather here is really interesting. About four days ago, we had ourselves a blizzard, a real blizzard. They had to cancel classes for two days because of the roads. It seems Ohio is a closed state. Travel advisories said that only four-wheel-drive vehicles could go on the road. It has been too much. We had practice, and we had loads of fun. We've had free time. I had two tests, one on Thursday and one on Friday cancelled. So tomorrow, Monday, I have to take them both probably. The great part is the fact that this has brought the students closer together. It's been fun just talking and playing parlor games, eating, and getting a great head start on New Testament survey. Also, I am able to write more letters.

Let me quickly illustrate for you my summer plans:

1. To get my driver's license
2. To get a job
3. To stay in shape
4. To work on ball handling drills and basketball in general
5. To read everything that I can pick up

I've learned two things, Mom and Dad. One, if you want something bad enough, you have to really work for it.

Second, studying is a yearly occupation. I have to close now because it is 11:30, and I have to go to bed. Well, parents, it is time to get to sleep. I hope that you *enjoy* the news from Cedarville from the eyes and the handwriting of Theodore DeSheilds Jr.

God bless you all.

Love,

Theo

Phillipians 4: 9–13, 19

P.S. This is my first birthday away from home. Please send a lemon meringue pie. Thanks. Ha Ha. I know that that is not going to work. I was only joking. Send cookies. That will do. Thanks, Teddy

In February, he wrote:

Dear folks,

How is everything? My birthday was really interesting. Thanks so much for the card, the letters, and the gifts. It was wonderful. The packages and the good common sense advice. I've been so busy, it's pathetic. I heard about your blizzard. It really slows things down, doesn't it? I hope that you are fine and haven't been down sick with anything. I really appreciate all of the concern when the blizzard hit us.

He spoke of his desire to get As and Bs and what a struggle it was the very first year to comprehend things that were coming at him from all directions. He tried to do well in his basketball as well as his school courses. He was always trying to find someone to help him with whatever he was having problems with and kept reassuring us that he was not going to give up and was going to keep on trying. After the Easter vacation, we were all looking forward to Teddy coming home to get a job doing the summer and to pull it all together. The plans that he had made for his improvement in school seemed to finally have come to fruition. He was going to make it. He thought that school was fun. He was enjoying himself and was looking forward to the very next year. Summer went swiftly. We did not realize how fast it went until it was time for him to go back to school in the fall. Now, he was a sophomore before we knew it. A year had gone by.

In October he wrote to us:

> Before I study for my first test in Baptist history, I want to write to you about several events and things that have happened to me around Cedarville. Yes, I received the package, and I thank you ever so much. I appreciate it. It has been helter-skelter around here. Of course, basketball is tough going. I have made some progress. I'm finally shooting a proper left-hand lay-up, Dad. This quarter has been so busy, and only two weeks have gone by. What can I say? I am certainly glad for a quiet dorm in which to study. That has been advantageous. Plus, my roommate, Doug, is showing me how to use my head on problems in quantitative analysis, and I think that the laboratory work is going well also. The fundamentals of English are finally sinking in.

He gave some examples in his letters that were so interesting, and he said, "If you do not understand the above statements, go on through the rest of the letter and just forget it." Then he talked about his dorm where they held a prayer meeting once a week. "It has really been a time for blessing. I have placed a request for the continued growth of our whole church. We have been praying together, which has just been great."

On October 6, 1978, Theo was able to take a trip to Stratford, Ontario, Canada. He attended the Shakespeare festival. They stayed at the Victory Inn in Stratford, and he wrote about it.

The trip was fabulous. I never had four Shakespearean plays come alive like that before. I would love to go back again. The plays were very good. We saw *Julius Caesar* and *Titus Andronicus* on Friday, and on Saturday we saw *Macbeth* and *The Merry Wives of Windsor.* The first three were tragedies, and the last one mentioned was a comedy. The least known play was *Titus Andronicus*, but it by far was the most brutal goriest tragedy I have ever seen performed. Even television couldn't beat out this play. The acting was superior. The entire weekend was capped off by the fact that most of the people there were English majors, which made it possible to get to know a different group of people from our school. By me playing basketball and being in pre-med, I do not often have time to talk to others who are in different majors. So it was a good experience. Now, enough about me. How is everyone doing? Is everyone healthy, spunky, and cheery? How's the church doing? I think it will be good if I can get a progress report.

Next week, the new president of the college will be inaugurated. The varsity and junior varsity players will serve as ushers. It will be a new experience for me. We are going to wear matching blue three-piece suits with the Cedarville emblem on them. They are quite sharp. With that, I must depart. Pray for me, God bless, and I hope to hear from you both soon.

Love,

Your Son

Psalm 1:12

November 27, 1978:

Dear folks:

How are you? I am doing well this Thanksgiving Day. I am just getting the chance to write. So much has happened in the last two weeks. I am really enjoying college much more now. Things are finally starting to come together. The only way that you can understand is if I tell you what the Lord has been doing for me. Let me start by telling you about my glasses. I've told you about how I broke my left lens. Well, it has been over two weeks, and I haven't been getting anywhere with the optician in Cedarville. So I called the optician at home and he, bless his soul, sent me the lens in four days. Now if I can just get the rest of the glasses back from Dr. Wheeler's office here in Cedarville, I will finally have my glasses problems straightened out. Folks, I think that we are going to have to discuss and consider contacts. Maybe next year.

I told you about how bad I had been doing in English fundamentals class. I went to the teacher and told him to please give me some good helps to prepare for the next test. I took the next test and, thanks be to God, with His help, I finally got a B. Things are finally beginning to perk up. I had a long talk with my adviser concerning my major and other important areas. First we discussed the entrance inventory exam that I took. He was interested in what the results would show. This test shows basic occupational interests in many different occupations. Some, including doctors, lawyers, nurses, etc. My interests lie in the medical-related field, but I do have some interests in arts and speaking. The doctor was very positive in that he said that the test should be where my interests lie and that there were many options open to me besides becoming a doctor. Simply, there are many things I can do if I have a BS in chemistry. He feels very strongly that I can graduate from Cedarville and maybe with a year or two in graduate school, could find a job in chemistry or medical work. Meanwhile, I am not going to change my major. I see that this field is very broad, and I really don't want to leave it no matter what. Besides, for the first time in my life I finally feel like I know where I am headed.

Thanks for your prayers, they have helped. I am looking forward to coming home for Christmas. The chapel services have been an inspiration to me. Dr. Paul Dixon spoke on Monday morning on the topic "Don't give up." It was just what I needed. That and my roommate, Doug, who by the way has been a blessing to me because we have devotions every day in the morning and it has really helped and has become a source of strength from God each day. Our study has been in Ephesians, and when we read Ephesians 3:20 and 21, I immediately tacked those verses up on the outside of our dorm room. God has been working in my life, Mom and Dad. I can see it and feel it, with joy and praises to Him. Thanks so much to you.

Well, how is the church doing? We are still praying for the church. I am looking forward to seeing everyone at home. I hope everyone is healthy and well at Thanksgiving. I wrote to some other relatives, and I hope they enjoyed receiving a letter from Ohio.

Well, before I close, I want to tell you about my social life. Things are better and I am meeting some nice young ladies. This is exactly what I wanted, so I am praising the Lord that things in my life are working out. You were right, time is a great healer. I hope to see you at the airport on the 19th of December. God bless you always.

Ephesians 3:16,20 and 21

Your Son,

Theo

January 2, 1978:

Dear folks: Greetings and happy New Year to you. I hope that Dad is enjoying his vacation. The rest of mine was both exciting, dramatic, and somewhat disappointing. Let me explain. The exciting part was the plane trip back to Ohio. When Walt left me off at the airport, he didn't realize, nor I, that the plane was going to not only be one hour late, but three hours late. The holdup was the fifteen inches of snow that had fallen in Albany, New York. Of course, the plane was coming from that city. Everything was so slow. While I was waiting, I read a couple of chapters in analytical chemistry and most of Josh McDowell's book, *Evidence that Demands a Verdict.* I also helped two men who were working on a crossword puzzle. I got back forty-five minutes til practice time which was at four o'clock. Well, so much for fast efficient flying service.

The tournament was good. Two of our players were outstanding, winning all tournament awards, and also one of our players was voted most valuable player. So much for the news that's good. Now for the good and cloudy stuff—my grades. Please understand one thing, I tried really hard. When you see the transcript, you will see that I missed a B in fundamentals and got a C in calculus. It looks sort of discouraging, doesn't it? I can only say that maybe this quarter holds better things. I sincerely thought that I could bang out a good quarter, but I am just doing average work. Please pray that I don't get discouraged and throw in the towel. I can and will, with God's help, finally do better. I know that you are tired of hearing me write or say that I must or will do better. You are waiting for action. Well so am I. I hope that I get it this time. I still can get the GPA up to 2.8 or so if I get a couple of good quarters, winter and spring. The goal is a 3.0 this quarter.

It seems so difficult, but the more I think about it, it seems that it is possible to do when I read Ephesians 3:20 and 21.

Well, my dear parents, I hope that you can understand my concern and my pain at this report, but this quarter, it was the best I could do, I guess. I am so hurt and disappointed by this and I hope that you can understand why. Well, I will close this letter and attempt to build again toward the goals that I set for myself. Mom and Dad, thanks for understanding, and I sincerely hope I will do better. I'm enclosing something that I wrote the last day of 1978. I hope that you will see the message in it, and I look forward to your reply to this letter.

Changes, so gradual and yet so sudden.

Once the frolicking of a kid used to be fun—

the jumping in the puddles of rainwater with good shoes on,

But now, what's happening to me? What's come over me?

Adulthood seems so far away, but yet it is around the corner.

Those years being seventeen and eighteen were great,

but now they must be left behind, now they must be a memory.

I long for those years, and yet I want with great expectation

to what the future holds for me.

Maybe growing up can be fun. What lies ahead?

I believe I'm becoming an adult.

Theo DeShields

Well, must go now. God bless, and remember me in your prayers. I will always remember you.

Love Theo

27

The Final Chapter

This chapter was written by Crawford Clark

I met Theo while attending college at Penn State University. We both were members of Campus Crusade for Christ, a Christian student organization that focused on helping students increase their understanding of biblical discipleship. There were only three African Americans who were part of Campus Crusade at the time. Theo, as I recall, did not come to every meeting because of his need to study. He was working on a master's degree in business administration and always put his schoolwork before all the other things that were going on in his life.

Theo was a naturally friendly person, and he regarded every person that he met as important. I had the opportunity to become his friend although I did not spend much time with him. I do not remember very many conversations that took place between us, but I do remember him telling me at one point that he wanted to become an alcohol and drug counselor because he wanted to help to bring hope to those who struggled with addiction. He wanted to be used as an agent of change. He had a real love for, and a heart deeply devoted toward people. He really believed the scripture in Luke 10:27: "You must love the Lord your God with all your heart and with all your soul and with all your strength and with all your mind; and your neighbor as yourself" (NIV).

The financial reality of most college students is that they do not have a lot of money. This was true also for Theo, but he would find a way to give gifts through his creativity. He would use his skill at calligraphy to make a card, and to top it off, he would use his other skill of photography to take pictures of flowers. He would incorporate the two skills together and produce a gift for a person, each one customized, of course, with an appropriate scripture the making of these gifts was time-consuming, but he seemed to find the time to make them for the numerous people he felt were important to him.

There is one person that I remember him telling me about who was a great treat for him. He had met Ms. Pennsylvania at the time and had become friends with her. Theo would get to know so many people, not only at Penn State, but everywhere he found himself. It was amazing how we both had similar temperaments. We loved Jesus, loved people, loved being around people, loved to help people, and if there were a need to be met, attempting to fulfill that need would come before other tasks that were before us.

We remained friends after college and would meet up at his mom's house when he came home from Penn State and, later, from the service. That is how I met his parents and eventually became friends with his mother. It was through his mom that I heard about Theo's death. Of course, I could not believe it was true. "How could someone who is twenty-eight years old who is in perfect shape die of a heart attack?" Theo, at the time, was the only male friend that I had, and suddenly, he was gone. His mother then became a wonderful friend to me. I even had the opportunity to redesign her front yard one summer. I had a landscaping business at the time, and she wanted the front yard changed. As I got to know her, I came to appreciate the value and the extent of the wisdom she possessed. She was a down-to-earth woman who loved Jesus and who loved her son dearly.

Theo died in 1987, and in my mind, his was much too short a time for a person to be on Earth. However, I realize that all of us have a divinely appointed life span, some short and some long. What we do within that time is of great value. Theo was able to maximize that time by filling his days with things that were of the greatest value. The love that his mother had for Theo was amazing, and she had a desire to share his story. Sadly, she herself became quite ill before she finished writing, and she passed away before she could finish. I sincerely hope that you have found what she wrote to be inspirational as well as encouraging. It truly is a great story of how God used Theo to fulfill His plan for Him in those twenty-eight years because Theo was a man who was *called according to his purpose.*

RESOURCES

Ten Special Needs Organizations You Should Know About

In case you aren't already aware, there's a plethora of organizations offering programs and services to the special needs community of families. Below you will find ten must-investigate organizations that offer services to all individuals with disabilities and special needs.

1. Easter Seals (https://www.easterseals.com)

What they offer: Resources for autism, seniors, children, adults, military, and veterans, employment and training, medical rehabilitation, camping and recreation, brain health.

2. Special Olympics (https://www.specialolympics.org)

What they offer: Real sports, community building, youth activation, healthy lifestyle promotion, leadership, research.

3. United Cerebral Palsy (https://ucp.org)

What they offer: My Child Without Limits, My Life Without Limits, family support, employment guides, health and wellness tips, housing help, financial assistance, international resources.

4. The Arch (https://thearc.org)

What they offer: Information and referral services, individual advocacy to address education, employment, health care and other concerns, self-advocacy initiatives, residential support, family support, employment programs, leisure, and recreational programs.

5. Friendship Circle International (https://www.friendshipcircle.org)

What they offer: Volunteer home visits, Torah circle for children, holiday programs, camp experiences, sports, sibling support, life skills.

6. Goodwill Industries International (https://www.goodwill.org)

What they offer: Financial coaching, savings and loan support, tax preparation, education programs, community services, financial aid, transportation, after school programs, housing assistance, clothing assistance, medical rehabilitation.

7. Parents Helping Parents (https://www.parentshelpingparents.org)

What they offer: Support groups, family and community services, crisis support, early intervention, assistive technology services.

8. Federation for Children with Special Needs (https://fcsn.org)

What they offer: special education center for parents, family support, health advocacy, family and community engagement, parent-professional leadership, summer camp, parent-to-parent support

9. Special Needs Alliance (https://www.specialneedsalliance.org)

What they offer: Connection to attorneys in your area that practice disability and public benefits law, covering special needs trusts and wills, Medicare, SSI, estate and tax planning, personal injury, health care, financial planning, guardianships, and conservatorships.

10. Family Voices (https://familyvoices.org)

What they offer: Family-centered care, partnerships, quality, access, affordability and acceptability, health systems that work for families and children, informed families/strong communities, and self-advocacy/empowerment.

Additional Organizations

Parent to Parent USA

Parent to Parent USA is a group that matches each parent with a fellow parent who has a child with the same special healthcare need, disability, or mental health concern, allowing each parent or family to have a contact for sharing information, receiving support, and creating new friendships.

National Youth Leadership Network

Led by young citizens, the National Youth Leadership Network works to build strength and "break isolation" among people with disabilities who are between the ages of sixteen and twenty-eight. They try to create a culture of full inclusion, sparking new ideas about how to measure success and ability and supporting youth with disabilities in leadership roles. The group hosts workshops around the country for young people to learn how to develop leadership skills.

National Collaborative on Workforce and Disability for Youth

NCWD/Youth focuses on young teens and helps them to learn how to cope with their disability and find their place in the workforce. The group also teaches kids to access the education they need. Once the young adults are able to achieve their educational and employment goals, NCWD/Youth works to assist them with living as independently as possible.

The M.O.R.G.A.N. Project

Making Opportunities Reality Granting Assistance Nationwide, established by parents Robert and Kristen Malfara, supports families in their journey of raising a child with special needs, be that child biological, adopted or within the foster care system. In addition to having a large library of resources and information on their website, the group also assists families with travel expenses for medical treatments and gifts of medical equipment that aren't covered by insurance, such as wheelchairs. It works to create a group of parents who are supportive of each other in difficult times.

Council for Exceptional Children

The Council for Exceptional Children is the largest international professional organization dedicated to improving the educational success of children with disabilities. By advocating for successful governmental policies, setting standards for professionals in the education industry, and providing professional development seminars, the organization helps teachers, administrators, parents, related students, and other educational support staff to best support and educate the children with special needs with whom they work.

Disabled Sports USA

Everyone deserves to have a fun time playing sports, according to Disabled Sports USA. Founded by injured Vietnam War veterans, the organization has expanded to anyone with a permanent disability who wants to play sports but hasn't been able to in a standard setting. Using sports as rehabilitation, many children and young adults with special needs gain confidence and dignity through their teamwork and active exercise. Disabled Sports USA also works with the United States Olympic Committee to help choose athletes to compete in the Paralympics.

Best Buddies

"Best Buddies is a great organization for helping kids with special needs develop friendships and stay social," says Dr. Jen Trachtenberg, a board-certified pediatrician in New York City. Best Buddies works to end the "social, physical and economic isolation of the 200 million people with intellectual and developmental disabilities" by helping them form meaningful one-to-one friendships with peers. Through these relationships, Best Buddies works to help those with special needs improve their communication skills, secure jobs and develop the necessary skills to live independently.

Forty-Five Great Websites for Parents of Children with Special Needs

The following are forty five great websites for parents of children with special needs. This list of resources is great for parents of children with special needs. The list contains links for associations, councils, centers, and societies. It also has links for conferences, financial aid and internships, and helpful websites, articles, and research. Blogs and Facebook pages are also on the list.

Autism Society: Since 1965, the Autism Society has been providing information for individuals on the spectrum, family members, and professionals.

Council for Exceptional Children: The Council for Exceptional Children provides information and resources about Special Education.

Family Hope Center: When children or adults have special needs, the Family Hope Center provides support to the entire family.

Family Resource Center on Disabilities: Training, assistance, and information are given to parents of children with disabilities by the Family Resource Center on Disabilities.

National Association of Parents with Children in Special Education (NAPCSE): Parents of Special Education students can learn how to be their child's best advocate.

National Council on Independent Living: NCIL promotes social change and strives to do away with disability driven discrimination.

National Center for Learning Disabilities: Children and adults with learning disabilities will benefit from the information and resources available from the National Center for Learning Disabilities.

National Collaborative on Workforce and Disability: NCWD for Youth provides strategies and development systems for youth with disabilities to join the workforce.

National Down Syndrome Society: The ndss supports people with Down Syndrome by providing resources such as wellness, education, and research.

Pacer Center: The Parent Advocacy Coalition for Educational Rights utilizes the idea of parents helping parents and provides support and resources for children and youth with disabilities and their families.

United Spinal Association: The United Spinal Association offers support, advice, and resources for those with spinal cord injuries.

Conferences

Closing the Gap Conference: The 32nd annual Closing the Gap Conference will take place in Minneapolis, Minnesota.

COPAA Council of Parent Attorneys and Advocates: The 17th annual COPAA Conference will take place in March of 2015 in San Diego California.

Disability Rights Education and Defense Fund: DREDF provides Special Education conferences in Northern California.

EPICS: The Native American Conference on Special Education has a conference in Albuquerque, New Mexico in March of 2015.

Professional Education Resources & Conference Services: PERCS will have its 18th annual Great Beginnings Conference in Worcester, Massachusetts.

Financial Aid and Internships

National Center for Learning Disabilities: The Anne Ford and Allegra Ford Thomas Scholarships are given to two graduating high school seniors who have been diagnosed with a learning disability to use for post-secondary education.

Possibilities: This is a financial resource for parents of children with disabilities.

Project 10: This site provides information about scholarships, grants, and financial resources that are helpful to those with disabilities.

Helpful Websites, Articles, and Research

Answers 4 Families: Families and professionals can find information and support from the Nebraska Department of Health and Human Services' Answers 4 Families.

Center for Parent Information and Resources: A training module for screening, evaluation, and assessment procedures for early intervention can be found here to help parents of babies and toddlers.

Center for Parent Information and Resources: 10 Basic Steps in Special Education explains the process special education services for a child.

Closing the Gap: Closing the Gap helps people learn how to utilize assistive technology to change lives.

Disabled Sports USA: Disables Sports USA provides recreation and sports opportunities to disabled youth, adults, and wounded warriors.

National Center for Learning Disabilities: The National Center for Learning Disabilities answers frequently asked questions (FAQ) on this page of resources.

Office of Disability Employment Policy: The United States Department of Labor offers many different disability employment policy resources that are categorized by topic.

Parent Training Information: Education topics and laws are presented on this site along with local information for those who live in Massachusetts.

Reading Rockets: Back-to-School Tips for Parents of Children with Special Needs is a great article to get the school year off to a good start.

U.S. Department of Education: The U.S. Department of Education provides many resources and research for parents of children with special needs.

Teaching Tips

Ability Path: Ability Path and Temple Grandin offer teaching tips for children and adults with autism spectrum disorder.

Autism Web: Autism Web gives parents and teachers tips for autism.

Help Guide: Help Guide offers advice for helping children with learning disabilities at home and at school.

LD Online: LD Online helps parents build a relationship with their child's teacher.

Children's Books

Children's Disabilities Information: The website provides a list of children's books that are about special needs and disabilities.

Explaining Special Needs to Your Child: 15 Great Children's Books: Special Needs Resources lists 15 great children's books that help explain special needs to children.

Institute for Humane Education: Characters with special needs take center stage in these children's books.

Blogs

Autism and Oughtisms: The mom of 2 autistic boys is the author of this inspirational and informative blog about autism.

Love that Max: A magazine editor mom of a special needs child writes this inspirational blog about parenting a special needs child.

My Special Needs Network: Learning solutions for kids with special needs can be found on this blog.

The Life Unexpected: Marianne Russo gives advice and information through The Life Unexpected and also through The Coffee Klatch Special Needs Talk Radio Network.

The Shut-Down Learner: Dr. Richard Selznick offers information and practical advice to parents of special needs children.

Facebook Pages

Community of Practice for Supporting Families with Disabilities: The Community of Practice for Supporting Families with Disabilities is a place to share resources and knowledge and to discuss issues.

Federation for Children with Special Needs: To benefit those with special needs or disabilities, Federation for Children with Special Needs provides support and inspiration.

Parenting Special Needs Magazine: This Facebook page gives inspiration and support to those with special needs and their families.

Parents of Special Needs Children: Family members of special needs children can find support and information on the page.

The Special Education Support Toolbox

(50+ Special Needs Resources)

Contributors: Peggy Ployhar and Donna Schillinger

THSC is committed to the homeschooling success of families with special needs. That's why we have developed a number of special education support resources especially for your family!

Additionally, there are many resources available through national organizations to aid in your parenting and homeschool journey. Finally, if one of these groups or services does not have what you're looking for, there's probably an app for that.

8 Resources THSC Offers to Families Homeschooling a Special Needs Student

National Resources

Special Education and Disability Law and State Offices

Free or Low-cost Therapy Options

Apps for Special Needs Support

Magazines and Websites for Special Needs

Eight Resources THSC Offers to Families Homeschooling a Special Needs Student

1. Special Needs Nook Blog. Stay informed every month with a new blog post addressing current special needs homeschooling issues. Simply sign up for email notifications.

2. "How Do I Start?" for special needs families. For parents in the initial stages of homeschooling a special needs child, our website highlights the tools and consulting services THSC offers.
3. Special Needs Curriculum Information. A newly revised list of "special needs parent-approved" homeschooling resources—a free PDF download.
4. Special Needs Consulting Services. THSC's Special Needs department provides one-on-one consulting services to special needs parents who need advice on how to advocate for your children, choose a curriculum, or develop an IEP to document your child's goals and need for accommodations or modifications to curriculum.
5. Helpful Hints. Recently added is a new, easy-to-access list of frequently asked questions under Special Needs on the THSC website, answering the most common special needs homeschooling questions.
6. Special Needs Glossary. Special needs parents quickly find they have a whole new language to learn! With special needs educational lingo being such a critical part of advocating for your special needs child, THSC also recently added an entire webpage dedicated to defining special needs terminology.
7. THSC Members get free use of a first-of-its-kind IEP Generator. Useful for many aspects of coordinating care and schooling, just complete the online form and our IEP Generator formulates your answers into a professional-looking and valid individualized education plan. Learn more about the IEP Generator.
8. Special Care at THSC Conventions. The Special Buddies program, which is THSC's special needs Convention program, offers unique help to parents attending the annual THSC Convention. Also, Buddy Helpers allows children that struggle with less severe disabilities to join our Kids Convention program.

What are we missing? If you have any ideas to share with us on how you would like THSC to further help in your special needs homeschooling endeavors, or how you would like to partner with THSC to help special needs homeschooling families in Texas, please contact us at specialneeds@ thsc.org.

Special Education and Disability Law and State Offices

Fortunately, our nation has a comprehensive consideration of physical and developmental disabilities in its laws and government. Here are some of the federal laws special needs families are most likely to encounter.

1. Section 504 of the Rehabilitation Act of 1973 protects the rights of individuals with disabilities in programs and activities that receive federal financial assistance, including federal funds.
   Section 504 provides that: "No otherwise qualified individual with a disability in the United States … shall, solely by reason of her or his disability, be excluded from the participation in, be denied the benefits of, or be subjected to discrimination under any program or activity receiving Federal financial assistance."
2. IDEA (Individuals with Disabilities Education Act) of 2004 governs how states and public agencies provide early intervention, special education, and related services to more than 6.5 million eligible infants, toddlers, children and youth with disabilities. (Understand the Differences Between Section 504 and IDEA.)
3. ADA (American Disabilities Act) of 1990 "ADA … makes it illegal to discriminate against people with disabilities at work, in school and in public spaces." Read this to discover how it applies to your child with special needs.
4. DARS (Texas Department of Assistive & Rehabilitative Services). As of September 1, 2016, programs and services previously administered or delivered by the former Texas Department of Assistive and Rehabilitative Services (DARS) have been transferred by the Texas Legislature to the Texas Workforce Commission or the Texas Health and Human Services Commission. (See how the former DARS services were divided between the two agencies.)
5. ESSA (Every Student Succeeds Act) reauthorized the Elementary and Secondary Education Act of 1965 (ESEA) and replaced the

No Child Left Behind Act. (Read this analysis of how ESSA intersects with disabilities issues.)

6. Guide to Disability Rights Law covers all of the above, plus applicable laws from Telecommunications Act, Fair Housing Act, Air Carrier Access Act, Voting Accessibility for the Elderly and Handicapped Act, National Voter Registration Act, Civil Rights of Institutionalized Persons Act, and Architectural Barriers Act

Free or Low-Cost Therapy Options for Special Needs Children

1. ABA (applied behavior analysis) therapy:
   - o Rethink first (ABA training)
   - o Spectacular kids (ABA training)
   - o PECS (ABA training and products)
   - o First path autism (ABA training)

2. Assistive technology:
   - o Great special ed apps and sites
   - o Common sense media – apps for special needs and learning difficulties
   - o Assistive technology selection guide for parents
   - o Assistive technology basics
   - o Enable mart

3. Occupational therapy (OT):
   - o Handwriting without tears (HWT), an OT approach to teaching handwriting
   - o the ultimate guide to ot therapy resources for kids
   - o The OT mom
   - o OT resources
   - o School OT

4. Speech therapy:
   - o Home speech home
   - o Super star speech
   - o Mommy speech therapy

- o Speech therapy at home
- o Super duper publications – speech therapy products

5. Visual and auditory processing therapy:
   - o Little giant steps
   - o Brain balance
   - o AWS learning skills program
   - o Auditory processing studio
   - o Eye can learn

Apps for special needs support

Therapy Tools

- Sixteen speech therapy apps
- Pediatric therapy apps to get kids moving
- Twenty occupational therapy apps
- ABA flash cards and games app

Diagnostic specific

- Ten ADHD friendly brain training apps
- Three apps for blind and visually impaired
- Best dyslexia apps for middle and high school
- Sounding board app for non-verbal communication
- Matrix game visual perception apps
- SnapType app for dysgraphia
- Best apps for down syndrome
- Apps for sensory processing disorder
- iHelp for autism

Organizational Tools

- Ten apps for teaching life skills
- Four free apps to increase attention and time management

Bonus Resources: Editor's top five magazines and websites picks for families with special needs students

1. Exceptional Parent Magazine
2. Audacity magazine
3. Interactive planner for special needs caregivers

Financial Assistance for Special Needs

Maybe it was in the maternity ward, when the doctor said, "There's a problem." Or after a few years, when you couldn't help but notice the lack of verbal progress or engagement with you.

Whenever you discovered that your child fell into one of the special needs areas, your love didn't change, but your dreams had to be altered. That realization is like being hit by a truck.

But there was another collision coming. A financial one.

In 2014, the U.S. Department of Agriculture estimated the cost of raising a child from birth to 18 years at $240,000 or about $13,333 a year. The Centers for Disease Control and Prevention said that it costs $17,000 more per year – about $30,000 — to raise a child with autism. Depending on how severe the child's birth defect or disorder, the cost of lifetime care can run well past $1 million, with occupational, behavioral and life skills therapy, private schooling and private caregivers among the expenses.

Take a deep breath. Help is out there. There are many benefits for parents of a disabled child available for special needs children through sources like the Social Security Administration, Medicaid, insurance, grants and educational assistance.

Will these sources cover all costs? No. But they can make a big difference.

Supplemental Security Income for Special Needs

Supplemental Security Income (SSI), a type of social security benefit, is the only source of federal income reserved for disabled children. SSI for a special needs child can be a lifeline that keeps the family out of poverty.

Not every child qualifies, and SSI is geared toward disadvantaged families, so there are income limits applied to the child and the family he or she lives with. Children on SSI received an average of $647 per month; the maximum payment for an individual is $771 per month. In most states, a child who qualifies for SSI will automatically qualify for Medicaid as well.

Receiving SSI requires proving the child suffers "marked and severe functional limitations" that must be established by medical evidence. Examples include Down syndrome, cerebral palsy, autism, intellectual disability and blindness. The maximum monthly amount of earned income a family can make for a disabled child to qualify for SSI is $3,209 for a one-parent family, $3,981 for a two-parent household assuming there are no other children in the home. (The amounts increase if there are other children.) If all income is unearned, the monthly limits are $1,582 and $1,968, respectively.

Health Care

Government programs and private insurance are primary ways to help offset the cost of treating children with special health care needs. In 2016, Medicaid and the Children's Health Insurance Program (CHIP) covered almost half of children with special health care needs. As with SSI, Medicaid and CHIP, which is run by states under federal rules, have financial eligibility limits, but they extend well above the poverty line. In January 2017, the median financial eligibility level for Medicaid and CHIP children was 255% ($52,989 per year for a family of three).

Medicaid covers many medical and long-term care services for special needs children, many of which are covered in limited amounts – if at all – in private insurance. In addition to doctor visits, hospitalizations, x-rays, lab tests and prescription drugs, it covers behavioral health, dental, hearing and vision care, physical, occupational and speech therapy and medical equipment and supplies. Medicaid also covers long-term care services, such as private duty nursing, that help children with special health care needs remain at home with their families, and non-emergency medical transportation to appointments.

Private insurance, on the other hand, often does not cover long-term care services and may offer limited coverage of other services important to children with special health care needs such as dental care, mental health services or physical, occupational, or speech therapy. By 2014, all but two states required insurance companies to cover autism spectrum disorders, but some coverage mandates are minimal. Visits to specialists often require the referral of the child's pediatrician, which increases expense and inconvenience. It pays to learn what your insurance does and doesn't cover, and you should be willing to challenge insurance companies when they deny payments or services.

Tax Credits for Special Needs Families

Tax breaks provide another important way to lessen the financial impact of caring for children with special medical needs. It begins with deducting unreimbursed medical expenses when filing your federal income taxes. You can deduct the amount that exceeds 7.5% of your adjusted gross income. If your adjusted gross income is $50,000, the threshold is $3,750. So, if you had $10,000 in medical expenses, you could deduct $6,250. The deductible expenses include more than just medicines and doctor bills: Medically required foods, mileage to and from health care visits and therapy supplies count, too.

The child and dependent care credit is a tax break for paying someone to care for your child while working or looking for work. There is no age limit if the child is disabled. Better news: It's a credit rather than a deduction, so it cuts your tax bill directly instead of just reducing your taxable income. The credit can be up to $3,000 per dependent, to a maximum of $6,000 for all dependents. Child-care, after-school programs, and day camp qualify for the credit. Keep good records and consult your accountant.

Another break is a 529A account, which are state-sponsored accounts that allow disabled people to save significant amounts without threatening their eligibility for need-based government help. Disabled people, their families and friends can contribute as much as $14,000 a year without putting federal benefits at risk. These are not deductible on federal taxes but are at the state level in some states. The permissible size of the account also varies by state.

Special Needs Grants

It may sound too good to be true, but there really are grants available to help people whose children have special needs. The need criteria and income requirements vary greatly, the funds are not limitless and a lot of people may be seeking the grants at the same time you are.

Grants for parents with special needs children

- Autism Cares Today SOS Program – Supports those impacted with autism who have an immediate need for treatment or support and whose safety is jeopardized if treatment is not found.
- Parker's Purpose Foundation Assistance – Provides financial assistance up to $1,000 to any family who has a minor with a life-altering illness or disability that is in an immediate financial crisis due to unforeseen medical expenses. Funding preference is given to Ohio residents, but is granted outside the state of Ohio if deemed eligible.
- First Hand Foundation – Provides funding for items to improve the quality of life of individuals with disabilities not otherwise covered by insurance.
- Ben's Fund – Provides grants up to $1,000 to families across Washington state who need financial assistance related to their child's autism spectrum disorder treatments.
- Autism Support Network – has an extensive list of grants available for autism related expenses

Education

A significant amount of financial aid is directed specifically toward students with special needs and learning disabilities. Here are several, ordered by disability.

Attention Deficit Disorder

Rise Scholarship Foundation – Five students diagnosed with ADD or ADHD and an additional learning disability receive this $2,500 award annually. Applicants must have a grade point average of 2.5 or higher to qualify.

Autism

Organization for Autism Research – Two nonrenewable, $3,000 scholarships for students on the autism spectrum who are full-time students working toward certification or accreditation in a particular field.

Learning and Cognitive Disabilities

Anne Ford Scholarship – The $10,000 scholarship ($2,500 per year over four years) goes to a graduating high school senior who will attend a four-year bachelor's degree program. Recipients must demonstrate financial need and be involved in school and community activities.

Landmark College Scholarships – Landmark College is one of only two colleges in the country specifically for students with learning disabilities. Multiple scholarships ranging from $5,000 to $34,000 are available for students and are based on financial aid and merit.

Visual Difficulties

Lighthouse Guild – Up to 10 merit-based scholarships are awarded each year to legally blind high school students getting ready to attend college.

General Disabilities

Microsoft Disability Scholarship – Awarded to promising high school students with financial need who plan to attend a vocational or academic college. This scholarship provides $5,000 per year up to a total of $20,000 and is designed for students who seek a career in the technology industry.

Max Fay: Max can be reached at mfay@debt.org. - Articles on Financial Assistance for Disabled Adults

Printed in the United States
by Baker & Taylor Publisher Services